# THE MYSTERIOUS
## BLACK MIGRATION
### 1800-1820

# THE MYSTERIOUS BLACK MIGRATION
## 1800-1820

### THE VAN VRANKENS
#### AND OTHER FAMILIES OF AFRICAN DESCENT IN WASHINGTON COUNTY, NEW YORK

## L. LLOYD STEWART

**To order additional copies of this book, contact:**
Xlibris Corporation
1-888-795-4274
www.Xlibris.com
Orders@Xlibris.com
127396

# TABLE OF CONTENTS

PAGE

List Of Charts And Tables ............................................................. 9
List Of Maps And Photos ............................................................ 10
Foreward .................................................................................... 13
Preface ...................................................................................... 15
Acknowledgements ................................................................... 19
Introduction ............................................................................. 21

## PART I

## WASHINGTON COUNTY, NY AND THE MIGRATION

CHAPTER I:
    History Of Washington (Charlotte) County, New York ........................ 31

    A.  History of Charlotte/Washington County ................................ 32

        1-  Overview ........................................................................ 32
        2-  Early General History .................................................... 40

    B.  Population Of African Descent ............................................. 43

CHAPTER II:
    The Migration ....................................................................... 46

    A.  African American History In Washington County, New York ........ 47
    B.  Causes And Rationale For The Migration
        Geopolitical Conditions ....................................................... 56

1- Revolutionary War Freedom Policies ..................................... 69

    A.  Enlistment Of Men Of African Descent........................ 69
    B.  Manumission During The Revolution ........................... 71

2- The New York State Confiscation And Forfeiture Laws ...... 73

    A.  Freedom Provisions........................................................ 75
    B.  Act Of Attainder ............................................................ 77
    C.  Attainder: Frederick Phillipse ...................................... 80

3- Washington County And The Confiscation Laws................ 83
4- Gradual Abolition: Manumission Provisions ....................... 86

    A.  The Gradual Abolition Act Of 1799 .............................. 88
    B.  Gradual Abolition In Washington County..................... 90

CHAPTER III:
  Economic Conditions In New York State And Washington County........ 106

  A.  The Economic Boom Of 1810 In Washington County............ 107

    1- Overview........................................................................ 107
    2- Economic History.......................................................... 109
    3- Agriculture & Industry ................................................. 110
    4- Economic Boom ............................................................ 111
    5- Washington County: chief agricultural and
       manufactured products ............................................... 114

  B.  Economic Downturn In New York State ................................. 138

    1- The Depression Of 1807-1814 ......................................... 138
    2- The Embargo Act of 1807 ................................................ 138
    3- Economic Recovery......................................................... 140
    4- Washington County And The Economic
       Depression Of 1807-1814............................................. 141
    5- Landowners of African Descent in Washington County....... 147

CHAPTER IV:
   Final Abolition........................................................................... 159

     A.  The Jim Crow Status Of "Freed" African
         Descendants After Emancipation ............................................ 162

         1-  The Politics Of Discrmination............................................ 164
         2-  Disenfranchisement ............................................................ 165

     B.  New York State Constitution Of 1821............................... 170
     C.  Perspective On The Politics Of Enslavement
         And Abolition In The United States.................................... 171

CONCLUSION........................................................................................ 179

# PART II

# THE VAN VRANKEN FAMILY

CHAPTER V:
   The History Of My Van Vranken Family............................................ 191

     A.  My Van Vranken Family History............................................. 192

         1-  Introduction ........................................................................ 192
         2-  The Van Vranken Family Chronology ............................... 193

     B.  The History of the Town of Half Moon, Saratoga
         County, New York .................................................................. 198

         1-  Early Settlement ................................................................. 198
         2-  Enslavement in Half Moon ............................................... 200
         3-  The Enslaved Labor Force ................................................ 200

     C.  Historical Premise For Placing My Van Vranken
         Family In Half Moon.............................................................. 206
     D.  My Van Vrankens Families' Arrival In Washington County ........ 211
     E.  My Van Vranken Family Settlement ....................................... 211

CHAPTER VI:
   The Van Vranken Family Genealogy ....................................221

   A.  Genealogy Of My Van Vranken Ancestors .............................222

       1-  My Van Vranken Descendant's Family Tree .......................243
       2-  List Of African Descendant Van Vrankens
           In Upstate New York ...........................................247

CHAPTER VII:
   The Van Vranken Burials In Washington County, NY ......................251

       1-  Historical Background .........................................252
       2-  Non-Traditional Landscapes ...................................253
       3-  The Burial Grounds Project ....................................253
       4-  Evergreen Cemetery ............................................256
       5-  Old Revolutionary War Cemetery Salem, New York ...............271
       6-  Washington County Poorhouse Cemetery ..........................275

## APPENDIX

APPENDIX A:
   Act Of Attainder October 1779 ........................................281

## BIBLIOGRAPHY

BIBLIOGRAPHY ............................................................299
INDEX ...................................................................309

# LIST OF CHARTS AND TABLES

CHARTS                                                                    PAGE

1- Population Washington County, 1790-1810 ................................... 42
2- Total "Free" And Enslaved African Descendants
   In Washington County, NY 1790-1820 .................................. 49
3- African Descendant Families In Washington
   County, N.Y. 1800-1820 ............................................. 52
4- Increases And Decreases In Free And Enslaved
   African Descendants In New York State, 1800-1810 ................... 58
5- Free And Enslaved African Descendants
   In New York State And New England 1800-1810 ....................... 62
6- Enslaved And Free African Descendants
   In New York State 1790-1820 ....................................... 66
7- Forfeiture Landowners With Persons Of African Descent 1810 ........... 112
8- Total "Free" Persons Of African Descent
   In Washington County 1810 ......................................... 127
9- Free African Descendants With White Families
   In Washington County 1810 ......................................... 129
10- 1810-1814 Census Washington County, NY ............................... 143
11- 1810-1814 Census Free And Enslaved Of African
   Descent In Washington County, NY .................................. 145
12- African Descendant Landowners In Washington County 1825 ............. 150
13- Afican Descendants With Van Vrankens Families 1800-1820 ............. 209
14- African Descendant Van Vrankens In Washington
   County 1820-1865 .................................................. 215
15- List Of African Descendant Van Vrankens In Upstate New York ......... 247

TABLES                                                                    PAGE

1- Phillipse Inventory ................................................... 82
2- Salem Town Minutes ................................................... 90
3- Washington County Manufacturing Table 1810 ......................... 116
4- 1790 Van Vranken Enslavement Record,
   Half Moon, Saratoga County, New York .............................. 203

# LIST OF MAPS AND PHOTOS

MAPS                                                                PAGE

1- 1683 Washington County, NY Map .......................................................... 35
2- 1772 New York State Map ................................................................. 36
3- 1786 Washington County, NY Map .......................................................... 37
4- 1800-1810 New York State Map .......................................................... 38
5- Present Day Washington County, NY ....................................................... 39
6- Map Of Evergreen Cemetery Salem, NY ................................................... 255
7- Section P African Grounds ................................................................. 259
8- Evergreen Cemetery, Salem, NY African Grounds, Section P ........... 261

PHOTOS                                                              PAGE

1- Original Condition Of African Grounds At Evergreen
   Cemetery Salem, NY .................................................................... 262
2- Refurbished Condition Of African Grounds, Section P
   At Evergreen Cemetery Salem, NY ..................................................... 264
3- New Freeman Gravesites With Headstones And Walkway ...................... 266
4- Betsey Freeman And Susan Robertson Freeman
   Headstones Evergreen Cemetery ....................................................... 267
5- New Van Vranken/Burk Gravesite And Walkway African Grounds ......... 268
6- Old Revolutionary War Cemetery Salem, New York ............................ 271
7- Sally Van Vranken And Mary Matilda Burk Gravesites Old
   Revolutionary War Cemetery Salem, New York ................................. 273

Note: Front Cover Photo has been cropped and graphics added.

# DEDICATION

*"If she were of Royal birth—She'd be the Queen."*

**—L. Lloyd Stewart**

For all of my life, she was the rock, the sage, the undisputed matriarch and the fountain of love and righteousness in my Life. When I was a child, she was the only real friend that I had. I would go to her house each day after school; to be taught and inspired. It was "at her feet" that I learned to dream and express my inner most feelings.

She helped me to find my Voice through hundreds of conversations with her. We became engrossed in conversation on my wants, wishes and dreams of my future life desires at a time when most elementary school children were engaged in conversations with adults on more mundane subjects like: How was school today? Or what are you going to do this weekend? She was able to guide me as we delved deeper into my evolving thought processes and thereby allowed me to think and respond to much more substantive subjects like: the development of my belief in God, our Family history and my future aspirations.

Granted these kinds of topics weren't responded to by me with a high degree of analytical or decidedly insightful observations but they began to establish the ground work for my later thoughts on life and my potential place within it!

I still remember those days; at times, as if they were yesterday. Not as simple moments in time but as the "Birth of my Soul." I remember how—when my sister, Judy and I used to run away from home—we ran to Mamoo's. She would warm us and dry our tears. She would console us and make the world a beautiful and wondrous place again. She would even call our mother down (we lived three blocks away) and scold her for upsetting her Babies.

She caused me to open a very closed and anger-dominated perspective on life! I will never be able to fully express my gratitude to her but I've always felt and still feel very special because of her Love and attention! She allowed me and encouraged me to see the whole world and to think to the Future. I will **always** remember those times, for without them and without her, my life would not have amounted to much.

This work is a continuing byproduct of genealogical research that I first began in the year 2000 as a special gift to Mamoo. As a result of oral family history, she was subconsciously aware of our long family history in New York State, and yet her actual conscious memory of our past was limited to just three generations. At the time of these very intimate, inspiring and enlightening conversations with her, she was a vibrant and spirited 93 years old.

I was able to present her a written labor of love, a preliminary copy of our family history, on Christmas 2001. She, unfortunately for all her family members and the community at large passed on November 1, 2002 at the age of 95.

I DEDICATE this work to my Grandmother, Anabel Puels: "Mamoo."

# FOREWORD

Americans seem to be living in an upside-down world in which myth and dream become reality and reality becomes a dream. They believe that a group of wise and holy men came down from Olympus and wrote a constitution which established the first great democratic government in the world, under an unprecedented written constitution. The reality, however, is that the organization of the political state which was put in place after the liberation of the colonies from British rule was a coalition government of two major factions. On the one hand was the slave political economy faction, primarily centered in the southern states, in which the African American was the private property of the land-owning slave master. Some of the savants who wrote the constitution were themselves major slave owners. Included among the chief architects of the new state were such outstanding men as the first and third presidents of the republic.

On the other hand the coalition government included a group of independent white landowners, traders, merchants, manufacturers who operated under a system of incipient capitalism in the northern states, with slavery playing a secondary, but important role.

African American slavery, which was in place since the beginning of the colonial era, was sanctioned by the great constitution once the republic was established. It continued for another eight decades until it was outlawed as a result of one of the bloodiest wars in American history. In the sequel, a system of Jim Crow second class citizenship, sanctioned by the great constitution, was put into place and functioned quite well for another century. By the middle of the 20th century African Americans became *bona fide* wage laborers, with attendant civil rights and the right to vote, but in practice relegated to the zero and lowest end of the wage distribution in most capitalist business firms and government employment. As a consequence their zero and low wages could only afford them the minimum goods and services required for their reproduction. Hence, poverty and economic deprivation are a major condition of their existence today . . . . still sanctioned by the great constitution.

Shortly after the formation of the republic many of the northern states began a process of gradual emancipation of their slaves. It was a process in which slave owners were treated with compassion by getting compensated for their "loss" of property; at the same time the complete freeing of the slaves was scheduled over a long period of time in which the former slave was subjected to a series of stringent restrictions which impeded the full exercise of freedom.

In most cases the very semblance of freedom set the freed people into migratory motion to pursue whatever better opportunities they believed to exist. A major segment of the freed slaves following on the end of the civil war was impounded into a system of sharecropping agriculture in the southern states. The rest immediately began a migration into the cities of the south. During World War I, the urban migration took a northern direction. When this movement ended in the middle of the 20th century, approximately one half of the African Americans had abandoned the southern cradle of their slave beginnings and settled in the large urban centers of the northern states.

This "great migration" of African Americans was presaged by the northern slaves who experienced gradual emancipation after the War of Liberation from Great Britain. Washington County in upstate New York exhibited in microcosm the great migration. Almost 3,000 freedmen moved into the county from other areas of New York State or from outside of New York State from 1800 to 1810. By 1820 they had disappeared from the census count of Washington County. From whence did they come, and why did they come in such great numbers over such a short period of time, why and where did they go in such an equally short period of time. These are questions posed in the present work.

A good understanding of these pioneering African Americans in an obscure county of one of the most important states in the union is made to be more grounded in reality when one heroic family among them is singled out for detailed analysis. The Van Vrankens come out of historical obscurity to provide a specific real life example of a people in their struggle for freedom and human dignity over the centuries of a living hell.

The historical research of the study sets the gold standard for works of this nature. The author scoured every conceivable record to uncover the facts of the case. More important is the skillful use of these sources to arrive at the conclusions of the study.

—LLOYD HOGAN, ECONOMIST

AUTHOR: *PRINCIPLES OF BLACK POLITICAL ECONOMY*

# PREFACE

Each year during Kwanzaa, I usually prepare a document or series of documents on our Family for my siblings, my children and grandchildren. I cannot continue to allow the missing history of our Family to exist as a series of shadowy images and figures or as some type of knowledge black hole or void that continues to impact our future existence as a whole and fully actualized family; replete with stories, legends and (he/she)roes. As I mentioned earlier, my Grandmother had a recollection of three generations of our Family's history. In actuality, our family (on my Grandmother's side) has resided, flourished and sustained itself in New York State for eleven (11) generations, as of this writing.

This family history begins in 1810 with church records from Cambridge, Washington County, New York and "officially" with census recordings of Francis Van Vranken (Van Woak) in 1820 in Jackson, Washington County, New York and his brother Johannes Van Vranken (Van Vrank) in the New York State Census of 1825 for Salem, Washington County, New York. These early family ancestors existed in New York State under conditions and circumstances that were purposely designed to limit and impede their growth and development as human beings and as a family unit. We have also been fortunate enough to establish the fact by way of DNA testing my Grandmother's family has its ancestral African origin within the Tikar People of Cameroon, West Africa.[1]

Somewhere out there in the ancient historical memory of time and space is the universal and physical evidence that links these two separated peoples hereditarily, culturally and spiritually over the vast and solemn journey of the infamous Middle Passage; and, the holocaust of enslavement and racial discrimination under which they suffered in this "new" world. It is indeed my intention to unearth those as yet "unforgotten" links and share, celebrate and proclaim them to my siblings, children and grandchildren. Until such time as

I am able to alleviate these feelings of futility and frustration that I feel, I will diligently endeavor to search for the remnants of my Families' "Black Box".

I was fortunate enough to be able to synthesize a portion of our family history into a larger expose' on enslavement and gradual abolition in New York State in a book entitled "A Far Cry From Freedom: Gradual Abolition (1799-1827) New York State's Crime Against Humanity," which was published in January of 2006. As I began the research on that book in 2001, it became eminently clear to me that my family's history in New York State was indeed extensive and that it required and deserved a more focused detailing and scholarly accounting. It was also evident that our family had unfortunately experienced a substantial portion of the chaotic and dehumanizing history of people of African descent in New York State during its first two centuries of existence.

It was during this initial research period that I was able to trace my ancestors back to the middle 1700s in New York State, and thus began the attempt to identify members of our family to the present day.

What **is** indisputable is that my family's history spans an extremely significant 200 year period of African American history in New York State. It encompasses the state's history of inhuman practices during the African "slave trade" and the resulting dehumanization and degradation of human enslavement; a protracted period of pre-emancipation in New York State called Gradual Abolition which resulted in the forced separation and bondage of African descendant children, which conceivably represents the beginnings of New York State's public policy initiative with respect to the institution of the foster care system; the final abolition of enslavement; and lastly, a period encompassing the disenfranchisement of "free" citizens of African descent and the implementation in New York State of a systemic code of discrimination and segregation often referred to in the southern states of America as "Jim Crow."

## REFERENCE NOTES

[1] The Tikar had a large population, sophistication in war, government, industry and the arts. The old Tikar dynasties dominated Central and West Africa for at least three centuries before they decline in the nineteenth century. We estimate that there were more than one million Tikar people. Today there are less than 100,000 in the French-speaking zone and 300,000 in the English speaking zone (Banso). They obviously met the criteria for "good slaves." They were attractive, learned quickly and had a tradition of slavery within their own society. The Tikar people attempted to abandon their traditional grassy savannahs and the plains, where they were easy slave trade targets with no natural protection. They were forced to leave their villages, with slave traders on the one side and four hostile tribes on the other side, seeking revenge.

One of the strategies they applied to fight off the enemy was to dig moats around villages; these still exist in at least five kingdoms. However this strategy failed and the survivors found refuge in the forest. The slave-trade during this period drained their brightest and most physically fit young people.

Having been weakened by war and the slave trade, they became vulnerable to neighboring tribes who had been ruled by the Tikar for several centuries. While much more could be known about the Tikar, very little scholarship has been invested in recounting their history; other than the fact that their ceramic techniques, architecture and iron smelting kilns were very advanced.

# Acknowledgements

**The author would especially like to give praise and thanksgiving to the Father/Mother God, THE ALL, for the blessings and love provided in pursuing this work. In addition, I'd like to also thank my Ancestors, known and unknown, without whose inspiration, instruction and sacrifices this work would not have been accomplished.**

Special thanks are given to the following individuals for their support and assistance in finalizing this work: To Economist Lloyd Hogan for his unwavering support, inspiration, direction, counsel and love but most importantly for his insightful and astute FOREWARD to this book. To Dr. Edward Cupoli, Professor and Head of NanoEconomics at the College of Nanoscale Science and Engineering at The University of Albany, SUNY, who provided much needed consultation with respect to the economic principles surrounding the state of the economy in Washington County, New York during the early 19th century. To Marcus Brown and the staff at the New York State Archives for their assistance in locating, acquiring and replicating important documents and records embedded with in this work, that were housed within the New York State Archives. Special thanks to my "Sister", Doris Bedell, whose professional editing skills and exceptional overall knowledge allowed me to transcend the last major hurdle to the completion of this work.

Special appreciation to Kenneth Perry, a very dedicated and prolific researcher and author of the history of Washington County and upstate New York, for his continued support and encouragement, and especially for his assistance and counsel in developing the storyline surrounding this work. Also special appreciation is given to Salem, New York Historian Al Cormier and Bancroft Library (Salem) Archivist, Peg Culver for their outstanding work and dedication with respect to the Evergreen Cemetery—African Grounds

Burial Project. Special recognition is also given to Washington County Archivist Dennis Lowery and County Historian Loretta Bates and her staff. Additionally, recognition is given to former Washington County Historian Joseph A. Cutshall-King, who was tremendously helpful with our research into the population of persons of African descent in early Washington County. Special appreciation and gratitude is given to Robert Arnold, a former historian, with the New York State Archives for his support and counsel; and finally to the Washington County Historical Society.

Most importantly, I'd like to acknowledge and thank my parents, Louis, Elizabeth and my Grandmother, Anabel Puels (Mamoo) who blessed me with unconditional love and encouragement and who graciously and lovingly allowed me to be my own person.

Ultimate Appreciation and love to my wife, Mitzi Glenn Stewart, for her unconditional love and her willingness at ALL times and hours of the day or night to discuss, argue, proof and edit this work from its very beginning and for her Cover concept. Special Appreciation is especially given to my children: Yusuf Ali, Malaika Amira, Tahirah Abeni, Rahsaan Alif-Iman, Jelani Isaiah (Facebook Page Design) and Jamal-Rami Anane (Designer of my Book's Cover), who have been extremely supportive of this work and for their financial investment in their Father's dream. Additional appreciation is given to my Brothers: Timothy Alan, Arthur-David and my Sister: Rachelle V. for their love and continued support and guidance; and to my ascended Sister and Brothers: Judith-Ann, Gary Edward and Steven Douglas, on the first anniversary of his transition. And, last but certainly not least, all of my Love to my soon-to-be 15 Grandchildren—the indisputable loves of my Life.

Finally, I'd like to acknowledge the numerous local historians and their staffs, who were willing to and instrumental in providing direction and access to local, county and state documents and records that helped address and authenticate the foundation and substance of this work within their respective counties, cities and towns.

# INTRODUCTION

## BACKGROUND

If asked about its past, most Americans could tell you that New York State was recognized as one of the leading colonies within our fledgling Nation, and that from its inception New York City has been the financial capital of America. They may even know that New York's economy had been sustained by the huge Port of New York, the Hudson River and the Erie Canal. Or that New York State had spawned the Empire State Building, at one time the tallest building in the world. They could tell you of the Twin Towers (The World Trade Center) and how they once dominated the skyline of lower Manhattan. But most significantly, they would solemnly inform you that it was the scene of the most horrific act of terrorism in our Nation's history and, of the fate of some 3,000 individuals who perished during that dark day in September 2001.

Little is known however, of New York State's long and shadowy history of enslavement and delayed abolition; nor of its sustained confusion of allegiance with respect to its historic relationship with people of African descent.

Unfortunately, this long hidden and often perplexing history has caused citizens of African descent to be marginalized in New York's rich and impressive history of accomplishments and achievements. This marginalization has resulted in the omission of countless phases, accomplishments and events of African descendant history including but not limited to: a major migration of thousands of citizens of African descent to Washington County in upstate New York at the turn of the 19th century.

The unrecorded story of people of African descent in New York history—and American history for that matter—compels us to pursue "courageous questioning" as a means of restructuring the true representation of this history. The where, when, how and why of people of African descent has suffered unprecedented misrepresentations, distortions and in some instances its literal corruption. This history has been often purposefully maligned and willfully ignored by the mainstream community of American historians, who comprise the memberships of the established academic departments and historical societies of this country. As a young student in American institutions of higher learning, I remember describing myself as *not* a historian or student of American history but more as a "*MYSTORIAN*": One who studies, researches, reconstructs and focuses on the—Mystery of My History!

The story that unfolds in this work is the manifestation of this pursuit of one of these historical mysteries that have plagued the true history of people of African descent in New York State. The impact of this disregarded history and its absence from the historical record of time has indelibly distorted the recollection and remembrance of a large segment of people of African descent who were trapped in the confinement of enslavement and discrimination in New York State during the turn of the 19th century. This period (1800-1820) represents a significant moment in both the history of New York State and in the existence of a community of people of African descent born, raised and toiling in the most extreme conditions of survival—*conditions not of their own making!*

As the State of New York began to alter its highly profitable economic system from an enslavement-based economy to a more capitalistic system of production based primarily on the exploitation of "free" labor; countless numbers of people of African descent within this paradigm struggled to find a means of navigating this economic transition with the clear goal of economic viability and sustainability.

# THE MIGRATION

They transported their families great distances for this period in history. They gathered their belongings and journeyed to whatever part of the State offered or even hinted at an opportunity for personal and/or economic enhancement. Newly disposed of the day to day oppression and brutality of enslavement, they struggled to find a more sustainable, prosperous and humane way to live.

They worked foreign fields in foreign towns, labored tirelessly on small farms and large plantations, sweat-shopped in fledgling factories and worked endlessly on canal sites and in road beds. Whatever the opportunity, up and down the State of New York, they did whatever was necessary to sustain themselves and their families with the dream of achieving and experiencing a better life. Their guiding purpose was not in searching for handouts or charity but to improve their opportunity for a future that would allow them to truly manifest the newly found "freedom" of which they now found themselves a part. They sought a life that would present them with the advantages that they were intimately aware of and desirous of—as "free" people.

They also sought the prospect of securing the upward mobility and social recognition that would provide them with the benefits associated with true citizenship. They didn't at this point in their journey desire to be treated as equals but, more importantly, as human beings—not property!

The quest for equality and full citizenship would come later. They would by example of their perseverance and dignity, first establish themselves as truly worthy. Given their previous circumstances and restrictive and suffocating living and working conditions, this new journey through life was not so unfamiliar; point of exception being the almost amorphous reality that they were pursuing it as "free" men and women.

They were attempting to provide as nurturing an environment as possible in which to raise their children, while at the same time attempting to promote and establish a "normal" existence that could sustain them beyond the restrictions and encumbrances of "second-class" citizenship. It should be made clear that the persons that we will be discussing in this work were in fact and in law "free" citizens of the State of New York during a period when New York State was still inextricably immersed in the institution of human enslavement. It wouldn't be until 1827 that the State of New York would legally abolish the enslavement of its people of African descent.

My own family's story is a manifestation of this "peculiar" period in New York State history and it is embedded within this corrupted matrix of human enslavement. This history becomes even more mysterious and compelling to those of us who hunger and search for the true representations of the accomplishments, struggles and survival of people of African descent in New York State and in America.

As a preview, this story of a community of people of African descent takes place in Washington County in upstate New York during the period of 1800 to 1820. A period in history, marked by the fact that New York State was still caught in the throes of human enslavement; and the dehumanizing and sordid practices of racial discrimination and inequity. A period that was markedly different from its preceding centuries. A period energized by an upheaval in the mechanics of production, the scales of economy, and the lifestyles and livelihood options of thousands of individuals of African descent attempting to evolve and make real this new concept and condition of Freedom.

Washington County, formerly Charlotte County, sits on the northeastern boundary of New York State and the states of Vermont, Massachusetts, New Hampshire and Maine. In fact, when it was established originally as Charlotte County, it included all or a portion of these not yet constituted states.

Washington County was a large county in geographical size during this period. It encompassed numerous evolving and constantly re-organizing towns and villages. Washington County would not impress the casual observer or even the inquisitive historian as a likely locale for a major event in African American history in New York State. This event, occurring during the early 1800s, highlights the migration of literally thousands of people of African descent who arrived at the borders of Washington County. As with most areas of upstate New York, Washington County's major claim to fame and its primary contribution to the economy of the state was agricultural production with a later development of sheep farming for wool production and home-textile manufacturing. Its reliance on farming and localized textile manufacturing would seem to represent the only serious attraction for a migration of *any* people to this remote area of the state.

Remaining within the traditional principles of journalism and reporting, the "*Who*" of our story to be explored is represented by a dynamic and statistically impressive migration of "free" people of African descent to Washington County during the turn of the 19th century. According to the Federal Census of 1800, Washington County registered a total population of 35,574 residents; of this number, the "Free Colored" population totaled one hundred and forty-four residents and its enslaved population totaled some eighty persons. These modest numbers would further reinforce the small farming community nature of this area. And yet, by 1810 with the total population of Washington County increasing to 44,289 residents; the number of the "Free Colored" population had dramatically and inexplicably increased to two thousand eight hundred and fifteen (2,815) "free colored" residents and its enslaved population had increased to three hundred and fifteen (315) persons. This unexplained increase in the "free colored" population in 1810 over a ten year period represented an incredible two thousand two hundred and sixty-five percent (2265%) increase over the 1800 census figure. Additionally, the enslaved population had also increased by some two hundred and ninety-three percent (293%) during this same period.

The fact is this population surge for Washington County in 1810 represents a significant increase under any circumstances. It is imperative to note and even more astonishing to report that this statistical increase in the "free" population of African descent took place at a time when the State of New York and Washington County respectively, were still fully engaged in their long history of the inhuman practices and policies of human enslavement.

The major initiator of this increase in the "free" population of persons of African descent in New York State can best be attributed to the passage of the State's Gradual Abolition Act. Its enactment in 1799, allowed New York State enslavers the option and authority to manumit (free) certain enslaved men and women, who they considered to be self-reliant and in no need of local government maintenance or financial support. The Law stipulated that:

> "... it shall be lawful for the owner of any slave immediately after the passing of this act to manumit such slave by a certificate for that purpose under his own hand and seal."

It is not surprising that the "*WHAT*" of this work becomes the most vexing and intriguing component. Within the story that follows, we will attempt to ascertain, "What" caused over two and one half thousand "free" African descendents to migrate 'en masse' to the "outlying" rural communities of Washington County in upstate New York?

What major transformative event or series of events caused "free" people of African descent to pack up their families and belongings and venture out to these relatively anonymous towns and villages of Washington County during a period in New York State history when enslavement was still actively enforced and vibrantly practiced? Was there some major yet undocumented, "free land" lottery as evidenced in the Oklahoma Land Rush? Or was there a major hiring initiative created in the county? What was the cause of this unprecedented exodus and migration to this rural and remote region of New York State?

The "*WHEN*" also presents a curious paradox within the context of this work. As mentioned earlier, even though New York State was still heavily involved in the institution of human enslavement during this period, the rumblings of "abolition" were beginning to sound. Several northern states had already begun the process of abolishing enslavement either through the courts or by way of modified (gradual) abolition, through their state legislative bodies. As stated earlier, in 1799 the State of New York had enacted its own Gradual Abolition Law after several unsuccessful attempts.

Although this Gradual Abolition Law did not abolish enslavement completely, it was viewed by abolitionists of the period as "movement" in the right direction. The fact remains however, that this law did not immediately emancipate anyone already bound by the dehumanizing practices of enslavement, nor did it immediately "free" the newborn children of enslaved mothers for whom the law was initially written. Instead, it created a "newly" legalized and state sponsored institution of human bondage—"statutory enslavement," that essentially indentured newborn children of African descent to bondage with the enslaver of their mother for 25 years if a female and 28 years if a male child.

The law did, however, allow for the manumission (freedom) of persons of African descent already in bondage, if they could demonstrate that their new found freedom would not cause any financial or other burdens on local authorities. The role that the Gradual Abolition Act may or may not have played in the development of this story will be discussed in greater detail later in this work.

The *"WHERE"* has already been answered in the Introduction—Washington County. One aspect of the "Where" that remains to be explained and explored is; *WHERE DID THESE "FREE" PEOPLE OF AFRICAN DESCENT COME FROM?* Over a ten year period, some twenty-seven hundred (2,700) persons left their existing places of residence to travel unrecorded distances to a region of upstate New York known for neither its high degree of economic opportunity nor for its remarkable hospitality to people of African descent.

The enslavement of people of African descent during this period was still very much a part of the economic and social life of the families and communities of Washington County. In fact, during this full-scale migration of "free" people of African descent, Washington County's enslaved population grew almost 300%. Therefore, the question remains; Where in fact did they come from—upstate, downstate, points east, like Vermont or New England? (There was in fact a major migration of New Englanders to upstate New York during and proceeding this period.) Or did they venture thousands of miles from the enslaved states of the south by way of the Underground Railroad or through their own individual initiatives and/or devices?

Finally, we will explore *"WHY,"* these "free" persons and families of African descent actually migrated to Washington County. At the conclusion of Part 1 of this work, I have included an example of a family that was intimately involved in this migration and actually the reason why I have undertaken this effort in the first instance—The Van Vrankens—*MY FAMILY*! They will serve as a mirror for the reader to visualize the personal and first-hand experience of these families of African descent in Washington County during the early part of the 19th century. As they strived and struggled to make sense of their new station in life—*FREEDOM*!

The Van Vrankens will serve as a baseline for the other 2,700 individuals and families that embarked on and joined in this arduous, complex and life-altering journey. Explicit in this recounting of my families' personal history, the reader will begin to bond with the realities and difficulties implicit in attempting to reconstruct a history that received very little attention and less documentation. My intention is to allow my Van Vranken family to illustrate and highlight the frustrations and accomplishments and the failures and successes that occur when one attempts to chronicle the history of people of African descent in New York State. Such issues, as origination and past enslavement, identities and names, family sizes and relationships, stories and personal accounts and the lack of cogent documentation. It has caused such research to further disguise and distort the contributions and accomplishments made by these unique and heroic people in the development and economic progress of New York State. Elements of this history of New York and Washington County are thus specifically outlined and emphasized by the history of the Van Vranken family, as they are well positioned to represent the experiences of the thousands of individuals of African descent who initiated this now "*RECORDED*" Migration at the turn of the 19th century.

*So, Let Us Begin The Exploration Of This Truly Unique And Mysterious Story Of These Individuals Of African Descent In New York State.*

*Ashe'*

# PART I

## WASHINGTON COUNTY, NY AND THE MIGRATION

# CHAPTER I

## HISTORY OF WASHINGTON (CHARLOTTE) COUNTY, NEW YORK

# HISTORY OF CHARLOTTE/WASHINGTON COUNTY

**When counties were established in New York State in 1683 (See Map 1), the present-day Washington County was part of Albany County. This was an enormous county, including the northern part of New York State as well as all of the present State of Vermont and, in theory, extending westward to the Pacific Ocean. On March 12.1772, the Legislature of New York split Albany County into three parts, one remaining under the name Albany County; the other two were called Tryon County (later renamed Montgomery County) and Charlotte County (later named Washington County). (See Map 2)**

## OVERVIEW

Charlotte County was named in honor of Queen Charlotte, wife of King George III of England in the 18th century. Charlotte County contained all of the present-day State of Vermont west of the Green Mountains and north of the northwest corner of the Town of Jackson, all of the present counties of Warren, Essex, Clinton and the eastern part of Franklin. This was the actual beginning of the County of Washington; the organization having been retained from that time forward, though both name and boundaries have been changed.

> *"On the east of the Hudson, the south line of the new county began at the mouth of Stony creek; ran thence east three miles and three-sixteenths; thence south to the Batten Kill; thence along that stream to the south line of Princetown; and thence east to the west line of Cumberland county, which was the summit of the Green mountains. From this point to Canada those mountains formed the eastern boundary of Charlotte county. From the mouth of Stony creek, the western and southwestern line followed the windings of the Hudson up to the northwest corner of the present town of Luzerne, in Warren county, ran thence west along the present north line of Saratoga county to its northwestern corner, and thence northwardly along the present west line of Warren county extended to Canada. The north line of Charlotte was of course the south line of Canada, or the forty-fifth parallel of north latitude."[2]*

The present towns of Easton, Cambridge, Jackson, White Creek, and the southwest part of Greenwich, remained in Albany County. Charlotte County and that part of Albany County now included in Washington County were principally settled by New Englanders, Scotch, and others of foreign birth. The former had almost all adhered to the precepts of the American cause, prior and during the

American Revolution, which many (though by no means all) of the latter were friendly to the king. Since the Americans were most of the time in possession of the territory in question, the New Englanders were largely in the majority among the dominant class.

## CHARLOTTE COUNTY BECOMES WASHINGTON COUNTY

*"The long and deadly struggle of the Revolution, with its accompaniments of invasion, house-burning, and Indian outrage, had naturally developed a very bitter feeling among the people, especially on the frontiers, against everything of English name or origin. Even the name of Queen Charlotte was not agreeable to the inhabitants of Charlotte county, whose farms had been devastated by the troops of Queen Charlotte's husband."[3]*

Accordingly, on the second day of April, 1784, the New York Legislature passed an act changing the name of Charlotte County. It was a model of brevity and precision, and the enacting clause, read as follows:

*'From and after the passage of this act the county of Tryon shall be known by the Name of Montgomery, and the county of Charlotte by the name of Washington."[4]*

The Legislature changed the name of Charlotte County to Washington not only due to its reference to the Queen, but probably more politically due to the bad feelings the "new" country had for England. (The present towns of Easton, Cambridge, Jackson, White Creek, and the southwest part of Greenwich still remained as part of Albany County.) Over the next few decades, townships formed and other counties broke off, thus leaving the County of Washington with the seventeen towns as we know them today.

# MAPS OF WASHINGTON COUNTY

# MAP OF NEW YORK STATE

## (When Counties were established in 1683)[5]

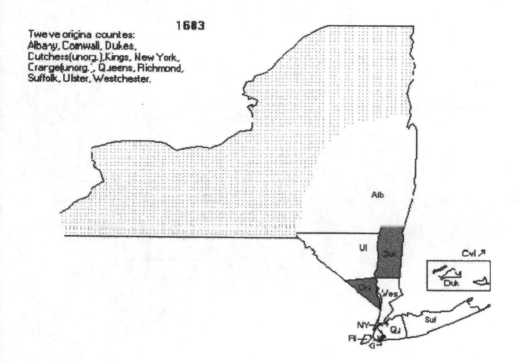

1683

Twelve original counties:
Albany, Cornwall, Dukes,
Dutchess(unorg.),Kings, New York,
Orange(unorg.), Queens, Richmond,
Suffolk, Ulster, Westchester.

Alb

Ul    Dut

Cwl

Duk

Ora   Wes

NY    Que    Suf

Ri    Kis

# MAP OF NEW YORK STATE
## WASHINGTON COUNTY BOUNDARY MAP
### 1772

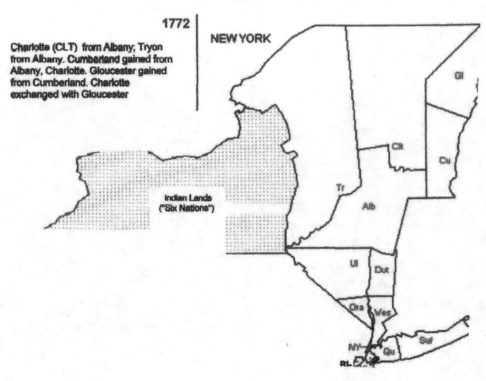

**1772**

Charlotte (CLT) from Albany; Tryon
from Albany. Cumberland gained from
Albany, Charlotte. Gloucester gained
from Cumberland. Charlotte
exchanged with Gloucester

NEW YORK

Gl

Clt

Cu

Tr

Alb

Indian Lands
("Six Nations")

Ul

Dut

Ora

Wes

Suf

NY

Qu

RL

# Washington County Boundary Map - 1786

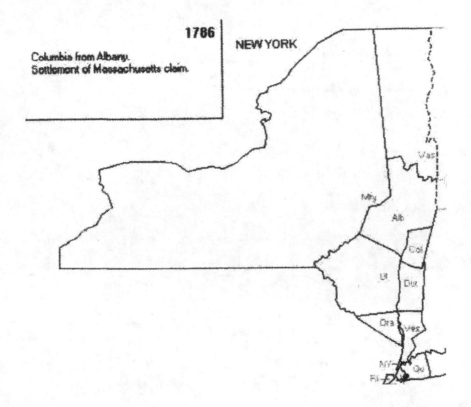

**1786**

NEW YORK

Columbia from Albany.
Settlement of Massachusetts claim.

# MAP OF NEW YORK STATE
## WASHINGTON COUNTY BOUNDARY MAP
### 1800-1810

**1800**

Greene from Ulster, Albany.
Rockland gained from Orange.

**1810**

Jefferson gained from Lewis

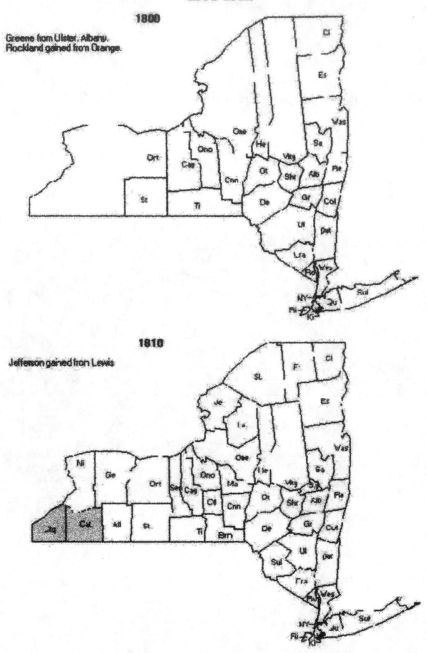

# PRESENT DAY
# WASHINGTON COUNTY

*Towns of Washington County*

Arqyle, Cambridge, Dresden, Easton, Fort Ann, Fort Edward, Granville, Greenwich, Hampton, Hartford, Hebron, Jackson, Kingsbury, Putnam, Salem, White Creek, and Whitehall

*Villages of Washington County*

Argyle, Cambridge, Fort Ann, Fort Edward, Granville, Greenwich, Hudson Falls, Salem, and Whitehall

## EARLY GENERAL HISTORY

## SETTLEMENT

In its earliest period, the area that is now Washington County was used for hunting by the Mohawks from the west and perhaps the Mohicans from the south, but it was largely uninhabited. By 1709, during the Queen Anne's War, the British built three fortifications in the area of Fort Saratoga at Easton, Fort Nicholson, and Fort Anne (now Fort Ann). The first European settler in what was to be Washington County was Col. John Henry Lydius, who built a house and a fur-trading post (ca.1730) near the ruins of Fort Nicholson to support his land claim. His settlement was later attacked and burned by the French in 1745.[6]

The French and Indian War was the defining event of the colonial period. In 1775, the British rebuilt Fort Anne and Fort Nicholson. The latter, was renamed Fort Edward, and proved to be the most important of the War's fortifications.

After the French and Indian War, some veterans of the war received land as bounties and with the end of hostilities in 1760, became permanent settlers of the area. The first important settlement in what was to become Washington County was Skenesborough (now Whitehall), founded by Major Phillip Skene in 1759.

Before the year 1783, there were few settlements in this region. Scots and Scots-Irish settled Argyle and New Perth (now Salem); German Moravians settled the Camden Valley; and those of Dutch descent settled in Easton. English immigrants and New England migrants settled throughout the county. By 1770, initial settlement had been made except in the northwestern towns of Dresden, Putnam and the interior Town of Hartford, all of which were occupied immediately after the Revolution. By the Revolution, most of the native people were gone. The few who remained were intermarried with non-Native Americans.[7]

During the Revolutionary War, the expedition of General Burgoyne forced the inhabitants to flee, as he destroyed their buildings and fences, and plundered their cattle and their property. After that event, the number of planters greatly increased, and they greatly advanced in prosperity and wealth. Settlement was rapid after the Revolution, with many soldiers returning with their families to take advantage of the rich land, abundant game and waterways they had observed during their military service. These settlers were mainly of English and Scottish descent who had first established themselves in the New England colonies. At this time there were thirty-five thousand inhabitants in Washington County, of which probably twenty-five thousand, or half the present number, were in the territory that is now Washington County, and the rest in present-day Warren County. The increase had been largely in the villages, which were then very few and very small. The farming population was probably two-thirds or three-fourths as large then as it is today. The amount of land cleared for settlement and farming was, however, very much less than now.[8]

Except in the villages, almost all the houses and barns were of logs. The inhabitants were predominately of Scotch and New England blood, with a few Hudson River Dutch intermingled. The raising of grain—wheat, oats, and rye—was the principal industry of the farmers, though considerable attention was also paid to the rearing of cattle. Sheep were raised so that wives and daughters could make the flannel and the "fulled-cloth" necessary for their own family.[9]

## POPULATION

In 1790, the County of Washington contained nine townships and 14,042 inhabitants; in 1800, sixteen townships and 35,574 inhabitants; and by 1810 twenty-one townships and 44,289 inhabitants resided there. Washington County's population increased steadily in the first half of the 19th century, peaking in 1870 at 49,568.[10]

| POPULATION OF WASHINGTON COUNTY TOWNSHIPS[11] | | | | | | | | |
|---|---|---|---|---|---|---|---|---|
| FOR SELECTED YEARS | | | | | | | | |
| | | | | | | | | |
| | | | | YEARS | | | | |
| TOWNSHIPS | | | 1790 | | 1800 | | 1810 | |
| | | | | | | | | |
| ARGYLE* | | | 2,341 | | 4,695 | | 3,813 | |
| EASTON | | | | | 3,069 | | 3,253 | |
| GREENWICH | | | | | 7,764 | | 9,818 | |
| CAMBRIDGE | | | 4,996 | | 6,187 | | 6.73 | |
| HAMPTON | | | 463 | | 700 | | 820 | |
| GRANVILLE | | | 2,240 | | 3,175 | | 3,717 | |
| WESTFIELD | | | 2,103 | | 2,502 | | 3,110 | |
| KINGSBURY | | | 1,120 | | 1,655 | | 2,272 | |
| FT. EDWARD | | | 4,228 | | 5,289 | | | |
| | | | | | | | | |
| | | | | | | | | |
| | | | | | | | | |
| *In 1790, Argyle included Greenwich and Easton. In 1800 Easton was separated and in 1810 | | | | | | | | |
| Greenwich was separated. | | | | | | | | |

# POPULATION OF AFRICAN DESCENT

# IN EARLY WASHINGTON COUNTY

The former Washington County historian Joseph A. Cutshall-King informs us that:

> *"One of the points I have made repeatedly, in my columns and elsewhere, is that there was an African population in this county from at least 1763, when Philip Skene brought thirty-three (33) slaves from Cuba to Skenesborough, now Whitehall, [Washington County]. Some of those people were freed and were living near Fort Ticonderoga at the outbreak of the Revolution. As the Revolution began to intensify here, Skene, who at first was in England, was then arrested upon return to America."[12]*

Cutshall-King continues;

> *"Skene's mills ended up being run almost wholly if not wholly by the blacks living in Skenesborough, the implication from the history I have read being that white Loyalists were not in enough number to help sustain the extensive holdings but that there were ample enough black people to do that."*

> *"Who were these people? Where did they live? The latter could be somewhat easily ascertained, and I think that the argument for their being nearer to Fort Ticonderoga than Whitehall is a substantial one, given that a freeman (of the [original] 33) lived on Lake Champlain by Six Miles Point. That's documented. It would seem that the iron manufactory and lumber mills under the direction of a man named Kane, in present day Fort Ann, would have been manned by these same black people. In other parts of the county, as you know, there were enslaved blacks. In short, between 1763 and 1777, when the area was finally engulfed in war, there was a population of an undetermined number"[13]*

The first and last statements of this Cutshall-King quote succinctly illustrates the most profoundly perplexing aspect of this work and our forthcoming adventure into the "Migration" of people of African descent to the County of Washington in the early 19th century. Where did they come from and how many actually migrated to Washington County? The latter portion of this mystery is addressed in great detail within this work. However, the question as to—Where these individuals of African descent came from is an aspect of this study that serves as the bedrock of the foundation of this work and haunts its focus throughout!

One example of African descendants in early Washington County is the story of Sylvia:

Dr. Asa Fitch reports that when Captain John Barnes and his Rangers went to Skenesboro (today's Whitehall) on May 9, 1775, to capture Tory Colonel Phillip Skene, Barnes returned to Salem with a young girl, 6 or 7 years old, named Sylvia, described as a "mulatto slave reputed to be the natural daughter of Col, Skene." When Colonel Barnes left Salem at the end of the Revolutionary War, he sold Sylvia to Major Thomas Armstrong who in turn sold her to Col. John McCleary.

Sylvia appears to have been Salem's first documented slave, and although no town records show that she was manumitted under the New York Manumission of Slaves Statute of 1785, Sylvia most certainly became free under the 1827 Emancipation Statute before she died in 1842. A *Salem Press* obituary of January of 1877 for Samuel Boston notes that his mother, Sylvia, was the wife of Quack Boston, and it "was believed that she was the daughter of Skene . . . a light colored mulatto woman—she may have been only a quadroon, and we think before slavery was done away with in this state, was owned by the late Col. John McCleary of this town."

Further proof of her place in Salem society is recorded by Fitch who states that she died in 1842 about age 75 and in 1861 was removed from the Old Burying Ground [*The Revolutionary War Cemetery]* and "reinterred in Evergreen Cemetery." Fitch goes on to note that "part of the inscription on her monument, which describes her story, reads as *follows.-" [Sylvia] **was noted as being intellectually superior to any of her race in the town, and won the kind regard and esteem of all who knew her.**"[14]

For some reason, Sylvia's name does not show up on Evergreen's African Grounds' burial list, and any other reference to her gravesite and gravestone, outside of Fitch's reference, is unknown.

# REFERENCE NOTES

[2]   Crisfield Johnson, History of Washington County, New York, Everts & Ensign: Philadelphia, 1878

[3]   IBID

[4]   IBID

**NOTE:** In 1788, Clinton County was split off from Washington County. This was a much larger area than the present Clinton County, including several other counties or county parts of the present-day New York State.

[5]   Anderson, Our County and its People, pg. 1; www.n2genealogy.com/newyork/ny-maps,html

[6]   Johnson

[7]   IBID

[8]   IBID

[9]   IBID

[10]  William Stone, "Washington County, New York, Its History to the Close of the 19th Century, 1904, pg. 300-314

[11]  IBID (Reformatted into a Chart.)

[12]  Joseph Cutshall-King e-mail to L. Lloyd Stewart, 6 May 2002

[13]  IBID

[14]  William Cormier, *Salem's Forgotten African Americans*, The Journal of the Washington County Historical Society, 2008, pg. 29-30

# CHAPTER II

## THE MIGRATION

# AFRICAN AMERICAN HISTORY IN WASHINGTON COUNTY, NEW YORK

It was here in Washington County that individuals and families of African descent chose to settle rather permanently after the passage of the Gradual Abolition Act in 1799. Although, we are unable to accurately document these individuals and families' participation directly in the Manumission Provisions of the Gradual Abolition Law, nevertheless it is evident that it did impact their status as "free" members of the Washington County community. It should be noted that in the early 1790s, the influence of the Dutch farmers in New York State began to decline both economically and politically. This shift in the economic and political landscape of New York State was essentially due to a relocation of its' chief agricultural center from the Dutch dominated southern regions of the state to upstate New York. The bulk of farm commodities were now sent to Manhattan for export from these upstate communities, like Washington County.

Washington County was settled by New Englanders, old opponents of enslavement. In 1796, a reapportionment of the New York State Legislature gave upstate New York greater political clout,[15] and resulted in a newly elected legislative body that was directly responsible for the passage in 1799 of the Gradual Abolition Act.

It should be noted that the opposition of New Englanders to enslavement was not based solely on the wholesale rejection of enslavement on purely moral grounds.

> *"New Englanders bought few slaves, in large measure because New Englanders did not have the capital to purchase them, in part because the land and the growing season did not return investments in chattel bondsmen and women."*[16]

We must be ever cognizant of the geopolitical reality of New York State's economy during this period. New York and the northern states were beginning to develop a more industrial economy in order to more successfully compete in the New World markets. A nascent manufacturing industry was developing there. While agriculture was still important in this era of New York, it was beginning to be exploited as capitalist farming to create commodities for sale, rather than for barter or other forms of exchange.

In Washington County, the population of residents of African descent, as documented in the various census reports for the period (1790-1820) allocates the "free" population of African descent as follows: 1790—three (3) "free" persons; 1800—one hundred and forty-four (144)[17] "free" persons; 1810—two thousand eight hundred and fifteen (2815) "free" persons; and, in 1820—two hundred and fifty-three (253) "free" persons of African descent in Washington County towns and villages. (See Chart 2: "TOTAL "FREE AND ENSLAVED AFRICAN DESCENDANTS IN WASHINGTON COUNTY, NY 1790-1820 CENSUS")

With respect to this population in Washington County during the beginnings of the 19th century, their total population of African descendants in 1810 amounted to an impressive total for upstate New York. This two thousand eight hundred and fifteen (2,815) person population according to the 1810 census represents a seventeen hundred and six percent (1,706%) increase over the "free" African descendant population in Washington County in 1800.[18] Its relevance is even more astonishing when we consider that the State of New York was still immersed in their centuries long holocaust of human enslavement during this period. In fact, New York State would not abolish enslavement for another seventeen (17) years on June 4th, 1827.

Hidden within these population statistics is the compelling reality that the combined Washington County census for 1800 to 1820 clearly manifests the settling of some forty-five "free" families of African descent totaling some one hundred and eighty-eight persons in the various towns and villages within the county. This early period in upstate New York history illustrates what could be described as a major "migration pattern." The settling of families of African descent elevates the status of this migration from a normal displacement of "migrant workers"—in their efforts to locate and secure seasonal work—to an actual and calculated "relocation migration."

# CHART 2

## TOTAL "FREE" AND ENSLAVED AFRICAN DESCENDANTS IN WASHINGTON COUNTY, NY
## 1790-1820

| TOWN | 1790 ENSLAVED | 1790 FREE | 1800 ENSLAVED | 1800 "FREE" | 1810 ENSLAVED | 1810 "FREE" | 1820 ENSLAVED | 1820 "FREE" |
|---|---|---|---|---|---|---|---|---|
| WHITEHALL | 1 | 1 | 1 | 6 | 3 | 155 | 1 | 8 |
| HAMPTON | 0 | 0 | 4 | 0 | 3 | 31 | 3 | 9 |
| SALEM | 22 | 1 | 6 | 7 | 36 | 227 | 24 | 41 |
| GRANVILLE | 0 | 0 | 6 | 11 | 3 | 274 | 7 | 20 |
| CAMBRIDGE | 0 | 0 | 79 | 7 | 82 | 612 | 27 | 31 |
| EASTON | 0 | 0 | 77 | 38 | 92 | 146 | 48 | 28 |
| GREENWICH | 0 | 0 | 0 | 0 | 8 | 132 | 6 | 11 |
| ARGYLE | 14 | 0 | 29 | 16 | 15 | 110 | 0 | 4 |
| KINGSBURY | 0 | 1 | 11 | 3 | 23 | 246 | 3 | 30 |
| QUEENSBURY | 1 | 0 | 2 | 0 | 6 | 69 | 0 | 0 |
| FT. ANN | 0 | 0 | 0 | 0 | 11 | 300 | 3 | 11 |
| HARTFORD | 0 | 0 | 1 | 3 | 11 | 185 | 0 | 3 |
| HEBRON | 0 | 0 | 13 | 1 | 11 | 267 | 2 | 1 |
| PUTNAM | 0 | 0 | 0 | 0 | 0 | 0 | 0 | 0 |
| HAGUE | 0 | 0 | 0 | 0 | 0 | 1 | 0 | 0 |
| JOHNSBURG | 0 | 0 | 0 | 0 | 2 | 14 | 0 | 0 |
| CHESTER | 0 | 0 | 1 | 7 | 2 | 2 | 0 | 0 |
| BOLTON | 0 | 0 | 0 | 11 | 0 | 4 | 0 | 0 |
| THURMAN | 0 | 0 | 2 | 7 | 0 | 2 | 0 | 0 |
| CALDWELL | 0 | 0 | 0 | 0 | 4 | 4 | 0 | 0 |
| FT. EDWARD | 0 | 0 | 0 | 19 | 0 | 0 | 0 | 19 |
| WHITE CREEK | 0 | 0 | 0 | 0 | 0 | 0 | 28 | 8 |
| JACKSON | 0 | 0 | 0 | 0 | 0 | 0 | 9 | 29 |
| WESTFIELD | 9 | 0 | 35 | 8 | 0 | 0 | 0 | 0 |
| LUZERNE | 0 | 0 | 0 | 0 | 3 | 34 | 0 | 0 |
| TOTAL | 48 | 3 | 267 | 144 | 315 | 2815 | 161 | 253 |

TOTAL "FREE" AND ENSLAVED AFRICAN DESCENDANTS
WASHINGTON COUNTY, NY
1790 - 1820 CENSUS

This form of migration embodies physical settlement, individual and family land purchases, and the establishment of business enterprises; in this instance: operational farms, trade labor development, and home-manufacturing, to name a few. It also speaks to the issue of formulating the foundations of family life development and thereby, establishing the beginnings of traditional historical family "roots." (See Charts 3: "AFRICAN DESCENDANT FAMILIES IN WASHINGTON COUNTY, N.Y. 1800-1820 CENSUS")

Another remarkable element of this explosion in the "free" African descendant population of Washington County is the fact that its population of two thousand eight hundred and fifteen (2,815) persons represented 11% of the entire "free" African descendant population of 25,333 in New York State in 1810.[19] This documented migration and population increase of 1706% for a single geographic area could easily be presented and classified as a "significant migration" under the most traditional of circumstances. And yet, very little about this migration is mentioned in the numerous written histories, books, articles or newspapers of Washington County during or after this period.

# CHART 3

## AFRICAN DESCENDANT FAMILIES IN WASHINGTON COUNTY, N.Y.
### 1800-1820

# "FREE" FAMILIES OF AFRICAN DESCENT
# WASHINGTON COUNTY 1800

| TOWN | NAME | GIVEN NAME | SEX | # IN FAMILY | |
|------|------|------------|-----|-------------|--|
| ARGYLE | | | | | |
| | HAMPTON | BILL | M | 4 | |
| | ROGERS | CATO | M | 4 | |
| | SENTEU | ANTHONY | M | 5 | |
| BOLTON | | | | | |
| | PALL | ANTHONY | M | 9 | |
| EASTON | | | | | |
| | CHARLES | HENRY | M | 7 | |
| | SCOONER | JOHN | M | 6 | |
| | ROGERS | CATO | M | 4 | |
| | VAN BUREN | HENRY | M | 7 | |
| | SCHUYLER | JIM | M | 5 | |
| | VAN SCHUYETS | PHILES | M | 4 | |
| GRANVILLE | | | | | |
| | PALMER | ABIATHER | M | 10 | |
| | BURNS | SAMSON | M | 1 | |
| HATFORD | | | | | |
| | KINCAID | JAMES | M | 1 | |
| SALEM | | | | | |
| | ARMSTRONG | THOMAS | M | 3 | |
| THURMAN | | | | | |
| | TURNER | BENJAMIN | M | 4 | |
| WESTFIELD | | | | | |
| | NYMHAM | HENRY | M | 4 | |
| | PETERS | PETER | M | 4 | |
| WHITEHALL | | | | | |
| | GOSEN | JAMES | M | 1 | |
| | BRISTOL | LONDON | M | 4 | |
| | MARSH | EPHRAIM | M | 4 | |
| TOTAL | 20 | | | 91 | |

# "FREE" FAMILIES OF AFRICAN DESCENT
# WASHINGTON COUNTY 1810

| TOWN | NAME | GIVEN NAME | SEX | FAMILY SIZE |
|------|------|-----------|-----|-------------|
| **BOLTON** | | | | |
| | CAMPE | AMOS | M | 1 MEMBER |
| **CAMBRIDGE** | | | | |
| | WHITESIDE | APHEY | M | 5 MEMBERS |
| **CHESTER** | | | | |
| | HOWE | ABNER | M | 1 MEMBER |
| **EASTON** | | | | |
| | SMITH | CAESAR | M | 8 MEMBERS |
| | BURNHAM | JACK | M | 10 MEMBERS |
| | SCHUYLER | JAMES | M | 9 MEMBERS |
| | VAN BUREN | HENRICK | M | 9 MEMBERS |
| | VAN SCHAICK | RUFS | M | 6 MEMBERS |
| **SALEM** | | | | |
| | BOSTON | QUACK | M | 4 MEMBERS |
| **GRANVILLE** | | | | |
| | NORTHRUP | MINTRUS | M | 5 MEMBERS |
| | GARDNER | ZEBEDEE | M | 4 MEMBERS |
| **JOHNSBURY** | | | | |
| | WHITMORE | JOSEPH | M | 1 MEMBER |
| | ROOSEVELT | JOHN T. | M | 1 MEMBER |
| **GREENWICH** | | | | |
| | WATROUP | POHNFS | M | 5 MEMBERS |
| **KINGSBURY** | | | | |
| | HAMPTON | WILLIAM | M | 8 MEMBERS |
| **QUEENSBURY** | | | | |
| | WING | GRAHAM | M | 1 MEMBER |
| **THURMAN** | | | | |
| | McDONALD | JOHN | M | 1 MEMBER |
| **TOTAL** | 17 | | | 61 |

# "FREE" FAMILIES OF AFRICAN DESCENT
## WASHINGTON COUNTY 1820

| TOWN | NAME | GIVEN NAM | SEX | FAMILY SIZE |
|---|---|---|---|---|
| **JACKSON** | | | | |
| | VAN WOAK | FRANCIS | M 45+ | 9 MEMBERS |
| | | | F | 45+ |
| | | | 3/M | 26-34 |
| | | | M | 14-25 |
| | | | M | Under 14 |
| | | | 2/F | Under 14 |
| **SALEM** | | | | |
| | SYLVESTER | | | |
| | | ROSEANNA | F | 45+ |
| | EPPES | | | |
| | | JOHN | M | 45+ |
| | | | F | 26-45 |
| | JACKSON | | | |
| | | RICHARD | M | 26-45 |
| | | | F | 26-45 |
| | | | F | 14-26 |
| | | | F | 14-26 |
| | | | M | 14-26 |
| | | | M | UNDER 14 |
| | DAILEY | | | |
| | | JOHN | M | 45+ |
| | | | F | 14-26 |
| | | | M | 14-26 |
| | | | M | 14-26 |
| | BOSTON | | | |
| | | QUACK | M | 26-45 |
| | | | F | UNDER 14 |
| | | | M | 14-26 |
| | AVERY | | | |
| | | CESAR | M | 45+ |
| | | | F | 26-45 |
| | | | M | 26-45 |
| | LATIMER | | | |
| | | JACOB | M | 45+ |
| | | | F | 26-45 |
| | | | F | UNDER 14 |
| | | | F | UNDER 14 |
| | | | F | UNDER 14 |
| | | | M | 14-26 |
| **TOTAL** | **8** | | | **36** |

# CAUSES AND RATIONALE FOR THE MIGRATION GEOPOLITICAL CONDITIONS

Truly the most exciting and at the same time, the most frustrating aspect of the research undertaken in the preparation of this work, was my inability to adequately resolve a number of the inherent mysteries of this migration story. In particular, answering the questions outlined in our Introduction—the *WHO, WHAT, WHEN, WHERE AND WHY,* all of which present their own unique and perplexing obstacles. Implicit in the "puzzle management" of these mysteries was the absence of specific and cogent documentation housed within the repositories and archives of New York State and Washington County itself. The mining of bits and pieces of intelligence for this work was severely compromised by centuries of natural and man-made disasters, as well as neglect and misappropriation, which is oftentimes a common occurrence in historical research that chronicles centuries old events. It often impedes one's ability to locate and secure important new and nuanced nuggets of information theretofore undiscovered. These data are frequently incorporated in the attempts by historians to establish new revelations or perspectives on historical events. However, in this instance, the "puzzle" that all historians struggle to solve and complete under normal circumstances has been neglected and corrupted.

Of particular consequence in the development of this work is the answer to the question—*WHERE?* Where did these two thousand six hundred and ninety-six (2,696) individuals and families of African descent migrate from on this historic journey to Washington County?

It is this author's considered opinion that these individuals and families migrated to Washington County primarily from counties within New York State that were experiencing an unprecedented increase in their population of "free" persons of African descent, due to the provisions of the Gradual Abolition Act and other state enacted "freedom initiatives." These newly "freed" individuals of African descent were struggling desperately to acquire a new method and model of survival, given the reality of the impending demise of the state's enslavement-based economy.

In the State of New York during this period (1800-1810), there existed various counties that would best manifest the criteria of "origination points" for this migration of "free" people of African descent to Washington County. In particular, these points would be those counties within the state that were experiencing the most immediate and economically unsustainable increases in newly "freed" African descendants after the passage of the Gradual Abolition Act. It would be logical to deduce that in any given county of New York, the initiator of any increase in the number of "freed" individuals would be the emancipation of members of the enslaved population. In other words, those counties which demonstrated a greater reduction in their enslaved population in 1810 due to emancipation policies or manumissions, versus the corresponding increase in their population of "free" persons of African descent, would support the premise that the numerical differentiation between these two population groups ("freed" and enslaved) would be the "freed" persons who were potentially available for relocation and/or migration.

Given the data included in various census reports, those New York State counties that would statistically support this hypothesis would include: Albany/Schenectady, Columbia, Dutchess, Suffolk, Ulster, Richmond and Clinton/Essex counties. (See Chart 4: INCREASES AND DECREASES IN FREE AND ENSLAVED AFRICAN DESCENDANTS IN NEW YORK STATE, 1800-1810) Between the years1800 to1810, these counties possessed a significantly mobile "free" African descendant population that could conceivably represent a substantial number of the two thousand six hundred and ninety-six (2696) individuals of African descent who migrated to Washington County. However, the reality is that this credible number of individuals within this data, who met these criteria for migration, does not represent the entirety of the total number of individuals who migrated to Washington County between 1800 and 1810. It is therefore, reasonable to surmise that a portion of these "migrants" came from outside of New York State, as well.

# CHART 4


## INCREASES AND DECREASES IN FREE AND ENSLAVED AFRICAN DESCENDANTS IN NEW YORK STATE, 1800-1810

| COUNTY | 1800 Free African Descendants | 1800 Enslaved African Descendants | 1810 Free African Descendants | 1810 Enslaved African Descendants | 1800-1810 FREE INCREASED | 1800-1810 ENSLAVED DECREASED |
|---|---|---|---|---|---|---|
| New York | 3499 | 2368 | 8137 | 1686 | 4638 | 1182 |
| Kings | 332 | 1479 | 735 | 1118 | 403 | 361 |
| Queens | 1431 | 1528 | 2354 | 809 | 923 | 719 |
| Suffolk | 1016 | 886 | 1373 | 413 | 357 | 473 |
| Richmond | 83 | 675 | 274 | 437 | 191 | 238 |
| Westchester | 482 | 1259 | 948 | 982 | 466 | 277 |
| Rockland | 68 | 551 | 503 | 292 | 435 | 259 |
| Clinton/Essex | 62 | 59 | 35 | 29 | -27 | 30 |
| Columbia | 490 | 1471 | 850 | 879 | 360 | 592 |
| Rensselaer | 113 | 890 | 362 | 750 | 249 | 140 |
| Ontario | 109 | 57 | 299 | 212 | 190 | -155 |
| Saratoga | 73 | 358 | 565 | 107 | 492 | 251 |
| Otsego | 44 | 48 | 133 | 74 | 89 | -26 |
| Delaware | 30 | 16 | 77 | 55 | 47 | 39 |
| Greene | 59 | 520 | 371 | 367 | 312 | 153 |
| Tioga | 33 | 17 | 39 | 61 | 6 | -44 |
| Steuben | 0 | 22 | 29 | 87 | 29 | -65 |
| Montgomery | 8 | 465 | 365 | 712 | 357 | -247 |
| Cayuga | 19 | 53 | 86 | 75 | 67 | -22 |
| Onondaga | 18 | 11 | 114 | 50 | 96 | -39 |
| Albany/ Sch. | 553 | 1809 | 1054 | 1090 | 501 | 719 |
| Herkimer | 8 | 61 | 77 | 64 | 69 | -3 |
| Oneida | 73 | 50 | 130 | 81 | 57 | -31 |
| Chenango | 40 | 16 | 76 | 13 | 36 | 3 |
| Washington | 119 | 80 | 2815 | 315 | 2696 | -235 |
| Schoharie | 11 | 354 | 235 | 316 | 224 | 38 |
| Dutchess | 931 | 1609 | 1124 | 1262 | 193 | 347 |
| Ulster | 336 | 2257 | 1066 | 1437 | 730 | 820 |
| Orange | 534 | 1145 | 927 | 966 | 393 | 179 |
| TOTAL | 10,374 | 28,614 | 25153 | 14739 | 14579 | 5853 |

By applying the same formula to states that surrounded Washington County and New York State and also calculating the reduction in the number of "free" African descendants in these state's population between 1800 and 1810; we can surmise that the opportunities which were developing in Washington County could have potentially attracted a number of out-of-state individuals of African descent. We would also propose that we include the actual reduction in the number of "free" African descendants in these states from 1800-1810, as a potential source for a portion of these Washington County migrants. This calculation would be based on the fact that several of these surrounding states had already abolished or were gradually abolishing enslavement prior to 1800. This occurrence would add an additional source to the potential number of migrates of African descendant to Washington County not residing within New York State, itself.

It should be further noted that during the period that Washington County was identified as Charlotte County, it included some or all of the States of Vermont, Massachusetts, Maine, and New Hampshire. Additionally, census records highlight the settlement of African descendants and others from New England to Washington County throughout the 17th and 18th centuries, other individuals also migrated to the county from Rhode Island, New Jersey and conceivably from Pennsylvania.

In fact, Washington/Charlotte County experienced a number of migrations of whites and African descendents and their families throughout its history. These migrations as documented in early census records and reports included New Englanders, who participated in the actual founding and settlement of the county. According to census data, several prominent families of African descent migrated to Washington County from outside of New York State during the Revolutionary War period and at the beginning of the 19th century. Included in this number were such families as the Hazzards, the Jacksons, the Haynes family, the Motts and the Northrups, to name a few.

Federal census records further inform us that a number of counties in states bordering Washington County and New York State met our newly established criteria for potential African descendants "migrants" during the period 1800-1810. These states and counties would include: 1—Massachusetts Counties: Barnstable, Dukes, Essex, Middlesex, Norfolk, Plymouth, and Worchester; 2—Rhode Island County: Washington; 3—Vermont Counties: Bennington and Orange; 4—Maine County: York; 5—New Jersey County: Bergen; and, 6—Pennsylvania Counties: Cumberland, Luzerne, Mifflin-Centre, Northampton, and Wayne. Each of these states reveal a significant reduction in the number of enslaved persons and an increase in "free" persons of African descent during this period. (See Chart 5: FREE AND ENSLAVED AFRICAN DESCENDANTS IN NEW YORK AND NEW ENGLAND, 1800-1810) [20]

Additional sources for potential migrants that should not be dismissed are those individuals of African descent who chose to escape the brutality of enslavement in the southern region of America and pursued freedom in the north. It should be remembered that the Fugitive Slave Law was not in existence during this period and Washington County would enjoy a highly respected reputation as a destination on the Underground Railroad to Canada, particularly after the passage of this Law.

So, whatever the original point of departure or the mode of transportation people of African descent ventured to Washington County, where opportunity was perceived as accessible.

Washington County, NY, which was bordered by several New England States, was replete with surplus land due to the redistribution of land confiscated during the Revolutionary War from British loyalists. With the selling and parceling of these lots into smaller portions to businessmen, large landowners and farmers, the prospects for increased agricultural production heightened. Consequently, this surge in production required an expediential and concomitant demand for cheap labor; and, the resulting migration of African descendants proved to be fortuitous to the county in sustaining this economic transformation.

# CHART 5

## FREE AND ENSLAVED AFRICAN DESCENDANTS IN NEW YORK STATE AND NEW ENGLAND
### 1800-1810

| YEAR STATE | 1800 Free African Descendants | 1800 Enslaved African Descendants | 1810 Free African Descendants | 1810 Enslaved African Descendants | 1800 – 1810 FREE INCREASED | 1800 – 1810 ENSLAVED DECREASED |
|---|---|---|---|---|---|---|
| New York | 10374 | 20614 | 25153 | 14739 | 14959 | 5596 |
| Connecticut | 5330 | 951 | 6453 | 310 | 1123 | 641 |
| Delaware | 8268 | 6153 | 13,136 | 4177 | 4869 | 1976 |
| Maine | 818 | 0 | 969 | 0 | 141 | 0 |
| Massachusetts | 6452 | 0 | 6737 | 0 | 285 | 0 |
| New Hampshire | 852 | 8 | 970 | 0 | 118 | 8 |
| New Jersey | 4402 | 12,422 | 7843 | 10,851 | 3441 | 1371 |
| Rhode Island | 3304 | 380 | 3609 | 108 | 305 | 272 |
| Vermont | 557 | 0 | 750 | 0 | 193 | 0 |
| Pennsylvania | 14,564 | 1706 | 22,492 | 795 | 7,928 | 911 |
| TOTAL | 54921 | 42234 | 62959 | 30980 | 33362 | 10775 |

We will learn that these "free" families of African descent migrated there in an effort to explore potential employment opportunities and to improve their economic and social living conditions. This migration further reinforced the fact that Washington County was becoming a Mecca for farming and textile manufacturing employment. Census records and reports for Washington County highlight the fact that the overall population itself increased by some ten thousand persons between the years 1800 and 1810 due to this economic transformation.

These "free" persons of African descent were thoroughly intent on re-establishing the reunion of family members separated during enslavement, while at the same time, this migration provided an opportunity to develop and sustain a new and "free" life, as well as a potentially secure foundation for themselves and their families. We will also learn that there existed within Washington County in addition to emerging opportunities for extended employment, the possibilities of land ownership for those who could manage to afford to do so.

# MAJOR TRANSFORMATIONS WITHIN THE AFRICAN DESCENDANT POPULATION

The reasons and circumstances that generated this migration and the major increase in the population of "free" persons and families of African descent in Washington County are directly related to those who acquired their freedom during and after the Revolutionary War in New York State.

From 1771 to 1786, the number of persons of African descent in the upstate counties (Albany, Ulster, Dutchess, Orange, Cumberland, Gloucester, Montgomery and Washington) rose from 7,882 to 10,275. This gain of 2,393 persons was registered while the southern six counties of New York State lost 3,407 persons of African descent. This loss in population resulted in a net loss of 1,014 persons of African descent statewide. Several of these upstate counties also displayed the same rapid expansion of their populations of African descent between 1786 and 1790. These counties collectively increased from 10,275 to 13,032 the population of African descent in those four years. Within this transformation, Albany County appears to have lost a considerable portion of its population from 1786 to 1790. However, this reduction in population can be attributed to the fact that five new counties (Montgomery, Washington, Columbia, Clinton, and Ontario) were formed from 1784 to 1791 from lands ceded by the county. [21]

The southern six counties: New York, Kings, Queens, Richmond, Suffolk and Westchester disproportionately lost their African descendant population in wartime compared to the rest of New York; thus resulting in the fact that upstate New York in 1771 represented 40.6% of the population of persons of African descent in New York; with 54.3% in 1786 and 49.7% in 1790. [22]

Chart 6 is a New York State county by county breakdown of "free" persons of African descent throughout the State of New York from 1790-1820. [23] You will notice that although Washington County represents the 2nd highest growth in the state in 1810 as relates to "free" persons of African descent, there is a very significant increase in "free" persons of African descent in several counties within the state during this same time period.

# CHART 6

## ENSLAVED AND FREE AFRICAN DESCENDANTS
## IN NEW YORK STATE
## 1790-1820

# ENSLAVED PERSONS AND FREE PERSONS OF AFRICAN DESCENT IN NEW YORK STATE*

| County | 1790 | | 1800 | | 1810 | | 1820 | |
|---|---|---|---|---|---|---|---|---|
| | Enslaved Persons | Free Blacks | Enslaved Persons | Free Blacks | Enslaved Persons | Free Blacks | Enslaved Persons | Free Blacks |
| Albany | 3,722 | 171 | 1,808 | 353 | 772 | 866 | 413 | 858 |
| Allegany | — | — | — | — | 21 | 0 | 17 | 12 |
| Broome | — | — | — | — | 23 | 30 | 25 | 63 |
| Cattaraugus | — | — | — | — | — | — | 2 | 4 |
| Cayuga | — | — | 53 | 19 | 75 | 86 | 48 | 191 |
| Chautauqua | — | — | — | — | — | — | 3 | 10 |
| Chenango | — | — | 16 | 40 | 13 | 76 | 7 | 189 |
| Clinton* | 16 | 16 | 58 | 62 | 29 | 32 | 2 | 96 |
| Columbia | 1,633 | 52 | 1,471 | 490 | 879 | 850 | 761 | 1,053 |
| Cortland | — | — | — | — | 0 | 2 | 3 | 48 |
| Delaware | — | — | 16 | 30 | 55 | 77 | 56 | 82 |
| Dutchess | 1,864 | 431 | 1,609 | 931 | 1,262 | 1,124 | 772 | 1,685 |
| Essex* | — | — | — | — | 0 | 3 | 3 | 28 |
| Franklin | — | — | — | — | 3 | 0 | 0 | 0 |
| Genesee | — | — | — | — | 11 | 14 | 35 | 82 |
| Greene | — | — | 520 | 59 | 367 | 371 | 134 | 637 |
| Hamilton | — | — | — | — | — | — | 1 | 1 |
| Herkimer | — | — | 61 | 8 | 64 | 77 | 72 | 188 |
| Jefferson | — | — | — | — | 0 | 40 | 5 | 135 |
| Kings | 1,482 | 46 | 1,479 | 332 | 1,118 | 735 | 879 | 882 |
| Lewis | — | — | — | — | 4 | 25 | 0 | 43 |
| Madison | — | — | — | — | 35 | 177 | 10 | 182 |
| Montgomery | 588 | 41 | 466 | 8 | 712 | 365 | 349 | 571 |
| New York | 2,373 | 1,119 | 2,868 | 3,499 | 1,686 | 8,137 | 518 | 10,368 |
| Niagara | — | — | — | — | 8 | 31 | 15 | 67 |
| Oneida | — | — | 50 | 73 | 81 | 130 | 9 | 368 |
| Onondaga | — | — | 11 | 18 | 50 | 114 | 59 | 195 |
| Ontario | 10 | 6 | 57 | 109 | 212 | 299 | 0 | 727 |
| Orange | 961 | 201 | 1,145 | 534 | 966 | 927 | 1,125 | 969 |
| Oswego | — | — | — | — | — | — | 0 | 32 |
| Otsego | — | — | 48 | 44 | 74 | 133 | 16 | 235 |
| Putnam | — | — | — | — | — | — | 49 | 166 |
| Queens | 2,308 | 819 | 1,528 | 1,431 | 809 | 2,354 | 559 | 2,648 |
| Rensselaer | — | — | 890 | 113 | 750 | 362 | 433 | 632 |
| Richmond | 755 | 127 | 675 | 83 | 437 | 274 | 532 | 78 |
| Rockland | — | — | 551 | 68 | 316 | 292 | 124 | 412 |
| Saratoga | — | — | 358 | 73 | 107 | 565 | 123 | 504 |
| Schenectady | — | — | — | — | 318 | 188 | 102 | 454 |
| Schoharie | — | — | 354 | 11 | 316 | 235 | 302 | 264 |
| Seneca | — | — | — | — | 101 | 44 | 84 | 180 |
| St. Lawrence | — | — | — | — | 5 | 17 | 8 | 14 |
| Steuben | — | — | 22 | 0 | 87 | 29 | 46 | 130 |
| Suffolk | 1,105 | 1,131 | 886 | 1,016 | 413 | 1,373 | 323 | 1,166 |
| Sullivan | — | — | — | — | 43 | 11 | 69 | 33 |
| Tioga | — | — | 17 | 33 | 61 | 39 | 104 | 32 |
| Tompkins | — | — | — | — | — | — | 6 | 66 |
| Ulster | 2,914 | 161 | 2,257 | 336 | 1,437 | 1,066 | 1,523 | 597 |
| Warren | — | — | — | — | — | — | 7 | 10 |
| Washington | 46 | 3 | 80 | 119 | 315 | 2,815** | 150 | 254 |
| Westchester | 1,416 | 358 | 1,259 | 482 | 982 | 948 | 205 | 1,638 |
| Total | 21,193 | 4,682 | 20,613 | 10,374 | 15,017 | 25,333 | 10,088 | 29,279 |

* The Encyclopedia of New York State, 2005, Syracuse University Press, pg. 1419

*Sources:* US Census; Inter-university Consortium for Political and Social Research (ICPSR).

*Notes:* Only counties created by 1820 are shown. Many counties did not have their present boundaries. Census takers often mistakenly enumerated free Blacks as slaves. The 1830 federal census counted 75 slaves in New York State: Albany Co, 2; Chenango Co, 3; Montgomery Co, 26; New York Co, 17; Oneida Co, 15; Putnam Co, 4; and Washington Co, 8. It is likely all of these people were free Blacks.

*In 1800 data for Clinton and Essex Cos were combined.

** This anomalous figure answered as such in the original census data.

A great deal of conjecture has existed with respect to this substantial increase in the "free" population of African descent in Washington County from 1800 to 1810. Assumptions and suppositions have been made with the objective being to qualify this recorded increase in the "free" African descendant population in 1810 as an anomaly or even a census collection error. However, Chart 6, which is composed of actual census data, disputes these allegations by illuminating the reality that several New York State counties also exhibited significant increases in their "free" African descendant populations in 1810.

Additional data that supports this 2815 figure of "free" individuals of African descent in Washington County in 1810 is presented in Chart 9—"FREE" AFRICAN DESCENDANTS WITH WHITE FAMILIES IN WASHINGTON COUNTY IN 1810" provided later in this work. This census data driven Chart clearly and definitively documents and authenticates the actual residences of this entire African descendant population.

What actions, policies or laws occurred in New York State that precipitated or were directly responsible for initiating and influencing this, heretofore, unrecorded and unprecedented advancement in the social and economic status of these persons formerly mired in the inhumanity of enslavement. The answers to these intriguing and important questions may well be attributed to three very significant and profoundly influential yet, not widely acknowledged or discussed initiatives undertaken by the State of New York

1- REVOLUTIONARY WAR FREEDOM POLICIES
2- NEW YORK STATE CONFISCATION AND FORFEITURE LAWS, AND
3- GRADUAL ABOLITION: MANUMISSION PROVISIONS

# 1- REVOLUTIONARY WAR FREEDOM POLICIES

## ENLISTMENT OF MEN OF AFRICAN DESCENT

During the Revolutionary War, the colonial forces held Albany, Ulster, and Dutchess counties, and parts of Orange, Tryon, and Westchester counties. The war, in addition to its destructive, chaotic and destabilizing nature uprooted the controlled institution of enslavement and thus, created new issues with respect to ownership. At the same time, it manufactured new opportunities for liberty for those enslaved. African descendants won freedom by military service with either the British or the Colonial armies.[24] While some enslaved families were further separated by the movement of their enslavers during the chaos of battle and army occupation, others used the conflict to permanently re-unite with their families members as free people.

On March 20, 1781, the American forces recruited men of African descent with the promise of freedom for either, three years of service or until regular discharge.[25] Any enslaver who delivered one or more of his able-bodied enslaved men to serve in a regiment was entitled to a land grant and were additionally exempt from any future maintenance of their former enslaved after they were freed.[26]

> **One such example was Solemon Close of Salem who received on August 26, 1777, a bounty for 2 1/2 months service to the army rendered by his enslaved man.[27]**

The number of enslaved who achieved freedom through service with the colonists is unknown. Many of those enslaved by Tories ran away to American controlled areas and many of those enslaved by colonials joined the army with their enslaver's consent.

> *"About 5000 men of African descent served in the Continental army. Those enslaved who fought in the Army for a set period were usually legally emancipated. Thousands more served in militia and state units."[28]*

Freedom was not the only consequence that people of African descent encountered during the War. Those enslaved were often captured for political advantage, private gain, and for military service by both the British and the Americans.

*"Westchester County's enslaved population was largely destabilized as a result of its occupation by both British and American armies, the plundering operations of both Tory and Colonial militia upon local property holders, the persecution of loyalists and sales of their property in colonial areas, and the flight of loyalists with their enslaved to British strongholds. The proximity of the British lines in New York City also encouraged Westchester's enslaved population to run away from their enslavers and seek freedom within the British camps. The number of those enslaved decreased by 63.7 percent from 1771 to 1786 in Westchester County. This lost population of African descent did not reappear in the 1790 census, as it did in the other southern New York counties."*[29]

New York's position as an active battleground during the American Revolution considerably enhanced and expanded opportunities for freedom to those enslaved locally, who were caught between the two opposing armies. Both British and American forces competed for the military services and allegiance of New York's enslaved population.[30]

As military resources, African descendants were useful as laborers, scouts, messengers, and spies. On June 30, 1779, Sir Henry Clinton, commander-in-chief of the British forces in America, issued a proclamation from his headquarters at Philipsburgh in Westchester County.

*"He granted liberty to any enslaved male or female who fled to the British lines and embraced the King's cause, this policy was in effect from its issuance until the signing of the Provisional Peace Agreement on November 30, 1782."*[31]

The number of New York enslaved and free persons of African descent who adhered to the British standard is unknown, but it is likely that large numbers sought freedom in this manner.

*"A Gravesend, Long Island slave testified in July 1776 that over eight hundred local persons of African descent had escaped into the British lines and would probably be made into a regiment."*[32]

Additionally, a survey of the labor resources of the Quarter Master General's Department, Commissary General's Provision Department, Forage Department, and the Barrack Master General's Department in New York, Staten Island, Long Island, and Harlem Heights on August 26-31, 1781, revealed that one guide, six drivers, and 116 "negro laborers" were in current service.[33] A total of 247 known former New York enslaved or freedmen were evacuated with the British between April 23 and November 30, 1783, according to ship registers which listed the names of 3,000 persons of African descent.[34] Many more New York enslaved persons may have been aboard unregistered private vessels for whom no records exist.[35]

As property, African descendants also risked being stolen or imprisoned by both colonial and Tory soldiers, militia of both sides, and civilians who either kept them or sold them to others for a profit.

And yet, many of those enslaved saw the confusion of war, occupation, enlistment and a disrupted enslavement system as an advantageous opportunity. These circumstances provided persons of African descent with a chance not only to escape their enslavers and seek freedom for themselves, but also to try to reunite their families. Some enslaved persons even participated in acts of self-liberation by escaping to other states where enslavement had already been abolished—Vermont (1777) and Massachusetts (1780).

## MANUMISSION DURING THE REVOLUTION

Occasionally loyalists, frustrated with the prospects of the loss of their worldly possessions and property and seeking to strike a personal blow at the arrogance and ruthless nature of the colonialists, manumitted their enslaved persons rather than abandon them to rebel confiscation, possession, and sale. One such loyalist Oliver De Lancey, whose name appeared on the October 22, 1779 list of persons whose estates were forfeited to New York State, freed his enslaved persons before joining the British forces as commander of a brigade of 1,500 loyalists. In a May 5, 1784 memo to the British government applying for compensation for his wartime losses, De Lancey stated that his house at Bloomingdale in New York was burnt down on November 26, 1777, by the rebels. At which time, he had twenty-three enslaved persons in residence on his property. Aside from a child of African descent killed in the fire, he gave all the rest but three "leave to work for their maintenance, and go where they pleased by which means they were lost to him."[36]

There were others who also manumitted those that they had enslaved. When Charles Theall of Rye wrote his will on September 17, 1778, he left his granddaughter "a negro boy now in the hands of Ebenezer Purdy, and sold to him by Commissioners as part of the estate of my son Ebenezer, and being then and is now my real property."[37] Still others like William Underhill of Westchester County refused to acknowledge the permanent loss of those enslaved persons confiscated during the Revolution. His estate inventory in 1784 listed;

*". . . a negro boy named Edward taken away in the time of war and now in possession of Israel Honeywell said to be sold to him by the commissioners of forfeitures worth 70," and "a negro man named Aaron taken away in time of war, also valued at 70."*[88]

These examples, although telling and informative did not constitute or represent in any way, a resounding commitment to the abolition of enslavement on the part of loyalists or colonialists, for that matter. The prospects of continued profits with enslaved labor resources still remained the primary focus of the majority of enslavers for post-war New York and America alike. It is inconceivable for rational minds to comprehend the fact that these principles, under which these individuals engaged in such a violent and protracted conflict, incorporated and celebrated freedom from oppression and the dignity of all men were being subverted in their very homes and communities. The fact that people of African descent were enslaved was inexplicably ignored and marginalized in this "New World Order of Hypocrisy." The fact is they were never considered because it was inconvenient and disruptive to the foundations of their economy and personal wealth.

## 2- THE NEW YORK STATE CONFISCATION AND FORFEITURE LAWS

The State's confiscation and forfeiture laws are another explanation and potential causation for this significant increase in "free" persons of African descent in New York State and this subsequent Washington County migration. It is firmly and squarely centered on Colonial and New York State public policies with respect to the legal confiscation and forfeiture of property and land of loyalists during and after the Revolutionary War.

## THE REVOLUTIONARY WAR

When hostilities broke out between British and American troops in 1775, New York had no provision for the regular compensation of its troops. The Provincial Congress adopted a militia bill on August 22, 1775 providing for payment to New York State Militia troops equal to that of Continental Army troops. The Treasurer, first appointed by the Provincial Congress in 1775 and continued by the State Constitution of 1777, was empowered to collect revenues as necessary and disburse funds in payment of the state's obligations. Additionally, the Office of Auditor-General, responsible for maintaining and reconciling the public accounts of the state, was established by resolution of the Provincial Convention on July 24, 1776.[39]

On March 6, 1777, the New York Provincial Convention appointed Commissioners of Sequestration for each of the counties not under British control. They were empowered to seize and sell the personal property of loyalists (including their enslaved men, women and children) and rent out their lands. Commissioners for Albany, Charlotte, Tryon, Dutchess, Ulster, Orange, and Westchester counties appropriated loyalist properties throughout the war until the termination of their powers on May 12, 1784.[40]

Commissioners of Sequestration were appointed to "take into their custody & possession all the personal property" of loyalists and sell the seized items at public auction. Loyalist families were only allowed to keep their clothes, some essential furniture, and three months' provisions. The lands of the Tories were to be leased at moderate rent, with preference for supporters of the American cause who had been displaced from their homes by the loyalists.[41]

The seized property of loyalists was sold to fill New York State coffers when funds became depleted during the War. A series of laws passed by the New York Provincial Congress and the Congress of the United States provided for this sequestration, and later confiscation of forfeited loyalist property.

*This act authorized "the speedy sale of the confiscated estates," writes Yoshpe, ". . . [it] systematized the confiscatory machinery and gave it impetus."[42]*

The Governor was ordered to appoint two Commissioners of Forfeitures for the four (4) designated Districts within New York State. The mechanism for paying troops was now in place, but the payments quickly fell far behind in its obligations and they had to make payments with inflated state and continental currency. The continuing lack of funds led to compensation for war service in land rights. In 1780, the Governor appointed three Special Auditors to settle accounts for back pay for enlisted men and the militia. The auditors issued certificates of debt bearing five percent interest. Soldiers or other creditors could use the certificates as payment for estates forfeited by loyalists, un-appropriated lands, or taxes.[43]

On October 4, 1780, the Provincial Congress issued an act stating that the certificates issued to pay New York troops defending the United States, in lieu of currency, would be accepted for the purchase of confiscated estates at the same value as specie.( Many of the soldiers who received such certificates, however, had been dubious of the fledgling government's ability to eventually redeem the bills, and therefore sold the certificates to speculators, who did not hesitate to take the State up on the offer to buy forfeited lands.

Sales of the estates set aside on June 15, 1780, and of other forfeited lands were authorized by the New York State Legislature on October 7, 1780. The Governor was to appoint commissioners to sell forfeited lands for gold, silver, or Congressional bills of credit, in order to pay off one-sixth the bills issued in pursuance of the Act of Congress of March 18, 1780.[44] These early transactions were not conducted by the Commissioners of Forfeitures, but rather by "Commissioners of Specie," who bridged the gap between the Commissioners of Sequestration and the Commissioners of Forfeitures. The majority of the forfeited estates, however, were not disposed of until after the conclusion of the war.[451)]

## CONFISCATION LAWS

On August 3, 1775, New York passed the first act which implied confiscation of loyalist property. As early as September 1, 1775, the Provincial Congress passed a resolution authorizing the seizure of property belonging to persons who had joined the British cause and on June 24, 1776, the Continental Congress declared that all loyalist property was liable to seizure, followed shortly thereafter by similar New York legislation.[46] Confiscation of loyalist property by local committees became more common after July 4, 1776 and finally, on

September 21, 1776, the Constitutional Convention ordered measures to be taken against British sympathizers, and loyalists were transported out of the state, jailed, freed on parole, forced to swear allegiance to the Americans, sent into the British lines, and/or executed for treason. Local committees enforced these policies against domestic enemies in all counties of New York not under British control.[47]

## FREEDOM PROVISIONS

**In New York State, enslaved persons of African descent were considered contraband of war by the British and colonials alike. Colonials confiscated and sold persons of African descent who belonged to loyalist enslavers and vice versa.**

The most significant aspect of these public policy directives stipulated that enslaved African descendants who had been abandoned on confiscated loyalist estates and who remained unsold on May 1, 1786, were to be freed by New York State.

# CHAPTER 58 OF THE LAWS OF 1786

An Act further to amend an act entitled, "An act for the speedy sale of the confiscated and forfeited estates within this State and for other purposes therein mentioned" passed the 1st of May, 1786, as stated below:

*"And be it further enacted by the authority aforesaid, that all negro slaves, become the property of the people of this State, by the attainder or, conviction of any person whomsoever and now in possession of the commissioners of forfeitures be, and they are hereby manumitted."*[48]

With respect to enslaved persons of African descent, these laws outside of actual enlistment in the Army or individual manumission by their enslavers provided the first state-sponsored instances for the actual and legal emancipation of enslaved persons of African descent in New York State. However, this Law only presented a narrowly focused action on the part of the state and established a public policy basis for the emancipation of only certain persons of African descent under specified and clearly defined circumstances.

Another condition of war involved the enslaved of loyalists and colonials, who were often stolen or imprisoned. African descendants enslaved by Tories were sold or transferred to new enslavers to avoid seizure by colonials. Many were appropriated and sold by either the Commissioners of Sequestration or

Commissioners of Forfeitures as confiscated loyalist property. Those who were left unsold by the Commissioners of Forfeitures in 1786 were now freed by New York State.

> *"The sale of one of her children motivated Zipporah to press for her own and the child's freedom though the auspices of the New York Manumission Society in 1802 based on her status as a former slave on the confiscated Floyd estate. Had she not been shifted to Peters's ownership, Zipporah would have been entitled to freedom if she had remained unsold by the Commissioners of Forfeitures in 1786 (when all such enslaved were freed by the state)."[49]*

Again, we are unable to determine the actual numbers of persons of African descent who were "freed" by this law and its policies. It should be noted that this law had provisions and stipulations that included the support by the state of those "freed" by the law.[50]

> *"Based on sums spent on the support of slaves who had belonged to John Rapalje, Daniel Kissam, Sr., Parker Wickham, Robert Bayard, Richard Floyd, and Frederick Philipse during the years 1786 through the end of 1796 outlined in the preceding pages, New York spent at least $1,976.75 (790.7.10) during this period.*
>
> *This sum represents in most cases only partial fragments of the real total spent on the former slaves of these six loyalists—some of the accounts located were burnt or illegible. Where gaps of either months or years appear in the payment record, it can be assumed either that support was intermittent or that the bills in question were not located. Often only a single bill per slave was found, reflecting what may have been but one out of several real years of support. This estimate of $1,976.75 paid by the state 1786 to 1796 is also severely limited in that it covers sums spent on the slaves of only six loyalists. It must be regarded as a bare minimum projection of the state-wide maintenance costs incurred by New York during this decade."[51]*

Numerous expenditure reports and records exist in the Journals of the New York State Assembly and Senate documenting the "support for slaves" allocated by the State of New York under the provisions of this Law.

# ACT OF ATTAINDER[52]

*". . . the losses of loyalists were as severe and Tories in the northern counties of the state as those suffered dearly from the harsh treatment. Out of 466 petitions filed by loyalists who had emigrated and claimed compensation for their confiscated property from the crown, Albany County furnished the largest number, followed by Westchester, Tryon, Dutchess, Charlotte, Orange, and Cumberland."[53]*

The Revolutionary War progressed and as funds for prosecuting the war became scarce, the real and personal property of loyalists was confiscated and sold to raise money for the State. In 1779, the New York State Legislature attainded 59 loyalists (abolished their civil rights) and declared their real property forfeited. A series of laws passed by the New York Provincial Congress and the Congress of the United States provided for this sequestration, and later confiscation of forfeited loyalist property. On October 22, 1779, "the Governor was authorized to appoint Commissioners of Forfeitures to dispose of the confiscated estates," allowing tenant farmers, "who had leased . . . and improved the land, first priority to purchase their tracts."[54(7]

The State was divided into four districts (Western, Eastern, Middle and Southern) and Commissioners of Forfeiture were appointed in each district to conduct sales of confiscated lands. Sales of confiscated lands were authorized by law in 1780 and again in 1784. Clear titles to lands purchased through the Commissioners of Forfeitures were often not obtained for decades due to claims against the forfeited estates, by widows and heirs of attainted loyalists. To settle these claims, in 1799 the state appointed commissioners to extinguish claims against lands sold by the state.[55]

Additionally, a law passed on March 10, 1780 called for the immediate sale of portions of the forfeited lands to pay for apparel and provisions needed by the troops. The United States Congress on March 18, 1780 passed a law which mandated the issuance of new currency, backed by the credit of the states to which the bills were allotted. Each state was to pay off one-sixth of the bills annually. On June 15, 1780, the New York State Legislature reserved the larger of the forfeited estates, including that of Frederick Philipse, as collateral for the redemption of the bills issued by New York in pursuance of this law. The Commissioners of Forfeitures, however, were not permitted to sell any of the mortgaged lands until further instructions from the Provincial Congress.[56)] Such orders came within a few months. "On October 4, 1780, the Provincial Congress issued an act stating that the certificates issued to pay New York troops defending the United States in lieu of currency would be accepted for the purchase of confiscated estates at the same value as specie."[571]On March

31, 1781, the right of tenants to preemption of purchase of their farms was again affirmed and the procedure for such sales further described.[58]

The English historian, Lecky, says that "Two-thirds of the property of New York was supposed to belong to the Tories." If this statement was intended to include the crown's lands, as well as the forfeited estates, it is undoubtedly true. Approximating the total sales from the partial sales which are left, it seems fair to conclude that the state received one million two hundred and sixty thousand pounds in standard money, or three million one hundred and fifty thousand dollars in Spanish coin, from the sale of forfeited real estate. The total loss for personal and real estate would be nearly three million six hundred thousand dollars."[59]

Exactly how much of a democratizing effect the Commissioners of Sequestration and Forfeitures had upon landowning in New York State is regularly debated by historians. Historian Harry B. Yoshpe holds that the immediate democratizing effect however, was not great, as most forfeited estates were bought up by well-off tenant farmers, wealthy businessmen, and speculators. The long-term democratizing effect however, was significant. Yoshpe further asserts that because many of the speculators eventually divided up their land into small lots to be sold to whoever would pay.[60(]

> *"Although the confiscation and sale of loyalist property was primarily a punishment for treason against revolutionary authority made good by war, still there was a result growing out of it of greater importance than the acquisition of property to the value of about $3,600,000 by the state. That result was the weakening of the feudal element in the social system of New York. The revolution was thus a democratic movement in land-tenure as well as in political rights. The ownership of the greater part of the lands of the state by a few aristocratic landlords like the De Lanceys, the Johnsons, the Skenes, John Tabor Kempe, the Jessups, Beverly Johnson, Roger Morris and others, now began to give way to ownership by their dependants and tenants."[61]*

Large manors, patents and estates were to an extent cut up into small lots and sold on easy terms to the common people. Although it was not uncommon for the widow or son of a loyalist to buy in his property, yet it was not the rule.

> *"The property of James De Lancey, for instance, in the southern district, went to about 275 different persons, and the 50,000 acres forfeited by Roger Morris in Putnam County were sold to nearly 250*

*persons. The large tracts in central and northern parts of the state were divided into farms of from one to five hundred acres and sold to poor farmers. The whole movement was leveling, equalizing and democratic, and left permanent social results in the new state.*[62]

The Commissioners of Forfeitures ceased operation on September 1, 1788, by an Act of the Legislature on March 21, 1788. They had sold nearly all the tracts of land entrusted to them, raising large amounts of revenue for the State of New York.

*"The Philipse Manor alone brought in $234,170.18s. The few remaining tracts of forfeited estates were then to be administered and sold by the Surveyor General. By 1782, the state had confiscated loyalist property in land value at £500,000, hard money."*[63]

## ATTAINDER: FREDERICK PHILLIPSE

As stated earlier, with the passage of an "Act of Attainder" passed on October 22, 1779, the revolutionary authorities moved from sequestration to actual confiscation of loyalist estates. The property of persons conspiring with or adhering to the enemy was declared forfeited to the state. Fifty-nine (59) persons were convicted of treason, other names were proposed for future indictment, and the governor was authorized to appoint Commissioners of Forfeitures to dispose of the real estate and other confiscated property.[64]

Since British troops occupied New York, Kings, Queens, Richmond, and Suffolk counties from September 1776 through November 1783, loyalist property there was neither confiscated nor sold during the war years. The Commissioners of Forfeitures began sales there in earnest only after the British withdrawal in November 1783 and after the passage on May 12, 1784 of enabling legislation.[65]

Among those attained was Frederick Phillipse, owner of the Manor of Phillipsburg, the largest tract of land in Westchester County. Several thousand acres of the Phillipse estate went to the tenant farmers who worked on the land. These farmers were not poor as one might expect. A combination of advantageous economic and geographical circumstances ensured that few Westchester County farmers had financial problems. Many were well-to-do and some agricultural families were quite wealthy. When tenant farmers could not afford or did not wish to purchase their lands, the tracts were sold to wealthy landowners, Revolutionary leaders, and businessmen from New York City. These landowners then sold portions of their newly acquired booty to smaller farmers or leased/rented portions to tenant farmers, respectively.[66]

The Phillipse Family had a long and sordid history with respect to persons of African descent and enslavement in New Netherlands and Colonial New York. Dutch privateers were known to traffic in enslaved Africans in the Indian Ocean. When they seized a group of thirty Africans and Indian Africans off the coast of New Spain in 1704, they delivered them to New York. How many Africans were brought to the colony by way of this formidable journey may never be known, for these "importers" never made a legal entry. Adolphus Philipse, Frederick's brother, a former Dutch patroon turned privateer, was described at the end of the century as returning on a ship from Madagascar with "nothing but Negroes."[67]

Adolphus Phillpse had acquired a large portion of land from the Wekquaesgeeks and Sint Sink Native American nations. He began his personal empire by securing both Dutch loans and a Dutch commission business in the fur, lumber, and human enslavement trades. Adolphus Phillipse and his brother Frederick understood the European system of exporting raw materials from the far-flung colonies for manufactured goods and other commodities and used enslaved labor as a means to increase production and expand their profits.

Frederick Phillpse also entered into the trading of Africans and land speculation. He had migrated to New Netherland in 1653 as a foreman of construction for the Dutch West India Company and became one of the richest men in the Colony. As a result of his trading in human lives between 1680 and 1750, most of the people that lived at Phillipsburg Manor were of African descent. These Africans and their descendants constructed, operated, and resided on a complex that consisted of a mill, manor house, bake house, a house for the enslaved, wharves, and a church. These enslaved Africans and their descendants labored as millers, bakers, sailors, dairy workers, coopers, and servants.[68] Table 1 is a reproduction of Adolph Phillipse's probate inventory. Notice that in the first column, the listing of his enslaved Africans and their descendants as property "on the Manor of Phillipsburgh." This document lists seven men, five women, three "men not fit for work" seven boys, and one girl among his "possessions" at the time of his death.[69]

Under the provisions of Chapter 58 of the Laws of 1786, the State of New York paid the Town of Yonkers $126.50 on May 26, 1802 for the support of an enslaved person "late the property of Frederick Philipse;"[70] and on May 3, 1803, the state paid Yonkers $126.50 for the "support of an ancient male slave formerly the property of Frederick Philipse. On May 29, 1804, Yonkers was reimbursed by the State for the sum of $126.50 for the support of a "male infirm slave" of Philipse for the April 2, 1803 to April 24, 1804 period.[71] This total excludes one of the bills for their support from April 4, 1791 (or May 1, 1791) to April 24, 1792.[72] These expenditures by the State further illustrate the subsidy provisions for "forfeited" enslaved African descendants, especially the support and maintenance provided by the State of New York to local governmental entities for the housing and care of former enslaved persons of the estates of attainders like Phillipse. Through the auspices of the Commissioner of Forfeiture for the Southern District several thousand acres of the Philipse estate went to the tenant farmers who worked on the land. Most of the buyers of confiscated estates were men. The only women to buy tracts of forfeited estates in the Southern District were either widows, administratrixes of estates or those who were pooling their resources with male family members to purchase land.

# ADOLPH PHILLIPSE PROBATE INVENTORY

On the mannor of Phillipsburgh

Negroe Viz

Men:
Ceaser ..
Dimond .
Sampson .
Keiser ...
Flip ......
Tom ....
Venture .

Women:
Susan .
Abigal .
Mary .
Dina ..
Sue ...

Men not fit for work:
James ..
Charles ..
Billy ...

Boys:
Tom abt 9 years old ...
Charles 9 D° ........
Sam 8 D° ........
Dimond 7 D° ........
Hendrick 5 D° ........
Ceaser 2 D° ........
Harry 1 & 4 months
Betty 3 years old A girl

Cattle Viz
6 worken oxen
12 Milch cows (old)

2 Silver Tankards ..
1 D° Mugs .......
6 New Silver spoons
6 old Ditto. .......
1 Silver teapott ....
6 Silver forks ......
1 D° pepper box ..

(In the Garrett) April 19th 1750
6 flax Spinning wheels
2 Woll ... D°
1 old gun
Some wool & Tow
a Miners pick Ax
4 Sithes & 2 handles
a flax Reel
a pr of old Scales and weights
Some old baskets and old Cask
a tin Cullender
1 small old brass kettle
1 d° skillett
1 old chafin dish & a small mortor

# 3- WASHINGTON COUNTY AND THE CONFISCATION LAWS

A large part of the land in Washington County had been owned by Tories and subsequently was forfeited, by various acts of the New York State Legislature. During the war there had been no sale for these lands, as they still remained in the possession of the State. However, a series of laws were passed by the New York Provincial Congress and the Congress of the United States to provide for this sequestration, and later confiscation, of forfeited loyalist property.

The state auditor, permanently established by statute in 1782, was empowered to receive from civil and military officers all accounts, vouchers, and other records needed to settle the state's accounts. In 1784, special auditors were directed to settle the accounts of New York troops in the service of the United States and to issue printed certificates dated January 1, 1782 and entitling the holder to receive a specified sum. Officers of the militia and levies, whose regiments saw actual service in the war, submitted unpaid accounts to the state auditor for settlement. The state treasurer was to issue certificates bearing five percent interest to each person named on the payrolls and accounts, preparing a receipt for each certificate issued. A Military Tract was laid out and land was granted to those eligible for bounty rights.

These special auditors were appointed for the purpose of liquidating financial obligations incurred by New York State during the War. Records were kept to document the service of and compensation due to soldiers and others who provided goods or services to the state during the war. Warrants to the state treasurer to pay creditors, account records, and receipts, and relate directly to the settlement of claims for reimbursement made between 1782 and 1794. Certificates by commanding officers, assignments of land bounty rights, several muster and pay rolls, and documentation of the seizure and sale of loyalists' lands were also issued.[73]

On the 12th of May, 1784, an Act was passed providing for the speedy sale of the lands in question by the Commissioners of Forfeiture. The three commissioners for the Eastern District were reduced, by the Act of May 12, 1784, to one Alexander Webster. Webster began to sell immediately. One of the oldest records in the Washington County Clerk's Office is Colonel Webster's register of the sales of forfeited lands. The "Report of Sales by the Commissioner of Forfeiture for the Eastern District of New York. It is headed as follows:

*"Registered for and by the direction of Alexander Webster, Esquire ommissioner of forfeiture for the eastern district of New York, in*

*pursuance of an act entitled an act for the speedy sale of the confiscated and forfeited estates within the State, and for other purposes therein mentioned, passed the 12th day of May, 1784."[74]*

One of the first records reads as follows:

*"Sold to Seth Sherwood the fee-simple of lot number thirty-nine in the Artillery patent, as it is distinguished by lot number thirty-nine in the map and field-book of said patent (special reference being thereto had), containing two hundred and forty-two acres of land, for the sum of four hundred and twenty pounds, on the twelfth day of October, one thousand seven hundred and eighty-four, forfeited by the attainder of Philip and Andrew P. Skene, late of Skenesborough, esquires."[75]*

The major attainder in Washington County was one Philip Skene (1725-1810). His career as a soldier eventually brought him to the New World, where he founded the settlement of Skenesborough (now Whitehall, NY) at the head of Lake Champlain in 1759. Skene worked hard to help this settlement flourish until it was captured by the Americans in 1775. Skene was taken prisoner and, after being exchanged as a prisoner of war, returned to England briefly in 1777. He then sailed again for America to aid the British army in the Revolution. After the recognition of independence, Colonel Skene was in London, and intended to return and begin again as an American citizen, but the State of New York attainted him and his son of high treason, and confiscated their estates. After the war, he returned to New York to recover his property, but was unsuccessful, and went back to England. The British government in 1785 granted him a pension of £240 per annum for life, and a sum of £20.000, with which he purchased the estate of Addersey Lodge, Northamptonshire.[76]

For many years, Skene tried in vain to regain his holdings in Skenesborough that had been captured. He did receive an annuity and a salary to compensate him for his losses and as payment for his services to the government. He returned to England and, in 1788, purchased Hartwell Manor, fifty-five miles northwest of London. He lived out his days there until his death in 1810.

No less than a hundred and sixty-two tracts of Andrew P. Skene's land were sold and registered, every one being declared forfeited by the attainder of Philip and Andrew P. Skene. Probably the elder gentleman had conveyed the land to the younger, in the hope of saving it from forfeiture, but the retribution of the old colonials was not to be ignored.

*"The elder Skene wrote from England to Elishama Tozer, of Whitehall, declaring that he had always been desirous of promoting the welfare of America, even when serving the king that he had no tie binding him to England, and desiring to learn whether there was any chance for him to resume his residence at Skenesborough, and regain his forfeited lands. But his efforts in this direction were without avail."[77]*

Besides the Skene's lands, a hundred and thirty-one tracts were registered as forfeited by Oliver DeLancey, ten by Edward and Ebenezer Jessup, three by Jonathan and Daniel Jones, three by Michael Hoffnagle, and one by John Tabor Kemp, ex-attorney-general in Washington County. Several tracts, amounting to about a thousand acres, had belonged to Donald Fisher. The largest number of tracts sold to any one person was to General John Williams, who purchased sixty-five, situated in all parts of the county. In a few cases the fee-simple was sold, but in most instances the Commissioner conveyed "the equity of redemption of the rent and reversion," the lands having been originally sold with the reservation of a quitrent to the crown."[78]

Up to that time they had sold 2,329 acres forfeited by Oliver DeLancey, 4,067 acres forfeited by Philip and Andrew Skene, and 2,000 acres forfeited by Edward and Ebenezer Jessup. In the standard money of the day these lots were worth about $50,000. From October 12, 1784 to August 29, 1788, the estates remaining of these same persons, and of John Tabor Kemp, John Rapelje, David Jones, Michael Hofnagle and Jonathan Jones, aggregating 62,000 acres, brought only £40,000 or $100,000, to the state. Later sales probably increased this amount considerably. The sums given above were equal to £60,000 sterling.[79]

# 4-    GRADUAL ABOLITION: MANUMISSION PROVISIONS

*"In one important respect the New York law did reflect a radical democratic approach: it conferred full civic rights on freedmen, allowing them to vote and bear arms. In this respect New York showed greater respect for republican equality than Massachusetts or Rhode Island where Blacks suffered legal discrimination."[80]*

This migration may have been the result of a Manumission Provision in the Gradual Abolition Act of 1799 passed by the New York State Legislature after numerous unsuccessful attempts. Given this possibility, I feel that it is incumbent upon us to discuss the provisions of this Law as it relates to the legal status of these people of African descent including the Van Vrankens to Washington County by way of this historic migration.

New York State's mandate for gradual abolition was a well wired and orchestrated compromise reached between the abolitionist and enslaver factions of the state and their respective representatives in the state legislature over the issue of compensating enslavers for the loss of their "property" to future abolition. It occurred at a time when Federalists "needed to prove that they were genuine friends of liberty." In this climate, the passage of an emancipation law could significantly assist Federalist leaders in re-establishing their rhetorical concern for civic freedom.

Furthermore, The Albany Argus, a leading Republican newspaper, had published articles ". . . which supported emancipation and warned that votes would be withheld from Republicans who failed to do so."[81]

A majority of both houses (Senate and Assembly) were clearly prepared to end enslavement in New York. And yet, opposition to gradual abolition still continued. Opponents argued that gradual abolition would become a burden on the community. They urged that gradual abolition would promote the notion that there should be a community of goods and an equal sharing of property.[82] It was also argued that the poor man was more dependent on his enslaved domestic than the rich, who were "wallowing in luxury" with armies of servants. It was also proposed that emancipation would rob widows and orphans of enslaved persons that were their only means of support.[83] Lastly, they argued that enslavers would see little benefit in raising enslaved children who would become free upon adulthood.

Interestingly enough, this compromise occurred during a period in time when Federalists and Republicans lived to oppose one another—an earlier version of the "red vs. blue" atmosphere of gridlock that exists in American politics today! And yet, gradual abolition attracted almost equal support from representatives of these two groupings. The extent of Republican support was remarkable considering the fact that New York abolitionism had heretofore been a Federalist cause.[84] This concept of gradual abolition which had already been legislated and adjudicated in other northern states, met little opposition in New York State legislative debates, as the bill was passed by a vote of 68 Federalists to 23 Republicans in the Assembly and 22 to 10 in the Senate.[85] After years of considerable debate over the last half of the 18th century, it was finally agreed by all factions that:

1- **African descendants already in bondage would remain so for the remainder of their natural lives, so that no investment would be lost;**
2- **Enslavers would have the option of manumitting any of their enslaved without having to pay any bond requirements; and,**
3- **Enslavers were given permission to abandon any and all of their infirmed, dependent, or aging enslaved persons without any financial obligation.**

As one-sided as these results might seem, the major concession that was made to the enslavers of New York State was centered squarely on *the fate of the Children*.

# THE GRADUAL ABOLITION ACT OF 1799

In 1799, New York State passed the Gradual Abolition Act which stipulated that:

1- any child born of an enslaved woman within the State after July 4, 1799, should "be deemed and adjudged to be born free;"

2- these same children shall be the servant of the legal "enslaver" of his or her mother until such child, if a male, reaches the age of twenty eight years and, if a female, the age of twenty five;

3- the enslaver of the mother and master or mistress of her enslaved child(ren) were required to register each child with the town clerk under the penalty of a fine;

4- should the enslaver of the mother choose to abandon his/her rights to the child's service, he/she was required to notify the town clerk;

5- town clerks would declare an abandoned child a pauper thus allowing the Overseers of the Poor (the predecessor of the Social Services and Corrections Departments) in that town to bound out the child to any interested parties;

6- the Overseers of the Poor were to be compensated or reimbursed by the state under this law at a rate of $3.50 per month per child for maintenance and support by the Comptroller and Treasurer of New York State until the child was contracted or bonded out to a new "employer;" and;

7- until the children were bound out to an "employer" by the Overseers of the Poor, these children were allowed to remain in the care of their mother's enslaver and these enslavers and not the Overseers of the Poor, were entitled to receive the full state allocated maintenance payment..[86]

The fundamental aspect of this new law revolved around the concept of "abandonment of responsibility" and its concomitant subsidy provision. This abandonment and subsidy option was a major concession to New York's enslavers to garner their support for the passage of the bill. In reality, it represented a thinly veiled scheme to provide for a state sponsored compensated abolition program. The Abandonment Program, as it has been referred to:

> *"had been inserted into the 1799 act to gain the cooperation of pro-enslavement forces in the passage of the bill. This disguised compensated abolition scheme permitted slaveholders to abandon children and then receive them back into their homes as boarders*

*until (and if) they were bound out to service—for which they would*
*receive monthly payments from local poor authorities.*[87]

The abandonment program of the Gradual Abolition Act of 1799 was amended in 1802 when the amount of monthly maintenance was reduced a second time from $3.00 to $2.00 per child per month. The duration of eligibility for this subsidy was also reduced to four years by this amendment. Now, abandoned children (abandoned at the age of one-year old) were to be bonded out by the Overseers of the Poor by the age of four (4) years old. After this period of time, the state would not be required to continue its subsidy for maintenance and support. The entire provision was later abolished in 1804 after five years of implementation and expense to the state.[88] Enslavers were now required to either abandon the young children of enslaved mothers without compensation or assume the cost of their upkeep through the ages of twenty-five for females or twenty-eight for males.

## MANUMISSION PROVISIONS OF THE GRADUAL ABOLITION LAW

The Provision of this Law that may be most relevant to the "free" status of our Van Vranken Family and the thousands of persons of African descent who migrated to Washington and other counties during the early 19th century, provides, that: ". . . it shall be lawful for the owner of any slave immediately after the passing of this act to manumit such slave by a certificate for that purpose under his own hand and seal."[89] This action on the part of enslavers, however, required certification by the Overseer of the Poor that these adults could support themselves independently of local expense. An amendment to the 1799 Law in 1804, stipulated that this process of manumission could occur once these young adults reached the age of twenty-one for males and females, the age of eighteen years.[90]

The 1799 law had also placed a moratorium on the posting of a bond of $250 by enslavers to ensure that no financial burden was placed on towns for the support of those manumitted. This bond had been an aspect of previous manumission requirements under various state laws. In its place, the statute provided that it was lawful for enslavers immediately after the passing of this law, to manumit an enslaved individual by certification and the seal of the owner. It would be interesting to research just how many of the more than 21,000 enslaved persons, who lived in New York during this period, were actually freed under the provisions of the Gradual Abolition Law of 1799; particularly with respect to the some two thousand and seven hundred "free" persons of African descent who migrated to Washington County between the years of 1800 and 1820.

## GRADUAL ABOLITION IN WASHINGTON COUNTY

The following narrative on Gradual Abolition in Washington County is meant to provide the reader with a true picture of the nature of Washington County and the political and social fabric of the county in which our Van Vranken Family and numerous other families of African descent chose to reside, raise their children and sustain their legally "free and independent" existence. The Gradual Abolition Act can be characterized as tantamount to this status.

Cities, towns and villages in counties throughout New York State judiciously followed the reporting and registration requirements of the Gradual Abolition Law of 1799. The small rural towns and villages of upstate New York and Washington County in particular provide a very clear example of this participation.

In the Town of Salem, "The Minutes of the Town of Salem" list the various reporting categories that were required by the 1799 Law. [91] Included in these official minutes outlined in Table 2 are the dispositions of various enslavement categories adhered to by Salem enslavers that required by law, certification and/or approval of the Town Clerk or Overseers of the Poor.

### TOWN MINUTES - SALEM, NY (1790-1826)

| Subject | Year | Month/day |
|---|---|---|
| Sabbath Day Keepers (Daniel Mathison, James Tomb, William McCoy, | 1790 | 4/1 |
| Sabbath Day Keepers (John Law, William Mathews, James Sawins, John Gage Jr. | 1790 | 4/1 |
| Sabbath Day Keepers (Robt. Stewart, William Harkness, William McFarland, | 1790 | 4/1 |
| School (annual reports for 1816 to 1834, 1837, 1840, 1841) | 1816 | 6/6 |
| Slaves (certificate by Poor Masters that slave, Lotte, is manumitted, by Edward Savage) | 1818 | 1/7 |
| Slaves (certificate of birth of Cato to slave, Amy. Owner Anthony Blanchard) | 1818 | 9/5 |
| Slaves (certificate of birth of male, Dick, to slave Violet, owner Margaret Warford) | 1807 | 10/1 |
| Slaves (certificate of birth of slave female, Nan. Owner John Savage, | 1818 | 9/21 |
| Slaves (certificate of birth of Sylvia; mother, Rose; owner Ebenezer Proudfit) | 1805 | 7/11 |
| Slaves (certificate of mulatto birth, male named Cuff, owner James Harvey) | 1808 | 3/24 |
| Slaves (certificate of ownership of child slave, Moses, to Ebenezer Russell) | 1803 | 8/17 |
| Slaves (certification of Peter, born to slave, Beck; owner Anthony Blanchard) | 1810 | 4/27 |
| Slaves (certification that manumitted slave, Amy, is capable of suporting herself) | 1820 | 11/29 |
| Slaves (Certification that slave Jack Becker or John Dean can support himself) | 1825 | 3/8 |
| Slaves (cetificate claiming slave child, Charles Woods. Owner Nathan Wilson) | 1821 | 5/11 |
| Slaves (John Williams abandons right to slave child, London, born of slave, Dina) | 1803 | 10/17 |
| Slaves (Poor Master certification that former slave, Flora, can provide for herself) | 1818 | 3/9 |
| Slaves (slave, Charles, of owner Nathan Willson Esq. is set free) | 1826 | 1/11 |

The initial category, the registration or certification of the birth of an enslaved child, is highlighted as "certified by the Town Clerk or Poor Master" in six instances between the years 1803-1818. One such registration is recorded as such:

> *Sir, my Negro woman Rose had a child on the third of April last whom she named Sylvia and who you will plan to record in the Town Book agreeable to Law.*
>
> *Ebinezer Proudfit, Salem July 1ˢᵗ 1805*

Another, record states:

> *I certify that a certain male Child born of a Negro wench a slave belonging to me was born on the 24ᵗʰ day of September 1807 in my family and that said Child is a Molato to which I have given the name of Cuff.*
>
> *Salem County of Washington, March 24ᵗʰ 1808 James Garvey*[92]

It would seem that Mr. James Garvey was attempting not only to register the birth of Cuff following the requirements of the Gradual Abolition Law, but at the same time, it can be argued that he was also making a statement with respect to the parentage of this young boy.

Town officials were also required to certify the official abandonment of the children of enslaved mothers. Table 2 identifies one instance of abandonment when John Williams abandons his rights to an enslaved child named London, born to one of his enslaved females named Dina Williams. Williams makes the following statement with respect to this abandonment:

> *"Pursuant to the Law of this State [posted] sp. this 8ᵗʰ of April 1801 I do hereby abandon my right of a Negro male child named London about ten months old which said Negro male child of a Female Slave purchased by me from one McGeorge Ashley of Whitehall named Dina.*
>
> *Salem Oct. 7ᵗʰ 1805 John Williams*[93]

In addition, these official records identify the instances of enslavers, Ebinezer Rupill and Nathan Wilson registering enslaved children Moses and Charles Woods, respectively. These two records provide another interesting insight into the provisions of the 1799 Law. Unlike John Williams, who abandons his rights to London, these two enslavers are asserting and receiving certification of their rights to ownership. Mr. Rupill's certification assumes the following form:

> *I Ebenezer Rupill of Salem in the County of Washington and State of New York do hereby certify in compliance to an Act of the Legislature of the State in such cases made and provided that I am the owner of a certain Male Negro Child named Moses aged eight months.*
>
> *Salem 17th August 1803 Ebenezer Rupill*

This statement of ownership reflects the newly acquired status of "ownership of the enslaved" sanctioned by the State of New York under the provisions of the Gradual Abolition Act of 1799. The 1799 Law also provided guidelines for the manumission of enslaved persons. The 1799 Law placed a moratorium on previous requirements of posting a bond of $250 by the enslavers to ensure that no financial burden was placed on towns for the support of those manumitted. These Salem Town minutes record five (5) instances of manumissions on the part of the town's enslavers. Recorded manumissions of Amy (1820), Jack Becker/John Dean (1825), and Flora (1818) address specifically the requirement of certification by the Poor Master [Overseer of the Poor] that they are capable of supporting themselves. In two other recorded manumissions, Lotte (1818) manumitted by Edward Savage is certified by the Poor Master while Charles (1826), owned by Nathan Wilson is just "set free." It would seem that in Lotte's case, the requirement of certification in the law had been met, even though it doesn't specifically speak to the issue of being able to support herself. Charles, on the other hand, probably qualified under an amendment of the law in 1802 that set manumission eligibility at twenty-one years of age for males instead of the original law's twenty-eight year requirement.

Even smaller Washington County communities maintained a dependence on enslaved labor. In 1790, in the small upstate town of Easton census records list the following residents as enslavers and the number of enslaved held:

> **"Martin Van Buren—2, Gerrit Van Buren—2, Abraham Widedale—3, Daniel Winne—10, Peter Becker—4, Simon DeRidder—5, Walter DeRidder—7, Gerrit Lasing—3, Jacob Van Schaick—6, Peter Van Woort—9, Cornelius Vandenberg—5. All of these slave holders were of Dutch descent and lived on, or very near, the River road."[94]**

Likewise in other Washington County towns like Hebron, town minutes record similar actions of the town enslavers and the Overseers of the Poor with respect to the required reporting and certification of African descendants and their "statutorily" enslaved children under the Gradual Abolition Act of 1799. [95]

Additionally, Gradual Abolition Act records were noted by Crisfield Johnson in his "History of Washington County" for the Town of Hebron:

### "BIRTH OF SLAVE CHILD

*1801.—Born on the 22d day of last August, a black negro male Bett; child's name is Antony. Said Bett is a slave to me Wm. McCracken. "Hebron, Feb. 1, 1801 "Entered on record May, 1801, per me "William McClellan, Town Clerk."*

Also recorded is:

### "EMANCIPATION OF A SLAVE..

*1814—This may certify that we, David Whedon and Samuel Livingston, overseers of the poor for the town of Hebron, having examined Tamar, a black woman, a slave to Thomas Gourley, and the said Thos. Gourley wishing to manumit her, or give her freedom, we the said overseers of the poor are fully of the opinion that the said Tamar is not of the age of forty-five years, and is of sufficient ability to provide for herself, agreeable to the statute of this State of New York, passed the 9th day of, 1813. "Dated the 5th day of Sept., 1814." [96]*

"The following items relative to the institution of enslavement in the "Old Town of Cambridge" have been extracted from the town records. It will be noticed that the sentiment against it produced the manumission of many servants"[97]:

*"Sept. 18, 1802, Austin Willis certifies to the birth of a female negro child named Jude.*

*Same date, Thomas Green certifies to the birth of a male negro child named Pomp."*

*"Jeremiah Stillwell certifies that Jan. 20, 1805, there was born of his female slave named Isabella, a female child named Harriet."*

*"Philip Smith manumits his negro man, 'Sam,' March 25, 1805."*

*"Wm. McAuley manumits his slave man named Samuel, April 8, 1810."*

*"Austin Wells manumits his slave woman named Hannah, Feb. 13, 1813."*

*"David Simpson manumits his negro man slave named Harry Van Schaick, Oct. 8, 1816."*

*"Henry Ham manumits his negro man slave, Thomas Thompson, March 24, 1819."[98]*

The following is recorded for the Town of Jackson:

*"Recorded May 6, 1818, the birth of a black female child, by the name of Diana, on the 10th of July, 1816, in the house of William McAuley, which he claims as his slave according to law."*

And,

*"Recorded Jan. 6, 1819, James, a black male child, born the 8th day of August, 1818, in the house of William McAuley, which said McAuley claims as his slave, according to law."[99]*

The Old Cambridge District also provides a telling version of life for those of African descent in Washington County. The following are excerpts from: "Up from . . . Slavery in the Cambridge Valley" by Dave Thornton.[100]

The following is the complete account of the Ashton slave purchase, as it appeared in The Washington County Post in 1873:

*"Received from James Ashton in cash and vallew (sic) to the amount of 55 Ib, one shilling and six pence, being in part for Shu the wench and child sould (sic) him I say, RCVD this 14th day of April, 1789. (signed) William Ferine, RCVD from James Ashton in cash and vallew (sic) to the amount of nineteen Ib, 18 shillings and 6 d (?) ₛ being in full for Shu the wench and child sold him, I say RCVD by me this 30th of March, 1790. (Signed) William Ferine"[101]*

Frank McClellan, who was an avid local historian, used his early family connections to gain access to Town of White Creek records that have since been lost. He borrowed the records from Henry Perry in December, 1940. According to Frank McClellan, "during colonial British rule it was common for men of property to own enslaved persons. One of the largest land owners in the Old Cambridge District was Philip Van Ness. His manor house stood near the John L. Pratt home (1940) at Buskirk's Bridge, According to the local census of 1790, six slaves lived on the Van Ness Manor. John Faulkner (location of house unknown) owned five slaves. Louis H. Veile, four; Peter Veile, two; and John Brott owned three.[102]

From the Old Cambridge Minute Book, other similar entries prove beyond doubt that slavery was an accepted practice among the early wealthy land owners of this area. The 1790 census reveals that there were 22 slave owners in Old Cambridge District. Among them were:

1- *William Whiteside, founder of one of the most prominent families in the history of West Cambridge and Easton and a major financial contributor to the local effort in the American Revolution, was also the owner of slaves. In the 1773 minute book of the Town, Whiteside "certifies that on the 10th day of Feb. 1802, a male child named Ben was born of a female slave owned by him"*

2- *Cornelius Wendell was a prominent local lawyer and judge. He served in the State Legislature. He also had a slave named Phillis that bore a Negro boy named Jack. and,*

3- *The Lake family, of early Dutch extraction, has been prominent in White Creek since before there was a White Creek. Gerrit Lake certified that: "on Jan. 15 1799, his female slave named Deyan was delivered of a female child . . . and on the 17th of Sept. 1802, the same slave was delivered of a male child named Harry."*

John Younglove was the leader of the local rebels of the Revolutionary War days and is buried in the front row of the old cemetery on Park St. After the Revolution, "Judge" Younglove decided who had been loyal to the cause and could return to his farm without paying taxes for the war years and who had not been sufficiently loyal and whose land should, therefore, be forfeited and given to one who had been a better servant of the Revolution.[103]

And yet, Younglove's passion for liberty did not extend to his own household. The Old Town Minute Book for the period reads, "On the 28th day of February 1801, was born a female child, of a slave named Nan the property of John Younglove Esq."

Even the clergy of Cambridge were involved in the inhuman practice of the enslavement of human beings:

*"Rev, John Dunlap was an early minister at the United Presbyterian Church. In 1813, Dunlap manumitted his slave named Nell. Richard Feus, who lives in the former Dunlap house on South Union St., has found records indicating that Nell continued on as the Dunlap house servant until she died."*[104]

The Old Cambridge Minute Book of 1773 also records the following practices of enslavement by prominent citizens of the area:

*"Jeremiah Stillwell is thought to have been a local patent medicine man. However he made his money, he was sufficiently affluent to afford slaves. Born on July 5 1805, his female slave (name not given) bore him a male child (name not given).*

*Cornelius Wendell, whose son, would grow up to be known as """the President's printer", was a prominent resident on the west end of Cambridge Corners. ^On the third day of July last" his slave Phillis gave birth to a "negroe" (sic) boy named Jack by his mother.*

*Austin Wells, of the only family named on the original Cambridge Charter to settle here, was also an owner of slaves. He certified that ". . . on the 28th of October 1801, was born in his house of a Negro slave of his named Nan, a female child named Dolly.*

*We know that Wells had more than one slave, and that he kept slaves for a number of years, because the old minute book holds a record of the birth of a female child to "Nan" on March I, 1807. Nan was owned by Austin Wells and the child, which would also belong to Wells, was named Sibbel.*

*In the record for 1803, Austin Wells again certifies that on the 18th day of Sept ". . . was born in his house of his Negro slave named Nan (another female Negro child", this one named Judy.*
*"Born in my house 30 March 1809 to my Necfro (sic) slave Nan, a female Negro child named Dina," so certified Austin Wells.*

*Again, on 17 May 1810, Austin Wells' slave Nan gave birth, this time to a child named Nell, evidently yet another female.* [105]

And,

*Wm. McAuley certified that on the sixth day of October, 1802 was born a male child named Dink of his slave named Mary."* [106]

Other families of prominence in Old Cambridge who participated fully in the institution of human enslavement included the following:

1- *"One of the oldest and most prominent families in early Cambridge history is the Greens. At least one, Thomas, owned slaves. The record indicates that on June 25, 1804 his slave "Jenn bore a male child named Pomp". On Sept. 20, 1808, Thomas Green's slave Jean bore a male child named Prince; also,*

2- *George Barber certified that on the 5 September 1803, was born to his female slave called "Dine" a male child named Andrew;*

3- *Peter Ferine had more than one slave and, based upon his transaction with James Ashton, perhaps bought and sold slaves as a business. On October 25, 1801, his female slave Rachel bore a male son named Charles. On December 30, 1804, his female slave Leney bore him a male child named Edenborough. Isaac Ferine, on 30 Sept. 1804, recorded that his female slave Bine was delivered of a female child named Margaret;*

4- *Joseph Gilberts reported that on 18 April 1805, his female child Almirer born to his female slave Nan; and,*

5- *The Cornell name is another 'old and prominent local family name that thrivesto this day. Indeed, the local Cornells are a branch of the family that founded Cornell University. But in 1804, at least one member of the family was a slave owner. Paul Cornell certified that on the 8th of November, . . . was born of his female slave Ann a female child named Fancy". And on the 9th of September, 1802 ". . . the same slave was delivered of a male child named Harry, and also on the 5 day April 1805 the same slave was delivered of a female child named Melinda".* [107]

Other examples included the following:

*"This may certify that born in the house and the property of James Fort a black male child named Han. Abraham T. Fort, guardian to James Fort.*

*Abraham Van Tuyl certified that on September 22, 1806, his female slave Rachel delivered a child, Susan. Van Tuyl was a farmer in the lower valley and a major slave-owner in the area. Abraham Van Tuyl certified that on 14 January, 1807 his female slave Rachel delivered yet another female child, Dean."[108]*

## LOCAL MANUMISSION OF ENSLAVED

John Younglove mentioned earlier, was one of those who sought to divest himself of his enslaved persons. The following record is also from an early Town of Cambridge Minute Book, 1773:

*"Whereas it is represented to us the subscribers being a majority of the overseers of the poor and two of the justice of the peace of the town of Cambridge, said county of Washington,—by John Younglove Esq., that he desires to manumit his Negro slave/ named Prince Acker, We therefore certify that he appears to be about the age of thirty-one and consequently under fifty years of age and in our opinion of sufficient ability to maintain himself.""Given under our hands in said Cambridge this 26th day of March, 1802, (signed) Reuben Pride and Jesse e Fairchild (overseers)Edmund Wells and James Towne (justices)"[109]*

Others who sought to manumit their enslaved persons included:

*"I Jesse Fairchild of the Town of Cambridge in the County of Washington State of New York . . . do certify that Jack a Negro boy to whose service I am entitled, was the PresbyterLan minister: "I, John Dun-lap, do hereby manumit my female slave named Nell S April 1813".*

Below is an excerpt concerning a curious account of a Washington County manumission:

### SALEM BEDEAU

One of the most interesting of the slaves of the community, just because we know something about his, life is Salem Bedeau (or Bedo). Salem was born at Seabrook, Connecticut about the year 1779. He was owned by Jeremiah Stillwell of Cambridge. Salem is described as being about 5 ft, 8 inches tall.

He was apparently manumitted by Stillwell 24 Aug 1810, although the record indicates that Stillwell tried to do it earlier:

> *I Jeremiah Stilwell . . . do hereby manumit my man slave named Salem Bedeau and my Negro woman slave named Arabella, his wife in pursuance of an act of the legislature of New York the eighth day of April, 1801. Jeremiah Stilwell, in the presence of David Simpson).*

Thereafter, Salem served as sextant, (or graveyard keeper) of the First Presbyterian Churchyard at Park and Main. Salem is buried in the extreme southeast corner of that burying ground, beneath a simple, recently repaired stone." [110]

The purpose for detailing this history of enslavement in Washington County is to assist the reader in understanding that the conditions and circumstances under which people of African descent lived and existed in Washington County were no different than those that existed throughout New York State during the time period that the state sanctioned and subsidized the enslavement of innocent human beings of African descent.

Therefore, without special considerations or customs; we are still confronted with the driving question as to: Why Washington County was chosen as the end point for the major migration of "free" African descendants?

# REFERENCE NOTES

[15] Burrows, Ewing and Mike Wallace, *Gotham: A history of New York City to 1898*, (Oxford Press, 1999) pg. 349

[16] Peter Charles Hoffer, Law and People in Colonial America, Revised Edition, (Johns Hopkins University Press, 1998) pg.124

[17] The Encyclopedia of New York State and other copies of the 1800 Census list this figure as one hundred and nineteen 119 "Free Blacks."

[18] 1810 Federal Census for Washington County, New York

[19] !810 Federal Census for New York State.

[20] !800 and 1810 US Federal Census

[21] 1790 Black Heads of Families, Bureau of Census, Century of Population Growth, Tables 98 & 99, pg. 183

[22] IBID

[23] The Encyclopedia of New York State, 2005, Syracuse University Press, pg. 1419

**NOTE**: You will notice that the listed numbers of "Free" and Enslaved Persons of African Descent in this Chart 6 and the corresponding numbers of "Free" and Enslaved Persons of African Descent in Chart 4 of this work are marginally different. Figures for Chart 4 have been compiled directly from the Federal Census of 1810 housed in the New York State Library in Albany, NY.

[24] For a list of over forty New York blacks who fought with the patriot forces, see National Archives and Records Service, General Services Administration, Debra L. Newman, comp., Special List No. 36, List of Black Servicemen Compiled From the War Department Collection of Revolutionary War Records (Washington, D.C.: National Archives and Records Service, 1974), pp. 1-29

[25] CHAPTER 32, LAWS OF THE STATE OF NEW YORK: "An Act for Raising Two Regiments for the defense of this state on bounties of inappropriate lands," March 20, 1781, 4th Session

[26] IBID

[27] See Vivivinne Kruger, Chapter 11, Reference note #: Ezekiel Hawley MSS, NYHS, possible paymaster, delivered the sum to Solemon Close

[28] Benjamin Quarles, Black Mosaic: Essays in Afro-American History and Historiography, 1988, ch 2-3.

[29] 1786 Census, Bureau of Census, Population Growth; The southern six counties disproportionately lost black population in wartime compared to the rest of New York. Whereas in 1771 60.4 percent of New York colony's black population lived in the southern six counties, only 45.6 percent lived there in 1786, and 50.3 percent by 1790. See table 1, p. above on the proportion of New York blacks resident in the southern six counties over time.

30   IBID
31   See Kruger, Chapter 11 Reference notes #21; Proclaimation by sir Henry Clinton, General and Commander-In-Chief," British Headquarters Papers, Document 2094, Manuscript Room, New York Public Library, published on July 3, 1779 in the Rivington's Royal Gazette
32   See Kruger, Chapter 11 Reference notes #22; Proclaimation by sir Henry Clinton, General and Commander-In-Chief," British Headquarters Papers, Document 2094, Manuscript Room, New York Public Library, published on July 3, 1779 in the Rivington's Royal Gazette
33   See Kruger, Chapter 11 reference note # 23, Collections of the New York Historical Society, Proceedings of a Board of General Officers of the British Army at New York, 1781
34   See Kruger, Chap. 11 Reference Note # 24, Book of Negroes Inspected on the 30th November 1783 by Capt. Gilfillan of Armstrong
35   Quarles, Benjamin, The Negro in the American Revolution (Chapel Hill: University of North Carolina at Chapel Hill Press, pg. 172
36   Yoshpe, Disposition of Loyalists Estates, pg. 17, 37
37   See Kruger, Chapter 11, reference Note # 15: Collections, New York Historical Society, Abstracts of Wills, 9:106
38   See Kruger, Chapter 11, reference Note # 16, William Underhill, Westchester Co., September 2, 1784, Inventories of Estates—New York City and Vicinity 1717-1844, NYHS; Scott and Owre, Genealogical Data from Inventories
39   New York State Comptroller's Office Revolutionary War Accounts and Claims, Overview of the Records New York (State). Comptroller's Office Revolutionary War accounts and claims,1775-1808, http://www.archives.nysed.gov/a/research/fa/A0200.shtml
40   IBID
41   Flick, Loyalism in New York,
42   IBID
43   New York State Comptroller's Office Revolutionary War Accounts and Claims, Overview of the Records New York (State). Comptroller's Office Revolutionary War accounts and claims,1775-1808, http://www.archives.nysed.gov/a/research/fa/A0200.shtml
44   Copy of Massachusetts Currency, n emission of £394,000 ($1,313,333) in legal tender bills of credit payable in Spanish milled dollars with 5% interest by December 31, 1786. This issue was authorized pursuant to the Continental Congress Resolution of March 18, 1780. Printed by Hall and Sellers in Philadelphia using paper watermarked "United States."

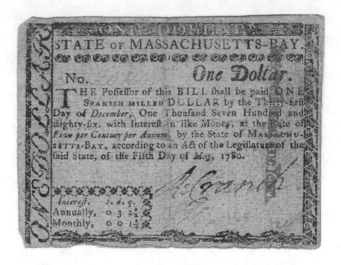

45  Flick, Loyalism in New York,
46  Chapter 64 of the Laws of New York State of 1784, "An Act for the speedy sale of the confiscated and forfeited estates within this state and for other purposes therein mentioned," May 12, 1784
47  Flick, Loyalism in New York, pg. 120-34, 136, 137-38
48  CHAPTER 58 OF THE LAWS OF 1786; "An Act further to amend an act entitled, "An Act for the speedy sale of the confiscated and forfeited estates within this state,' May 1, 1786, 9th Session
49  See Kruger, Chapter 11 Reference Note #37: New York Manumission Society—Reports of the Standing Committee, April 24, 1802, microfilm reel 1 and 2, pg. 218
50  Chapter. 45 of the Laws of 1816: "An Act concerning the maintenance of certain persons, formerly slaves," March 22, 1816, 39th Session,
51  See Kruger, Chapter 11, reference Note #137
52  CHAPTER XXIV OF THE LAWS OF THE STATE OF NEW YORK, PASSED IN THE THIRD SESSION OF THE LEGISLATURE, HELD AT KINGSTON, IN ULSTER COUNTY; *An Act for the Forfeiture and Sale of the Estates of Persons who have adhered to the Enemies of this State, and for declaring the Sovereignty of the People of this State, in respect to all Property within the same.—Passed 22d October, 1779.*
53  Yoshpe, Disposition of Loyalist Estates, p. 187.
54  Ratner, Vivienne L. "The Hastings Men." *The Westchester Historian.* 48 (Summer 1972). Pg. 56
55  IBID
56  IBID
57  IBID

58 IBID
59 Flick, Loyalism in New York, pg. 158
60 Yoshpe, Disposition of Loyalists Estates, pg.
61 Flick, Loyalism in New York, pg. 159-160
62 IBID
63 IBID, pg. 150
64 Yoshpe, Disposition of Loyalists Estates, pg.
65 Flick, Loyalism in New York, pg.145-50, 153-57
66 Yoshpe, Disposition of Loyalists Estates, pg.
67 Hugh Thomas, *The Slave Trade*, (NYC: Touchstone, 1997), 203; also see Ira Berlin, Many Thousands Gone, (Boston: The Belknap Press of Harvard University Press, 1998) 48
68 *The Dutch Imprint,* Cross Roads & Cross Rivers: Africans at Phillipsburg Manor, Upper Mills, (*www.hudsonvalley.org*)
69 Adolph Phillipse's Probate Inventory, 2 February 1750, New York Public Library
70 Office of the State Comptroller, Albany, Day Book No. 2, August 13, 1801 to January 8, 1803, p. 145.
71 Office of the State Comptroller, Albany, Day Book No. 4, November 10, 1803 to January 9, 1805, p. 231. All three Day Books are catalogued as Manuscript No. 310, New York State Library, Albany, N. Y.
72 Office of the State Comptroller, Albany, Day Book No. 3, January 11, 1803 to November 9, 1803, p. 113.
73 New York State Comptroller's Office Revolutionary War Accounts and Claims, http://www.archives.nysed.gov/a/research/fa/A0200.shtml
74 Report of the Sales by Commissioner of Forfeiture for the Eastern District of New York; Alexander Webster Commissioner, Oct. 1784, New York State Archives.
75 IBID
76 Edited Appletons Encyclopedia, Copyright © 2001 StanKlos.com™
77 C. Johnson, History of Washington County, pp 63
78 IBID
79 Flick, Loyalism in New York during the American Revolution, pg. 153
80 Zilversmith, 176-82, McManus, Black Bondage in the North, 171-8

**NOTE:** This seemingly positive act of civic rights, however, would be vehemently challenged and revoked by Republicans during the gradual abolition years.

81 Blackburn, Robin, *The Overthrow of Colonial Slavery*, Verso( New Left Books, 1998) 273
82 Ibid, 274
83 Blackburn, 273
84 Ibid

[85] *N.Y. State Senate Journal*, March 25, 27, 1799; *N.Y. State Assembly Journal*, March 28, 1799

[86] Chapter 62 of the Laws of 1799 of New York State as detailed in "A Far Cry From Freedom: Gradual Abolition (1799-1827) by L. Lloyd Stewart, AuthorHouse, 2005

[87] Kruger, pg. 822

[88] Chapter 40 of the Laws of the State of New York of 1804

[89] Chapter 62 of the Laws of the State of New York of 1799

[90] Chapter 40 of the Laws of New York State of 1804

[91] Town o Salem Minutes 1790-1826, Washington County Clerk's Office, 1992

[92] Ibid

[93] Ibid

**NOTE:** The fact that these declarations were handwritten leaves some translation to individual interpretation but the guest of these records is accurate with respect to this abandonment information.

[94] Washington County Historical Society, *History of Washington County, New York; Some Chapters in the History of the Town of Easton, N.Y.*, 1959, 07-112

**Note:** A few of those enslaved in Easton remained in the town for three and four generations. As late as 1957 the remains of two of their descendants were sent from a distant city for burial in the family lot in the Greenwich Cemetery.

[95] Hebron (Washington County) Town Record Book, 1784-1845, Office of Town Clerk, 11/28/75, NY State Archives

[96] History of Washington County, New York, by Crisfield Johnson, New York, Everts & Ensign, Philadelphia, 1878, pg 390

[97] IBID, pg.256

[98] IBID

[99] IBID, pg 410

[100] Dave Thornton, Up from . . . Slavery in the Cambridge Valley, Historical Perspectives, Cambridge, NY, 2002

[101] Ibid, pg.30

**NOTE:** *Thomas B. Ashton's comment:* **"I feel thankful that should the iniquity of the fathers be visited upon the children it extends only to the third and fourth generation.**

[102] IBID

[103] **NOTE:** This passage refers to the NY State Forfeiture Law of 1786 which will be discussed in greater detail later in this work.

[104] IBID, pg. 19

[105]  IBID, pgs. 22-23
[106]  IBID, pg. 23
[107]  IBID, pgs. 23-24
[108]  IBID, pg. 24
[109]  IBID, pg. 25-26
[110]  IBID, pg. 30-31

# Chapter III

## ECONOMIC CONDITIONS IN NEW YORK STATE AND WASHINGTON COUNTY

# THE ECONOMIC BOOM OF 1810 IN WASHINGTON COUNTY

## OVERVIEW

The geopolitical conditions that jumpstarted and sustained this economic resurgence and subsequent "migration" of "free" persons of African descent to Washington County represents only a part of the vector of this re-populating of Washington County. The major, and I would suggest—the primary initiator of this mass relocation centers squarely on the changing economic realities and conditions that were fundamentally transforming the economy in Washington County during the early 1800s. While these growth conditions encompassed a fifteen (15) to twenty (20) year period, particular emphasis in this Chapter will be placed on the "boom" year of 1810. Census and economic data chronicle a significant advancement in the economy of Washington County's towns and villages during this period.

The year 1810, a federal census year, is uniquely documented in the Federal Census of 1810 with the publication of two supplemental economic data studies never attempted before by the United States in prior censuses. These supplemental records entitled: "A Statement of the ARTS AND MANUFACTURES OF THE UNITED STATES OF AMERICA, for the year 1810: Digested and Prepared by: Tench Coxe, Esquire, of Philadelphia[111] and "A Series of Tables of the Several Branches of AMERICAN MANUFACTURES, Exhibiting Them in every County of the Union;"[112] provide the primary source documentation necessary to track and reconstruct this seemingly transformative economic revitalization in Washington County.

It is by way of this federal documentation that we have been able to strengthen and enhance our research with respect to the answers to the question, *WHY* was Washington County chosen as the destination point for this major migration of "free" persons of African descent from across New York State and the region? This documentation also provides a very concise and cogent depiction of the ever increasing vitality in the economy of Washington County in 1810 and most specifically, it emphasizes the economic realities supporting and sustaining this migration.

As the Manumission Provisions of New York State's Gradual Abolition Law were providing the establishment of what proved to be a truly significant advancement in the social/economic status of persons of African descent in New York State; simultaneously, in Washington County, an economic boom created an unprecedented opportunity for these newly "freed" citizens to solidify and actualize their dreams of freedom and prosperity.

The prospects of "free" status would prove meaningless without the opportunity to provide for and sustain a family and children by way of real and substantive employment. Washington County therefore, provided the foundation for just such an effort to secure upward mobility and independence for a largely unskilled and semi-skilled yet, highly motivated and ambitious people.

*SO THEY CAME!*

# ECONOMIC HISTORY

*"A few men of more than usual enterprise, and actuated by a most commendable public spirit, endeavored, it is true, to increase the wealth of Washington County by originating various schemes, nearly all of which, from the causes I have stated viz.. : the stoical indifference of the farmers—were total failures."[113]*

Washington County, according to Crisfield Johnson in his "History of Washington County, New York," had had a long and marginally successful history of agricultural production and home-manufacturing (primarily focused on the production of cloth for clothing and other necessities of life).[114]

The Champlain Valley became the major transportation route connecting New York City and the Middle Atlantic States to the south with Montreal and Quebec City to the north. The completion of the Champlain Canal in 1823 from the Hudson River at Fort Edward to Lake Champlain in Whitehall played a large part in Washington County's economy and continued population growth. It provided a swift water route to New York City, to eastern Canada and connecting with the Erie Canal near Albany, to the developing cities to the west.

Farm creation required at least as much labor as capital, plus a good measure of endurance and some luck. Labor involved all able-bodied members of a family and, when larger tasks or those requiring special skills were involved, neighbors. Within a few years of establishment, pioneer farms were largely self-sustaining in terms of clothing and food. A family of six was said to be able to feed itself on 12 acres of crops. Nevertheless, significant amounts of cash were needed for items that could not be locally grown or made and for payment of debts. The largest of which were outstanding land payments and the accompanying compound interest. Earning cash required a ready market and an efficient means of transporting products to it.

The main market for exports from Washington County was at Montreal, by way of Lake Champlain. For Hudson and Mohawk Valley farmers, access to the Port of New York was comparatively straightforward via bateaux and sloops on the respective rivers. Residents transported not only the surplus grain of farmers but large quantities of pot and pearl ashes, made from the timber which they were glad to get rid of in order to clear their land. Potash, in fact, was one of the main resources of the pioneers of Washington County. Due to its ease of transportation in proportion to its value, it would always bring cash, while grain could sometimes hardly be sold for enough to pay the cost of freight.

More cost effective than shipping surplus crops was hauling the more highly valued forest products to markets closer to home: such as potash to

Ithaca, where the price in 1821 was $90 per ton. Alternatively the ash could be sold to a local merchant at $2.50-$3.00 per 100 pounds. There was also a local market at Lansingburg (Troy was not yet in existence), where small sales and purchases were made, especially in the winter when Lake Champlain was closed by ice. Another option was to drive cattle, swine, turkeys, and geese to stockyards and slaughterhouses in Albany, Catskill (Greene Co), and other Hudson River towns.[115]

The Northern Turnpike Company, the first operated within this county, was incorporated on the 1st day of April, 1799. It had for its object the building of a turnpike from Lansingburgh, through Cambridge, Salem and Hebron, to the house of Hezakiah Searling in the town of Granville.[116] The company immediately built the road to the designated point, but continued it northward through Hampton to the state line, connecting with a similar road to Burlington, Vermont. This company also built a branch from Salem northwestward to the state line and another from Granvilie to Whitehall. Routes that existed in colonial times as trade routes became toll roads in the early 19th century. Additionally, beginning in 1809, a steamboat connected Whitehall with the north end of Lake Champlain. The natural water routes were improved by the Champlain Canal (1823) from Whitehall to Waterford (Saratoga County). This effort gradually shifted the economic and political power to canal towns, especially Fort Edward, Kingsbury, and Whitehall.[117]

## AGRICULTURE & INDUSTRY

Agricultural, mineral and timber-related industries had consistently made up the largest sectors of the economy of Washington County. Industry was shaped by available resources and abundant waterpower for sawmills and gristmills. By 1785, wing dams were constructed on the Hudson River at Sandy Hill and Fort Edward for power. Later dams diverted water to the canal system and attracted paper mills, foundries and machine shops. Clearing the forests in the 18th and 19th centuries created a thriving lumber industry, especially in the areas near the Hudson River and Lake Champlain, where logs could be rafted to market. Early industry in Washington County also included iron ore mining and smelting.[118]

Although flax, grain, cheese, wool and lumber were first produced for local consumption, they soon went south to Lansingburgh and north to Whitehall for shipment. Wool from Cambridge, Salem and Granville was the county's chief export until the 1840s. In Granville, Hampton, Hebron, Kingsbury, Salem and Whitehall, slate and other stone quarries emerged. There was still a great deal of home-manufacturing. Not only were "fulled-cloth" and flannel, tow-cloth and linen made in nearly every Almshouse, but hats, caps, and shoes were made in every little village.[119]

## ECONOMIC BOOM

The early 19th century ushered in a new economic boom and created a major shift in the fortunes and production capabilities of Washington County, as a whole. With newly acquired land from Albany County that was included in the renaming and restructuring of Charlotte County into Washington County in 1784, New York State through negotiated land settlements with Massachusetts and Vermont significantly restructured the boundaries of the county. In addition, the parceling of the thousands of acres of forfeited land acquired after the Revolution from British loyalists into smaller portions and lots for sale or rent provided a seemingly endless resource for increased production in agriculture and home-manufacturing.

The "Report of the Sales by Commissioner of Forfeiture for the Eastern District of New York, October 1784 to August 1788", documented the sale of Washington County land made available by the State of New York through the "Act of Forfeiture."[120] The Report records the sale of some 450-500 lots or some 62,000 acres of land to large, mid-sized and smaller farmers. These transactions enhanced the state coffers in an amount equal to £60,000 sterling.

This Record provides us with some insight into the economic development of Washington County during the beginning of the 19th century. The lands sold under the auspices of forfeiture legislation and documented in the Commissioner's Report were still producing in 1810 during Washington County's "boom" period. If we track these original sales and purchases in 1784-1788 recorded by Commissioner Webster in his Report and project them to family members still operating in the county in 1810, we can begin to piece together the impact that these forfeited lands had on the economic boom in 1810 and, their subsequent role in the migration of persons of African descent to Washington County. It also highlights the manner in which these "free" men and women of African descent began to establish a foothold in upstate New York.

Chart 7—"FORFEITURE LANDOWNERS WITH PERSONS OF AFRICAN DESCENT, 1810" details the descendants of some of these families that were involved in the original sales of these forfeited lands in Washington County. It also documents the number of "free" persons of African descent who worked these properties in conjunction with these descendant family members during the early 19th century, particularly during the year 1810.

# CHART 7

## FORFEITURE LANDOWNERS
## WITH PERSONS OF AFRICAN DESCENT
## 1810

# FORFEITURE LANDOWNERS IN 1784-85
## WITH FREE AFRICAN DESCENDANTS
### 1810

| SURNAME | GIVEN | Date of Sale | ACRES | Sale Price | 1810 DATA NAME | Town | "FREE"AFRICAN DESCENDANT |
|---|---|---|---|---|---|---|---|
| Harrington | Peter | 26 May 1785 | 172 | 112.5,9 | Harrington, Pete | Hebron | 4 |
| Stone | Abner | 1 Aug. 1785 | 84 | 30 | Stone      Abner | Salem | 6 |
| Simpson | Alexander | 1 Aug. 1785 | 84 | 30 | Simpson Alex | Salem | 3 |
| Williams | John | 12 Oct. 1784 | 242 | 320 | William John | Salem | 4 |
| Thompson | Willis | 28 Dec. 1784 | 100 | 65 | Thompson, Will | Whitehall | 3 |
| Hubbard | Salman | 26 May 1785 | 130 | 84.1 | Hubbard, Salma | Greenwich | 3 |
| Bowen | James | 1 Aug. 1785 | 168 | 60 | Bowen       John | Cambridge | 5 |
| Wilson | Thomas | 6 Oct. 1785 | 60 | 39 | Wilson      Robert | Hebron | 3 |
|  | Joseph | 1 Aug. 1785 | 84 | 30 | Wilson      Giles | Hebron | 3 |
|  |  |  |  |  |           James |  | 7 |
| Sturdafant | C. | 28 Dec. 1784 | 150 | 97.1 | Sturdafant Freelove | Kingsbury | 8 |
| Clark | Robert | 1 Aug. 1785 | 84 | 30 | Clark       George | Ft. Ann | 6 |
| Cleveland | B. | 1 Aug. 1785 | 84 | 30.2 | Cleveland Abel | Cambridge | 3 |
| Wray | George | 25 May 1785 | 1000 | 320 | Wray        John | Ft. Ann | 3 |
| Stockwell | Levi | 20 Dec. 1784 | 203 | 66.19 | Stockwell John | Hartford | 4 |
| Harris | Moses | 25 May 1785 | 185 | 278 | Harris      Samuel | Kingsbury | 3 |
| Scott | John | July 1785 | 100 | 65 | Scott      Abraham | Hebron | 3 |
| Johnson | Edon | 26 May 1785 | 103 | 66.18 | Johnson  Luther | Kingsbury | 3 |
| Hopkins | Sam | 1 Aug. 1785 | 84 | 30 | Hopkins James | Granville | 3 |
| **TOTAL FAMILIES** |  | **18** |  | **TOTAL AFRICAN DESCENDANTS** |  |  | **77** |

## WASHINGTON COUNTY: CHIEF AGRICULTURAL AND MANUFACTURED PRODUCTS

Washington County seized upon this opportunity to increase production and expand its economic position within the state. This increase in production was focused on four primary areas (products) all considered labor intensive industries with respect to their successful enterprise. These products include the increased production of flaxen goods; wool goods; cotton goods; and the measured production of fulling mills.

Table 3 indicates that in 1810, Washington County ranked #1 in New York State in the production of flaxen and woolen goods (yards) and # 2 in the state in the production of cotton goods (yards) and in the production of Fulling Mills (yards produced). Washington County also ranked # 3 in the State of New York in production from Hatteries (hats) and Tanneries (calf skins).[121]

The key to this major augmentation in production and the heightened advancement in the economic status of Washington County in New York State can be illustrated partially by the increase in the availability of land, as mentioned earlier; but, even more important is Washington County's major boost in available labor, particularly its fortuitous increase in the population of laborers of African descent. All of the textile production increases, cited above, are fundamentally attributed to labor intensive production. Without a significant labor force for production and processing, Washington County would have remained only as marginally successful as it had been prior to the turn of the century.

Examples of this labor intensive nature of production are highlighted in the following descriptions of Washington County's chief agricultural and manufactured products (Table 3):

# TABLE 3

## WASHINGTON COUNTY
## MANUFACTURING TABLE
### 1810

| Manufacture → | Cotton (yards) | Flaxen (yards) | Wool Goods (yards) | Carding Machines (pounds) | Fulling Mills (yards) |
|---|---|---|---|---|---|
| **New York State** | | | | | |
| Total Measure | 216,013 | 3,372,645 | 3,257,812 | 1,881,596 | 1,811,005 |
| Value | $ 69,124 | $ 2,014,742 | $ 2,850,585 | $ 940,798 | $ 2,263,756 |
| Total Mfg. Plants/Equip | 26 | - | 33,069 | 413 | 427 |
| **Washington County** | | | | | |
| Total Measure | 51,141 | 350,754 | 384,359 | 107,000 | 135,600 |
| Value | $ 16,365 | $ 129,779 | $ 334,392 | $ 53,500 | $ 169,500 |
| Total Mfg. Plants/Equip | 1 | - | 2,200 | 13 | 18 |
| | | | | | |
| Rank in State | 2 | 1 | 1 | 4 | 2 |
| % of State Total | 24% | 10% | 12% | 6% | 7% |
| % of State Value | 24% | 10% | 12% | 6% | 7% |
| % of Mfg. Plants/Equip | 4% | 0% | 7% | 3% | 4% |

| Manufacture → | Hatteries (Hats) | Forges (tons of iron) | Tanneries (hides) | Tanneries (calf skins) | Spirits Distilled (Gallons) |
|---|---|---|---|---|---|
| **New York State** | | | | | |
| Total Measure | 104,014 | 1,684 | 151,165 | 210,445 | 2,107,243 |
| Value | $ 260,035 | $ 168,400 | $ 659,079 | $ 235,698 | $ 1,685,794 |
| Total Mfg. Plants/Equip | 124 | 48 | 867 | | 591 |
| **Washington County** | | | | | |
| Total Measure | 7,900 | 199 | 10,000 | 14,000 | 23,263 |
| Value | $ 19,750 | $ 19,900 | $ 43,600 | $ 15,680 | $ 18,610 |
| Total Mfg. Plants/Equip | 11 | 6 | 37 | | 2 |
| | | | | | |
| Rank in State | 3 | 4 | 4 | 3 | 20 |
| % of State Total | 8% | 12% | 7% | 7% | 1% |
| % of State Value | 8% | 12% | 7% | 7% | 1% |
| % of Mfg. Plants/Equip | 9% | 13% | 4% | | 0% |

# FLAX

*"Flax had previously been produced only in small quantities, such as could be manufactured by the "little wheel" and the loom of each family; every farmer usually sowing a few square rods."*[122]

In May, 1812, when the country was preparing for the War of 1812, which was declared the next month, and when prices were rising in consequence. Mr. James Whiteside of Cambridge, sowed three acres in flax. All of his neighbors were astonished, and predicted that the labor of raising and dressing it would be so great as to more than use up any price which could be obtained. These forebodings were false. Despite all such awful prognostications, the value of the flax constantly continued to rise until dressed flax was sold at an unprecedented sum of eighteen and three-fourths cents per pound—thus providing the raiser a handsome profit.[123]

As a consequence, the raising of flax very soon became an important industry in Washington County, especially in its southern part. Even when prices after the War of 1812 fell, its cultivation was still found profitable, attaining a magnitude of no small importance, by becoming a resource to local county farmers. As the value continued to rise and returned a handsome profit, several of Mr. Whiteside's neighbors embarked in the same business. Flax-raising soon became an important industry in the southern part of Washington County. Even when prices went down after the war, it was still found profitable and attained a magnitude of importance.[124]

The war, however, was very influential to the financial interests of the county, especially as the demands created by the necessities of the general government changed this stagnation to an unusual business activity.

An example of this was the culture of flax. While the flax plant is not difficult to grow, it flourishes best in cool, humid climates and within moist, well-plowed soil. The process for separating the flax fibers from the plant's woody stock is laborious and painstaking and must be done in an area where labor is plentiful and relatively inexpensive. It is remarkable that while there is some mechanization to parts of the fiber preparation, most fiber preparation was done by hand as it had been for centuries. This may be due to the care that must be taken with the fragile flax fibers inside the woody stalk, which might be adversely affected by mechanized processing.

Both wool and linen were tremendously important fibers in the New World. Relatively easy to grow, American settlers were urged to plant a small plot of flax as early as the seventeenth century. While flax is easy to grow, settlers knew all too well the tedious and highly laborious chore of processing the woody stalks for its supple linen. Before the industrial revolution, much sturdy, homemade clothing was woven from linen cultivated, processed, spun, dyed, woven, and sewn by hand. It may be argued that until the eighteenth century, linen was the most important textile in the world. Linen yarn is spun from the long fibers found just behind the bark in the multi-layer stem of the flax plant *(Linum usitatissimum)*. In order to retrieve the fibers from the plant, the woody stem and the inner pith (called pectin), which holds the fibers together in a clump, must be rotted away. The cellulose fiber from the stem is spinnable and is used in the production of linen thread, cordage, and twine. From linen thread or yarn, fine toweling and dress fabrics may be woven. Linen fabric is a popular choice for warm-weather clothing. It feels cool in the summer but appears crisp and fresh even in hot weather. Household linens become more supple and soft to the touch with use, thus, linen was once the bed sheet of choice.

All that is needed to turn flax fiber into linen is to spin and weave the linen fibers into linen fabric. The process for separating the fibers from the woody stalk can use either water or chemicals, but these are ultimately washed away and are not part of the finished material. The manufacture of linen yarn requires no special design processes. All that has to be determined prior to manufacturing is the thickness of the yarn to be spun. That will depend on the grade of linen in production and the demands of the customer.

By the 1850s, linen production had virtually been abandoned in the United States because it was so much cheaper to buy the factory-made cotton. Some New Englanders of Scottish or Irish background continued to cultivate some flax for processing into linen used for fancy domestic linens such as bed sheets, toweling, and decorative table clothes, as their ancestors had for centuries. However, most Americans abandoned the cultivation of the plant in this country and instead chose cheap cotton that was carded, spun, woven, and roller-printed for just pennies a yard.

# WOOL

*"The woolen manufacture also continued to flourish. Under a [New York] State law of the period a premium of forty dollars was paid in 1813 to Scott Woodworth, of Cambridge, for the best woolen cloth made in the county, and another of thirty-five dollars to Adam Cleveland, of Salem, for the second best. The next year the first premium was carried off by Alexander McNish, and the second by Reuben Wheeler, both of Salem."[125]*

The production of wool in Washington County steadily increased during the early 19th century and an expanded labor force again contributed greatly to the expanded production of wool and woolen products. In 1825, Isaac Bishop of Granville began buying wool to send out of the county, the average price that year being fifty-two cents a pound. The business continued to increase, and for thirty years wool-raising was one of the leading industries of Washington County. Granville, Salem, Cambridge, and one or two other points became so favorably known as wool-markets that large amounts of the product were brought there to be sold from the State of Vermont and from the adjoining counties of New York State.[126]

The branch of the agricultural industry, which up to this period, had been little regarded but soon became one of the most important in the county was the raising of sheep. Dr. Asa Fitch's "Survey of Washington County," informs us that throughout the 18th century farmers raised only sheep enough to supply their families with home-made clothing, and they thought themselves lucky if they could circumvent the wolves with sufficient shrewdness to do that. The few that were raised were long-legged animals with light, coarse fleeces, and were inveterate rovers over hill and dale. Their principal good quality was the hardiness with which they withstood the severities and changes of this variant climate.[127] But during the first years of the 19th century, the wolves were pretty well thinned out, and at the same time a few manufacturers began to spring up in the country, affording a market for wool. Through the efforts of New York State's Chancellor Livingston, a beginning was made in the importation of fine-wooled sheep. The first cross of the common sheep of the county was with an English variety, which produced a great improvement. The fleece being heavier than that of either parent; and the mutton being more plentiful and of equally good quality. The change immediately obliterated the roving propensities of the common breed.[128]

The first Merino sheep in Washington County were brought into the present town of White Creek (then Cambridge) in 1809. The next year a flock was begun in Salem. Nathan Wilson, co-founder of the *Register Newspaper* and a United State's Representative, is credited with introducing Spanish Merino sheep into the county.[129] Spanish Merinos improved domestic quality and allowed the American woolen industry to compete with the best imports. The Merino sheep, in particular, with their deeply wrinkled folds producing large quantities of wool, caused a stir among American farmers in the early part of the 19th century. A few "gentlemen farmers" avoided Spanish export restrictions and imported some Merinos. As wool prices rose during the Embargo of 1807, a "Merino craze" occurred that pushed the price of fine wool and pure bred animals to record levels. Then, in 1810, an American diplomat arranged the importation of 20,000 purebred Merinos, and the woolen industry from Vermont to Pennsylvania to Ohio was changed forever.[130]

# THE MANUFACTURING PROCESS

The mechanization of the woolen cloth industry provides an example of the extent of 19th century industrial change. Every step of the process, except shearing the sheep and sorting the wool into different grades, was mechanized between 1790 and 1890. Only the organic aspects of shearing live animals and the value judgments required of human sorters resisted mechanical replication until the twentieth century.

The major steps necessary to process wool from the sheep to the fabric are: shearing, cleaning and scouring, grading and sorting, carding, spinning, weaving, and finishing.

### Shearing

Sheep are sheared once a year—usually in the springtime. A veteran shearer can shear up to two hundred sheep per day. The fleece recovered from a sheep can weigh between 6 and 18 pounds; as much as possible, the fleece is kept in one piece. Most sheep are still sheared by hand.

### Grading and sorting

Grading is the breaking up of the fleece based on overall quality. In sorting, the wool is broken up into sections of different quality fibers, from different parts of the body. The best quality of wool comes from the shoulders and sides of the sheep and is used for clothing; the lesser quality comes from the lower legs and is used to make rugs. In wool grading, high quality does not always mean high durability.

## Cleaning and scouring

Wool taken directly from the sheep is called "raw" or "grease wool." It contains sand, dirt, grease, and dried sweat (called *suint);* the weight of contaminants accounts for about 30 to 70 percent of the fleece's total weight.

To remove these contaminants, the wool is scoured in a series of alkaline baths containing water, soap, and soda ash or a similar alkali. The byproducts from this process (such as lanolin) are saved and used in a variety of household products. Rollers in the scouring machines squeeze excess water from the fleece, but the fleece is not allowed to dry completely. Following this process, the wool is often treated with oil to give it increased manageability.

## Carding

The fibers are passed through a series of metal teeth that straighten and blend them into slivers. Carding also removes residual dirt and other matter left in the fibers. Carded wool intended for worsted yarn is put through gilling and combing, two procedures that remove short fibers and place the longer fibers parallel to each other. From there, the sleeker slivers are compacted and thinned through a process called *drawing*. Carded wool to be used for woolen yarn is sent directly for spinning.

## Spinning

After being carded, the wool fibers are spun into yarn. Spinning for woolen yarns is typically done on a mule spinning machine, while worsted yarns can be spun on any number of spinning machines.

Thread is formed by spinning the fibers together to form one strand of yarn; the strand is spun with two, three, or four other strands. Since the fibers cling and stick to one another, it is fairly easy to join, extend, and spin wool into yarn. Spinning for woolen yarns is typically done on a mule spinning machine, while worsted yarns can be spun on any number of spinning machines. After the yarn is spun, it is wrapped around bobbins, cones, or commercial drums.

## Weaving

The wool yarn is woven into fabric. Wool manufacturers use two basic weaves: the plain weave and the twill. Woolen yarns are made into fabric using a plain weave (rarely a twill), which produces a fabric of a somewhat looser weave and a soft surface (due to napping) with little or no luster. The napping often conceals flaws in construction.

Worsted yarns can create fine fabrics with exquisite patterns using a twill weave. The result is a more tightly woven, smooth fabric. Better constructed, worsteds are more durable than woolens and therefore more costly.

## Finishing

After weaving, both worsteds and woolens undergo a series of finishing procedures including: fulling (immersing the fabric in water to make the fibers interlock); crabbing (permanently setting the interlock); decating (shrink-proofing); and, occasionally, dyeing. Although wool fibers can be dyed before the carding process, dyeing can also be done after the wool has been woven into fabric.

> *"Great excitement was manifested at this period, and the streets of the villages before mentioned were thronged at the wool-selling period with eager buyers, and many an industrious farmer or enterprising speculator thought he was about to secure unbounded wealth from the merinos sheep nurtured on the slopes of the Washington County hills. But the excitement went down with many others of that inflated period, and though wool-growing continued to be an important industry, prices never rose so high again until the great ascension caused by the war."[131]*

There were, of course, many fluctuations in the price of woolen products, and fortunes were lost or made in the business. In 1825, as before stated, the highest price was fifty-two cents and in 1827, it had fallen to thirty-six cents. In 1831, it ranged from sixty to seventy-eight cents for common grades, while for the finest merino the price was a dollar a pound. In 1835, common wool sold at from forty to sixty-five cents per pound, while the best quality brought eighty-three cents.

# COTTON

Cotton was the initial bumper crop of Washington County in the 17th and 18th centuries and it remained at the top of the list of production as the county moved into the 19th century. It also provided the makings of a specialty crop for local county farmers who had just acquired new land rights or rented lots from the surplus land available entering the 1800s. The influx of labor by way of persons of African descent migrating to Washington County provided the workers necessary for this labor intensive crop.

Washington County in 1810 was responsible for approximately one-quarter (1/4) of New York State's total cotton production and approximately one-quarter (1/4) of the entire state's revenue from cotton production This accomplishment could be considered outstanding given the fact that Washington County only possessed one (1) cotton manufacturing establishment.[132]

Two developments spurred the cultivation of American cotton: cotton spinners and the cotton gin. The cotton gin, developed by Eli Whitney in 1793, easily removed tenacious cottonseeds. Cotton plantation owners began planting cotton as a result of these innovations, using large labor forces for harvesting the cotton.

Most steps involved in the production of cotton have now been mechanized, including seeding, picking, ginning, and baling. Samples are taken from the bales to determine the quality of the cotton. Harvesting is now done by machine in the United States, with a single machine replacing 50 hand pickers. This ratio is very informative to our research with respect to the labor intensive force that was necessary to promote Washington County's production of cotton to #2 in the state in 1810. Most American cotton was harvested using pickers. Pickers must be used after the dew dries in the morning and must conclude when dew begins to form again at the end of the day. This aspect of the production process would also demand a tremendous commitment of labor. Not all cotton reaches maturity at the same time, and harvesting may occur in waves, with second and third pickings.

Most American cotton is stored in "modules," which hold 13-15 bales in water-resistant containers in the fields until they are ready to be ginned. The cotton module is cleaned, compressed, tagged, and stored at the gin. The cotton is then cleaned to separate dirt, seeds, and short lint from the cotton. At the gin, the cotton enters module feeders that fluff up the cotton before cleaning. After cleaning, cotton is sent to gin stands where revolving circular saws pull the fiber through wire ribs, thus separating seeds from the fiber.

Cleaned and de-seeded cotton is then compressed into bales, which permits economical storage and transportation. The compressed bales of cotton are banded and wrapped. The wrapping may be either cotton or polypropylene, which maintains the proper moisture content of the cotton and keeps bales clean during storage and transportation. The bales remain there until they are sold to a mill for further processing.

## FULLING MILLS

Although Washington County ranked #2 to Columbia County (22 Mills) in the production of yards of cloth through the Fulling Process (135,600 yards), it only operated eighteen (18) Fulling Mills. There were six other counties in New York State that operated more of these mills than Washington County and yet produced less product.[133]

The Fulling or Tucking process consists of the closing together of the threads of newly woven woolen fabric with the assistance of soap or acid liquor, with the end purpose of producing a grease free cloth of the correct thickness for future use, including dying. After a piece of woolen cloth has been first woven, the fibers of its fabric are loose, airy and unmeshed, and similar in texture and appearance to a piece of cheesecloth or sackcloth. The cloth, clinging to its fibers, still retains a significant amount of oil or grease introduced during the weaving process. Since oils and grease will inhibit the binding action of the dyes, these need removing. Fulling was one in a sequence of important processes involved in the production of woolen cloth, and fulfilled two functions that were necessary for the proper finishing of the cloth, namely scouring and consolidation of the fibers of the fabric. Woven cloth straight from the loom has a rather open, loose texture and the woven threads needed closing or tightening. The fulling process intended to consolidate and thicken the structure of the fabric by knitting the fibers together more thoroughly and by shrinking them, which transformed the cloth from a loose 'net' of threads into a compact, tight, textural whole.

Scouring, using water and a cleaning agent, helped rid the cloth of any natural oils and greases. This process involved the use of a number of different agents such as fuller's earth, stale urine or soapwort. Fuller's earth, with its ability to absorb dark organic matter from oils and greases was particularly valued for its de-greasing and decolorizing properties. It is a non-plastic, fine clay, containing over half silica and it was from its use in the fulling process that it got its name.

# EXPANSIVE LABOR FORCE

This economic boom that precipitated the increase in production and manufacturing was stimulated by the fact that Washington County's extraordinary rise in production was directly attributed to its high state ranking in production mills, plants and related equipment. Washington County in 1810 ranked first in the number of woolen looms (2,200); 7th in the number of fulling mills and 10th in the number of carding machines in New York State. Additionally, Washington County also ranked 3rd in the number of hatteries; 4th in the number of Forges and 4th in the number of tanneries for hides.[136]

The operation of these various production apparatuses necessitated a concomitantly large number of machine workers and a significantly high number of laborers. This substantial labor force was readily available due to the major influx of individuals of African descent. This new labor force included the "free" families of African descent listed in Chart 8 "TOTAL "FREE" PERSONS OF AFRICAN DESCENT IN WASHINGTON COUNTY, 1810" and the number of "free" individuals of African descent who labored for the descendants of the original purchasers of these forfeited lands (See Chart 5). These individuals and families represented the backbone of the economic transformation of Washington County.

As stated earlier, the labor intensive nature of the production of flax, wool and cotton, and the processing mechanism involved in the manufacturing of "fulled-cloth" required a massive labor force in order for Washington County to lead the State in such production. Individuals of African descent fulfilled this requirement and also began to develop the means of enhancing their own individual and family economies through farm labor production and home-manufacturing of various products like linen, cotton and wool.

Chart 9—"FREE" AFRICAN DESCENDANTS WITH WHITE FAMILIES IN WASHINGTON COUNTY IN 1810" illustrates clearly and concisely the distribution of persons and families of African descent who ventured to Washington Counties' towns and villages up to and including its peak population explosion of 1810. In fact, 1810 represents the apex of persons of African descent in the county during this migration and economic boom era. Charts 8 and 9 delineate the total number of African descendants in Washington County by town and village according to the 1810 Federal Census for Washington County; and record the total population of each town, the total number of individual African descendants, and, the total number of families of African descent in the county and in each town. Further, they record for each town the distribution of individual African descendants who resided with white families Chart 9 further records the individual white families by town who housed "free" individuals of African descent and the number of African descendants with each family according to the number of white families with one, two or three or more African descendants residing in their homes or on their farms. Finally, it represents the number of independent families of African descent in each town. The total of these categories reflects the total population of African descendants in each of the towns of Washington County.

This major influx of individuals and families of African descent also resulted in the development of "free" communities of African descent. One such community in Washington County was Slyboro. Slyboro was a fully formed community of African descendants by 1800 and was situated in the Town of Granville. Not much has been written on Slyboro other than a passing reference in "The Encyclopedia of New York State."[137] However, Slyboro and other "forgotten" communities of African descent in upstate New York can easily be equated to the "*Township*" phenomenon of the Republic of South Africa. There townships are fully segregated, engaged and attached to cities and towns with the primary function of providing labor for the various industries located within these respective localities. Slyboro and the other "forgotten" communities of persons of African descent existed in much the same manner as Soweto and Alexandria do today, as attached townships to Johannesburg, South Africa.[138]

# CHART 8

## TOTAL "FREE" PERSONS OF AFRICAN DESCENT IN WASHINGTON COUNTY
### 1810

| TOWN | | | TOTAL "FREE" AFRICAN DESCENDANTS | | | | |
|---|---|---|---|---|---|---|---|
| WHITEHALL | | | 155 | | | | |
| HAMPTON | | | 31 | | | | |
| SALEM | | | 227 | | | | |
| GRANVILLE | | | 274 | | | | |
| CAMBRIDGE | | | 612 | | | | |
| EASTON | | | 146 | | | | |
| GREENWICH | | | 132 | | | | |
| ARGYLE | | | 110 | | | | |
| KINGSBURY | | | 246 | | | | |
| QUEENSBURY | | | 69 | | | | |
| FT. ANN | | | 300 | | | | |
| HARTFORD | | | 185 | | | | |
| HEBRON | | | 267 | | | | |
| PUTNAM | | | 0 | | | | |
| HAGUE | | | 1 | | | | |
| JOHNSBURG | | | 14 | | | | |
| CHESTER | | | 2 | | | | |
| BOLTON | | | 4 | | | | |
| THURMAN | | | 2 | | | | |
| CALDWELL | | | 4 | | | | |
| LUZERNE | | | 34 | | | | |
| | | | | | | | |
| TOTAL | | | 2815 | | | | |

# CHART 9


## FREE AFRICAN DESCENDANTS
## WITH WHITE FAMILIES IN WASHINGTON
## COUNTY
## 1810

# 1810 FREE AFRICAN DESCENDANTS
## WHITE FAMILIES IN WASHINGTON COUNTY, NY

| WASHINGTON COUNTY | Total Pop. | Total # Free African Descendants | # Free Families African Descent |
|---|---|---|---|
| | 44289 | 2815 | 19 |

| TOWN | | | |
|---|---|---|---|
| Whitehall | 2110 | 155 | 0 |

| Individual Family Names | # Free African Descendants (3 or more Individuals) |
|---|---|
| Smith, Justin | 5 |
| Evans, Daniel | 3 |
| Foster, Abel | 5 |
| Shaw, John | 3 |
| Searl, Gideon | 3 |
| Jackway, Isaac E. | 8 |
| Rock, Nathony | 5 |
| Simmons, Shubel | 4 |
| Mygatt, Ezra | 4 |
| Boyton, Elijah | 3 |
| Downs, Samuel | 8 |
| Thompson, Isaac | 3 |
| Thompson, Willis | 3 |
| Subtotal | 57 |

| | |
|---|---|
| Families w/ 1 African Descendant | 82 |
| Families w/ 2 African Descendants | 16 |
| Total Free African Descendant Family Size | 0 |

| TOWN | Total Pop. | Total # Free African Descendants | # Free Families African Descent |
|---|---|---|---|
| SALEM | 2833 | 227 | 1 |

| Individual Family Names | # Free African Descendants (3 or more Individuals) |
|---|---|
| Clara, Thomas W. | 3 |
| Allen, Ephraim | 4 |
| Williams, John | 4 |
| Archibald, Robert | 7 |
| Blossom, John | 3 |
| Wood, William | 12 |
| Becker, Catherine | 4 |
| Murray, Robert | 6 |
| Simpson, Alexander | 3 |
| Rowan, Stephen | 9 |
| Stone, Abner | 6 |
| Hathan, William | 3 |
| Crawford, James | 3 |
| Stevens, Theodorus | 4 |
| Crosier, William | 3 |
| Subtotal | 74 |

| | |
|---|---|
| Families w/ 1 African Descendant | 116 |
| Families w/ 2 African Descendants | 33 |
| Total Free African Descendant Family Size | 4 |

| TOWN | Total Pop. | Total # Free African Descendants | # Free Families African Descen |
|---|---|---|---|
| Granville | 3717 | 274 | 2 |

| Individual Family Names | # Free African Descendants (3 or more Individuals) |
|---|---|
| Hamilton, James | 3 |
| Parker, Nathaniel | 4 |
| Haff, Samuel | 4 |
| Donald, Lewis W. | 3 |
| Robards, Daniel | 3 |
| Frisby, Ambrose | 4 |
| Hamilton, Henry | 6 |
| Hitchcock, Horace | 3 |
| Northrup, Mintus | 5 |
| Gardner, Zebeder | 4 |
| Morrison, Samuel | 3 |
| Thorn, Stephen | 3 |
| Hopkins, James | 3 |
| Wheadon, Ansel | 3 |
| Tracy, Riel | 3 |
| Wheeler, Timothy B. | 4 |
| Frank, Nathaniel | 4 |
| Frank, John | 3 |
| Leavers, Hezekiah | 4 |
| Steel, Johnathan | 5 |
| Mars, Johabid | 3 |
| Shephard, Zebulon R. | 4 |
| Beckwith, Henry | 3 |
| Atwater, Stephen | 3 |
| Standish, Samuel | 3 |
| Everts, Levi | 4 |
| Fulton, Robert | 3 |
| Subtotal | 97 |

| Families w/ 1 African Descendant | 130 |
|---|---|
| Families w/ 2 African Descendants | 38 |
| Total Free African Descendant Family Size | 9 |

| TOWN | Pop. | African Descendants | African Descen |
|---|---|---|---|
| Cambridge | 6730 | 612 | 1 |

| Individual Family Names | # Free African Descendants (3 or more Individuals) |
|---|---|
| Wright, Josiah | 3 |
| Lee, John | 3 |
| Norton, Elijah | 4 |
| Pulman, Jonathan | 3 |
| Cowell, Lathan | 7 |
| Miller, John | 3 |
| Hay, Henry | 5 |
| Dole, John W. | 3 |
| Green, Thomas | 3 |
| Maxwell, William | 5 |
| Coulter, George | 3 |
| Lauderdale, Edward | 4 |
| Johnson, Mathais | 3 |
| Bullyon, Alexander | 3 |
| Stevenson, William | 3 |
| Small, Edward | 3 |
| Rich, Jesse | 3 |
| Olcott, Oliver | 3 |
| Shindler, Andrew | 4 |
| Cleveland, Abel | 3 |
| Frazier, John | 5 |
| Shaler, Timothy | 4 |

| TOWN | Pop. | African Descendants | | African Descen |
|---|---|---|---|---|
| Cambridge | 6730 | 612 | | 1 |

| Individual Family Names | # Free African Descendants (3 or more Individuals) |
|---|---|
| Bessey, Ebeaoga | 3 |
| Sanger, Arhbel | 3 |
| Simpson, Nathaniel | 3 |
| Bowen, John | 5 |
| Richardson, James | 3 |
| Horton, Elijah | 3 |
| Barber, Thomas | 4 |
| Priede, Eliakein | 3 |
| Stewart, Joseph | 3 |
| Allen, Christopher | 3 |
| Allen, John | 3 |
| Rubel, Humphrey | 3 |
| Evans, Edmond | 7 |
| Van Woert, Peter | 5 |
| Hathaway, Phillip | 3 |
| Welly, Timothy | 3 |
| Durham, Ezra | 5 |
| Quackenboss, Peter | 4 |
| Duel, Job | 5 |
| Welly, Joseph | 3 |
| Gifford, Caleb | 3 |
| Rundle, Abel | 3 |
| Cornwell, Govett | 3 |
| Allen, Nathan | 3 |
| Subtotal | 248 |

| | |
|---|---|
| Families w/ 1 African Descendant | 286 |
| Families w/ 2 African Descendants | 73 |
| Total Free African Descendant Family Size | 5 |

| TOWN | Total Pop. | Total # Free African Descendants | # Free Families African Descen |
|------|-----------|----------------------------------|-------------------------------|
| EASTON | 3253 | 146 | 5 |

| Individual Family Names | # Free African Descendants (3 or more Individuals) |
|-------------------------|----------------------------------------------------|
| Starbuck, Charles | 3 |
| Van Schnnick | 4 |
| Anthony, John | 4 |
| Vandernen, Isaac | 3 |
| Rogers, Nathan | 3 |
| Moway, Willaim | 3 |
| Subtotal | 23 |

| | |
|---|---|
| Families w/ 1 African Descendant | 75 |
| Families w/ 2 African Descendants | 16 |
| Total Free African Descendant Family Size | 32 |

| TOWN | Total Pop. | Total # Free African Descendants | # Free Families African Descent |
|------|-----------|----------------------------------|-------------------------------|
| Greenwich | 2752 | 132 | 1 |

| Individual Family Names | # Free African Descendants (3 or more Individuals) |
|-------------------------|----------------------------------------------------|
| Kingon, David | 3 |
| Hubbard, Salman | 3 |
| Brewer, Peter | 7 |
| Mdane, Thomas | 5 |
| Gilbert, Jedathan | 7 |
| Button, Shubal | 3 |
| Van Derwerken, James | 5 |
| Page, Stephen | 3 |
| Poatt, William | 3 |
| Sarfford, Joseph | 3 |
| Becker, John P. | 4 |
| Hoffman, Anthony | 3 |
| Rocker, Ephraim | 3 |
| Eillis, John | 3 |
| Subtotal | 59 |

| | |
|---|---|
| Families w/ 1 African Descendant | 44 |
| Families w/ 2 African Descendants | 24 |
| Total Free African Descendant Family Size | 5 |

| TOWN | Total Pop. | Total # Free African Descendants | # Free Families African Descen |
|---|---|---|---|
| KINGSBUR | 2292 | 246 | 1 |

| Individual Family Names | # Free African Descendants (3 or more Individuals) |
|---|---|
| Stindivant, Freelove | 8 |
| Rhades, samuel | 3 |
| Jones, Elisha | 8 |
| Sherad, Darris | 4 |
| Wing, Daniel W. | 8 |
| Cole, Russel | 3 |
| Conkling, David | 3 |
| Padden, Benjamin | 3 |
| Barret, Oliver | 6 |
| Platts, Nehennah | 3 |
| Johnson, Luther | 3 |
| Curtis, Levi | 3 |
| Bird, Thomas C. | 3 |
| Surkuder, Christian | 7 |
| Pitcher, Nathanial | 3 |
| Phillips, Reed | 3 |
| Litle, William | 4 |
| Catlin, Aza | 3 |
| Finch, Jeremiah | 3 |
| Sprague, Arna | 3 |
| Freeman, Aldolphus | 3 |
| Paddon, John | 7 |
| Harris, Samuel | 3 |
| High, Rue | 3 |
| Bentley, Benjamin | 4 |
| Luce, Mory | 4 |
| Beadle, Joseph | 3 |
| King, Solomon | 3 |
| Dawley, Elijah | 3 |
| Subtotal | 117 |

| | |
|---|---|
| Families w/ 1 African Descendant | 91 |
| Families w/ 2 African Descendants | 30 |
| Total Free African Descendant Family Size | 8 |

| TOWN | Total Pop. | Total # Free African Descendants | # Free Families African Descen |
|---|---|---|---|
| FORT ANN | 3200 | 300 | 0 |

| Individual Family Names | # Free African Descendants (3 or more Individuals) |
|---|---|
| Blackman, Anthony | 4 |
| Draper, Johnathan | 3 |
| Lloyd, Francis | 3 |
| Rowe, Roderick | 3 |
| Barney, James | 4 |
| Clark, George | 6 |
| Cook, Samuel | 4 |
| Crosby, John | 3 |
| Parish, Ezra | 3 |
| Nichols, Elisha | 3 |
| Cotton, Aaron | 7 |
| Cone, Ella | 5 |
| Otis, Joel | 4 |
| McClellan, Gardener | 5 |
| Dayton, Jehiel | 3 |
| Jacques, John | 4 |
| Smith, Ebenezer | 3 |
| Cornwell, Benjamin | 3 |
| Brown, Nathan | 3 |
| Day, Erastus | 3 |
| Barney, Charles | 5 |
| Barney, Frank | 5 |
| Mason, Shubel | 3 |
| Jenkins, Beer | 3 |
| Wray, John | 3 |
| Smith, Abijah | 5 |
| Hewitt, George G. | 3 |
| Blackman, Elisha | 3 |
| Clemons, Henry | 3 |
| Weed, Abraham | 5 |
| Copland, Benjamin | 5 |
| Winegar, Samuel | 3 |
| Bacon, Winthrop | 3 |
| Branch, Liberty | 5 |
| Goodell, Asa | 3 |
| Subtotal | 138 |

| | |
|---|---|
| Families w/ 1 African Descendant | 135 |
| Families w/ 2 African Descendants | 37 |
| Total Free African Descendant Family Size | 0 |

| TOWN | Total Pop. | Total # Free African Descendants | # Free Families African Descent |
|---|---|---|---|
| HARTFORD | 2389 | 185 | 0 |

| Individual Family Names | # Free African Descendants (3 or more Individuals) |
|---|---|
| Sherman, Christopher | 3 |
| Hyde, Benjamin | 4 |
| Cowan, Joseph | 4 |
| Smith, John | 4 |
| Ruggles, Amosa | 5 |
| Austin, David | 3 |
| Goodin, Seth C. | 4 |
| Love, Thomas | 3 |
| Furman, Enoch | 6 |
| Dickson, John | 3 |
| Davis, William | 6 |
| Hall, Elisha | 3 |
| Clara, Isaac W. | 3 |
| Brown, Elisha | 7 |
| Stockwell, John | 4 |
| Subtotal | 65 |

| | |
|---|---|
| Families w/ 1 African Descendant | 94 |
| Families w/ 2 African Descendants | 26 |
| Total Free African Descendant Family Size | 0 |

| TOWN | Total Pop. | Total # Free African Descendants | # Free Families African Descent |
|---|---|---|---|
| HEBRON | 2436 | 267 | 0 |

| Individual Family Names | # Free African Descendants (3 or more Individuals) |
|---|---|
| Wilson, Robert | 3 |
| Stearay, Isabel | 5 |
| Nelson, Robert | 4 |
| Adams, Ebenezer | 3 |
| Nelson, John R. | 3 |
| Crage, Joseph | 6 |
| Jenkins, George | 4 |
| Dix, John | 4 |
| Livingston, William | 4 |
| Johnson, Hugh | 3 |
| Stolacker, James | 3 |
| Webster, George | 5 |
| Duncan | 6 |
| Ely, Isreal | 8 |
| Carpenter, Mary | 8 |
| Scott, Abraham | 3 |
| Smith, Aaron | 7 |
| Smith, Nathan | 7 |
| McCloud, John | 4 |
| McColl, Hugh | 3 |
| Case, Samuel | 3 |
| Hestchingon, Peter | 4 |
| Bockus, Peter | 3 |
| Wilson, Giles | 3 |
| Litle, Mary | 4 |
| Wilson, James | 7 |
| Hopkins, David | 3 |
| Dutton, Peter | 4 |
| Hyde, Amos W. | 3 |
| Smith, Christopher | 3 |
| Subtotal | 133 |

| | |
|---|---|
| Families w/ 1 African Descendant | 114 |
| Families w/ 2 African Descendants | 20 |
| Total Free African Descendant Family Size | 0 |

| TOWN | Total Pop. | Total # Free African Descendants | # Free Families African Descent |
|------|------------|----------------------------------|----------------------------------|
| Queensbury | 1948 | 69 | 1 |

| Individual Family Names | # Free African Descendants (3 or more Individuals) |
|-------------------------|----------------------------------------------------|
| Gardner, Delwgry | 3 |
| Darby, John | 3 |
| Wing, William | 3 |
| Sherwood, Thomas A. | 3 |
| Subtotal | 12 |

| | |
|---|---|
| Families w/ 1 African Descendant | 46 |
| Families w/ 2 African Descendants | 10 |
| Total Free African Descendant Family Size | 1 |

| TOWN | Total Pop. | Total # Free African Descendants | # Free Families African Descent |
|------|------------|----------------------------------|----------------------------------|
| ARGYLE | 3803 | 114 | 0 |

| Individual Family Names | # Free African Descendants (3 or more Individuals) |
|-------------------------|----------------------------------------------------|
| Bane, James | 7 |
| Hoffman, Anthony M. | 3 |
| Merchant, John | 3 |
| Switzer, Charles | 4 |
| Eillis, John | 3 |
| Subtotal | 20 |

| | |
|---|---|
| Families w/ 1 African Descendant | 78 |
| Families w/ 2 African Descendants | 16 |
| Total Free African Descendant Family Size | 0 |

| TOWN | Total Pop. | Total # Free African Descendants | # Free Families African Descent |
|------|------------|----------------------------------|----------------------------------|
| Lazerne | 1015 | 34 | 0 |

| Individual Family Names | # Free African Descendants (3 or more Individuals) |
|-------------------------|----------------------------------------------------|
| Looker, Samuel C. | 3 |
| Parmenter, Isaiah | 3 |
| Welch, John | 3 |
| Subtotal | 9 |

| | |
|---|---|
| Families w/ 1 African Descendant | 21 |
| Families w/ 2 African Descendants | 4 |
| Total Free African Descendant Family Size | 0 |

**\* ADDITIONAL FREE FAMILIES OF AFRICAN DESCENT**

| Town | # Families of African Descent | Total Size of Families |
|------|-------------------------------|------------------------|
| Bolton | 1 | 1 |
| Chester | 1 | 1 |
| Johnsbury | 4 | 4 |
| Thurman | 1 | 1 |

# ECONOMIC DOWNTURN IN NEW YORK STATE

## THE DEPRESSION OF 1807-1814

As is the case with numerous economic booms, they are often preceded or followed by economic recessions or depressions. Such was the case in our story of New York State and by association Washington County. However, the particular economic depression we are about to discuss was a major occurrence that had national and international implications and repercussions. The Depression of 1807-1814 was a public policy disaster that adversely affected the overall stability of the economy of the United States and involved the major global powers of Great Britain and France. The United States became embroiled in an international conflict that threatened the very survival of the nation, and further severely challenged the future stability of its fledgling economy and potentially its existence as an independent nation.

## THE EMBARGO ACT OF 1807

The most likely reason for the Depression of 1807-1814 was the trade embargo imposed by President Thomas Jefferson in his attempt to keep the United States from becoming involved in the war raging in Europe. Britain and France had become engaged in yet another struggle for primacy in Europe. One of Jefferson's fears was that American shipping to both countries could be interdicted and thus, adversely affect the economic viability of the U.S. He was also concerned that these circumstances would require a U.S. military response. Jefferson felt that by keeping American shipping out of the war zone that the U.S. could avoid being brought into this dangerous political and economic conflict. The British were making the situation even worse by treating American sailors as British citizens, who could be, and were in some instances, impressed into their military service.

A major result of the Embargo was the disappearance of export demand, which closed down many important industries in the United States. The trade embargo also significantly disrupted and consequently reduced American imports. In principle, this potential loss of foreign markets to U.S. business could have been compensated for by a shift to production for domestic markets. However, such a shift would have taken time and the resulting economic recession created by the Embargo had reduced domestic demand.

The trade embargo was obviously proposed by Jefferson as a temporary policy and therefore, investment in markets that would be difficult to retain once the Embargo was lifted was not viewed as an attractive option. As a result, the predictable economic reaction to the trade embargo was recession.

The Embargo Act of 1807, upon passing through Congress, absolutely devastated the shipping industry of the U.S. The Act prohibited trade with the countries of Great Britain and France, resulting in what President Thomas Jefferson clearly ignored—a complete failure of the American export economy, which was hugely dependent on Great Britain at the time, for its survival. The Embargo was also imposed in response to flagrant violations of U.S. neutrality, in which American merchantmen and their cargo were seized as contraband of war by the belligerent European navies. The British Royal Navy, in particular, resorted to impressments, forcing thousands of American seamen into service on their warships.

Great Britain and France were engaged in a life and death struggle for control of Europe and rationalized the plunder of U.S. shipping as incidental to war and necessary for their own economic survival. *COLLATERAL DAMAGE*! The deliberate diplomatic insults and presumptuous official orders issued in support of these actions by European powers were widely recognized as grounds for a U.S. declaration of war.

President Jefferson initially acted with restraint as these abuses mounted, calculatingly weighing public support for diplomatic options or ultimately retaliation. He finally recommended that Congress respond with commercial warfare, rather than with military mobilization.

The Embargo was a financial disaster for the United States due to the fact that the British were still able to export goods to America. Loopholes in the law overlooked the unintended smuggling by coastal vessels from Canada, whaling ships and privateers from overseas, and enforcement difficulties due to widespread disregard of the law.

The anticipated effect of this drastic measure was economic hardship for the warring nations and it was expected to chasten Great Britain and France, and force them to end their molestation of American shipping, respect U.S. neutrality, and cease the policy of impressments. The Embargo turned out to be impractical as a coercive measure, and was a failure both diplomatically and economically. As implemented, the legislation inflicted devastating burdens on the U.S. economy and the American people. The Embargo virtually prohibited merchant vessels from sailing from United States ports and ultimately forbade commerce with any foreign nation. It adversely affected all regions of the United States and all segments of the economy. However, it severely hit the New England shipping interests, resulting in major hardships for many coastal towns. With cotton prices falling by fifty percent, it also hit the South very hard, forcing many planters out of business. The resulting depression all but paralyzed the United States' economy.

The Embargo's intended purpose was to impose economic restrictions on the British and French economies but this did not happen. It had virtually no affect on the British economy especially considering the fact that Brazil and the Spanish colonies were opened to British trade at about the same time that the Embargo was implemented. These new trading partnerships had the effect of offsetting any impact the loss of American trade might have had on the British economy. In fact, the Embargo actually helped British policy in many ways and it precluded any assistance the French may have received from American shipping.

The failure of the Embargo precipitated a tremendous political blow to Jefferson and his Republican supporters; while it had the effect of encouraging smuggling along the Canadian border. Its effects on the maritime capabilities of the nation were disastrous. The merchant fleet was rotting in port, while American seaman sought work where they could find it. This quite often meant the Royal Navy, itself.

Many Americans who worked in the shipping industry lost their jobs, resulting in tremendous suffering for their families. Businesses also suffered through the loss of considerable profit, particularly in large sea-faring towns where unemployment ravaged the local economies.

Just as importantly, the Embargo undermined national unity, provoking bitter protests, especially in New England commercial centers. The issue vastly increased support for the Federalist Party and led to huge gains in their representation in Congress in 1808. It also had the pernicious effect of simultaneously undermining American citizen's faith that their government could execute its own laws fairly, and strengthened the conviction among America's enemies that her republican form of government was inept and ineffectual. At the end of 15 months, the embargo was revoked on March 1, 1809, in the last days of Jefferson's presidency.

As a result of Jefferson's failed strategy, the U.S. was drawn ultimately into a new conflict, the War of 1812, during which the U.S. capital of Washington was burned.

I have chosen not to elaborate in any great detail on the War of 1812 other than to briefly reference its impact on the economy of the U. S. and particularly Washington County, New York. Numerous and exhaustive volumes have described this period in United State's history. With the war's end and the end of the trade embargo the U.S. economy began to recover.

## ECONOMIC RECOVERY

The Embargo, which lasted from December 1807 to March 1809, effectively throttled American overseas trade and consequently all areas of the United States economy suffered. In commercial New England and the Middle Atlantic states, ships remained grounded, and in the agricultural areas, particularly in the South, farmers and planters could not sell their crops on the international market. For New England and especially for the Middle Atlantic states there was some consolation; the scarcity of European goods meant that a definitive stimulus was given to the development and expansion of American industry.

The War of 1812 coincidentally gave a dramatic boost to the manufacturing capabilities of the United States. The British blockade of the American coast created a shortage of cotton cloth in the United States, leading to the creation of a cotton-manufacturing industry, beginning at Waltham, Massachusetts. The war also spurred construction of the Erie Canal project, which was built to promote commercial links yet, was also perceived as having military uses should the need ever arise. Seven years after the marked beginning of this depression in 1814, the economy was considered by most economic historians to be recovered, and progressing towards a growing trend.

## WASHINGTON COUNTY AND THE ECONOMIC DEPRESSION OF 1807-1814

> *By 1812, Washington County was struggling with an economic depression, but "the war was a most excellent thing for the financial interests of the county, especially as the demands created by the necessities of the general government changed this stagnation to an unusual business activity."[139]*

The War of 1812-1815, between the United States and Great Britain found Washington County struggling under the same depression which affected the agricultural and textile industries throughout the nation.

Specifically, the war caused the price of flax, Washington County's major crop and the product that represented the county's major economic generator, to plummet. Conversely, as sheep raising first spiked between 1810 and 1815 in conjunction with hostilities with Britain, the establishment of domestic woolen mills, and the consequent demand for quality fleece increased. The crash that followed cost many farmers dearly as their investments in Spanish merino stock proved shortsighted. Beginning in the 1820s, the wool market started a recovery and once again this occurrence prompted hill country farmers bordering the Hudson Valley to turn to wool and tallow as surplus crops.

We learn however, that this depression period in Washington County caused tremendous turmoil throughout the county, such to the point that by 1814 the population of the county had begun to decrease by some seven thousand five hundred (7500) individuals due to the effects of the depression (See Chart 10). It can be surmised that this reduction in population was caused by these depression related conditions and the need for individuals and their families to seek employment opportunities in other parts of the state and in the western regions of the U. S. It was during this period that a nationwide mass movement of citizens began, both toward western New York and points further west due to the newly acquired Louisiana Purchase.

Development in western New York was in a fledgling state of progress. However, opportunities were beginning to materialize, particularly in the construction of roads and canals and, the clearing of western lands for settlement and other opportunities relating to westward expansion began in earnest.

# 1810 - 1814 CENSUS
## WASHINGTON COUNTY, NY

| TOWN | 1810 TOTAL | | | 1814 TOTAL | CHANGE |
|------|-----------|---|---|-----------|--------|
| WHITEHALL | 2110 | | | 2016 | -94 |
| HAMPTON | 820 | | | 861 | 41 |
| SALEM | 2833 | | | 2955 | 122 |
| GRANVILLE | 3717 | | | 3863 | 146 |
| CAMBRIDGE | 6730 | | | 6599 | -131 |
| EASTON | 3253 | | | 3253 | 0 |
| GREENWICH | 2752 | | | 3138 | 501 |
| ARGYLE | 3803 | | | 3962 | 159 |
| KINGSBURY | 2292 | | | 2216 | -76 |
| QUEENSBURY | 1946 | | | 0 | -1946 |
| FT. ANN | 3200 | | | 1840 | -1360 |
| HARTFORD | 2389 | | | 2466 | 77 |
| HEBRON | 2436 | | | 2737 | 301 |
| PUTNAM | 499 | | | 453 | -46 |
| HAGUE | 398 | | | 0 | -398 |
| JOHNSBURG | 651 | | | 0 | -651 |
| CHESTER | 937 | | | 0 | -937 |
| BOLTON | 726 | | | 0 | -726 |
| THURMAN | 1330 | | | 0 | -1330 |
| CALDWELL | 560 | | | 0 | -560 |
| LUZERNE | 1015 | | | 0 | -1015 |
| | | | | | |
| TOTAL | 44289 | | | 36833 | -7456 |

Note: The Towns listed above with zeros in their population columns represent various mergers of these towns with other existing towns in the county.

The settling of the western United States was also in full bloom and under extreme development as the U. S. began to stretch its boundaries.

The consequences of the 1807-1814 Depression also had an incredible impact on the plight and livelihood of African descendants in Washington County. Forced by the conflicting circumstances of independence and their newly found freedom, African descendants began to develop a more "migrant worker" mentality and behavior due to the financial realities associated with their participation in the transition from a system of enslavement to a more capitalistic approach to production. Families of African descent were now faced for the first time with the reality of searching for employment opportunities, wherever possible. Those that had not been able to develop a sustainable environment of subsistence farming or in securing manufacturing labor were now in constant search of temporary and/or subsistence employment. This dramatic change in lifestyle, constantly in search of employment, caused great hardships within the African descendant community. It must always be remembered that racism and discrimination were still the underlying actuality of life for people of African descent in New York State and the nation for that matter. The specter of being relegated to the most menial of jobs and the constant competition for employment with newly arriving European immigrants forced African descendants to the bottom of the social and economic ladder; thus, precipitating a standard where they were often forced to accept wages below those of their European immigrant counterparts.

As this Depression progressed, it became imperative for survival purposes that a large number of individuals and families of African descent left Washington County in an effort to preserve their economic existence as independent and viable citizens—not beholding to others for their support and maintenance. (Chart 11) It becomes obvious to the student of this period in New York State history that the depressive conditions that affected the economy of Washington County and its various towns had an even harsher economic impact on the African descendant population than the total county population.

# 1810 -1814 CENSUS
## "FREE" AND ENSLAVED AFRICAN DESCENDANTS
## WASHINGTON COUNTY, NY

| | 1810 | | 1814 | | DIFFERENCE | |
|---|---|---|---|---|---|---|
| | ENSLAVED | "FREE" | ENSLAVED | "FREE" | ENSLAVED | "FREE" |
| WHITEHALL | 3 | 155 | 2 | 4 | -1 | -151 |
| HAMPTON | 3 | 31 | 3 | 11 | -3 | -20 |
| SALEM | 36 | 227 | 19 | 18 | -17 | -209 |
| GRANVILLE | 3 | 274 | 4 | 22 | +1 | -252 |
| CAMBRIDGE | 82 | 612 | 26 | 59 | -56 | -543 |
| EASTON | 92 | 146 | 36 | 66 | -56 | -80 |
| GREENWICH | 8 | 132 | 12 | 4 | +4 | -128 |
| ARGYLE | 15 | 110 | 8 | 74 | -7 | -36 |
| KINGSBURY | 23 | 246 | 3 | 28 | -20 | -218 |
| QUEENSBURY | 6 | 69 | | | -6 | -69 |
| FT. ANN | 11 | 300 | 4 | 4 | -7 | -296 |
| HARTFORD | 11 | 185 | 4 | 5 | -7 | -180 |
| HEBRON | 11 | 267 | 12 | 6 | +1 | -261 |
| PUTNAM | | | | | | |
| HAGUE | 0 | 1 | | | 0 | -1 |
| JOHNSBURG | 2 | 14 | | | -2 | -14 |
| CHESTER | 2 | 2 | | | -2 | -2 |
| BOLTON | 0 | 4 | | | 0 | -4 |
| THURMAN | 0 | 2 | | | 0 | -2 |
| CALDWELL | 4 | 4 | | | -4 | -4 |
| FT. EDWARD | 0 | 0 | | | | |
| WHITE | 0 | 0 | | | | |
| JACKSON | 0 | 0 | | | | |
| WESTFIELD | 0 | 0 | | | | |
| LUZERNE | 3 | 34 | | | -3 | -34 |
| | | | | | | |
| TOTAL | 315 | 2815 | 138 | 301 | -177 | -2514 |

Note: The Towns listed above with blanks in their population columns represent various mergers of these towns with other existing towns in the county.

Consequently, the total population of Washington County was reduced by seven thousand four hundred and fifty-six (7456) residents or 16.8% from 1810 to 1814 due to the negative economic conditions imposed by the 1807-1814 Depression. Of greater consequence, for this work were the effects of this Depression literally decimating the population of African descent in the county. In 1810, the total "free" population of African descent amounted to 2815 residents. As mentioned earlier, this figure was the high point of the population and migration of individuals and families of African descent at the turn of the century. However, in an 1814 New York State Census, the figure representing the total population in Washington County of people of African descent was a remarkably low three hundred and one (301) individuals. This figure represents a reduction in the total population of African descent of eighty-nine percent (89%) over the four year period of 1810-1814.[140] These numbers reflect a considerably higher rate than that for Washington County's white population of 16.8%.

It should also be noted that the enslaved population of Washington County was reduced in the same period by fifty-six percent (56%) from three hundred and fifteen (315) to one hundred and thirty-eight (138) individuals.[141] This population reduction may have more to do with the economics of enslavers maintaining enslaved workers than with any moral statement against the institution of enslavement, itself. Negative economic conditions were more likely to cause enslavers to cut expenses in every manner possible. Thus, enslavers in Washington County essentially cut their losses during the Depression by selling or "freeing" their enslaved African descendants. It would make good business sense, especially if they were unable to meet their support and maintenance costs. And yet, they were probably able to find individuals in neighboring counties that could afford the purchase of enslaved men, women and/or children. At the very least, these transactions provided the possibility for profit. This reduction in the enslaved population may also simply reflect their relocation with their enslavers to other parts of New York State and beyond.

The provisions of the Gradual Abolition Act were also still in effect during this period, if this option of sale did not readily present itself. The provisions of this law, as outlined earlier, allowed enslavers to manumit any of their enslaved individuals under their own seal as long as they did not create a financial burden to localities.

Thus, these circumstances ended the major period of the "Migration" of people of African descent to Washington County that had begun in 1800. Just as the year 1800 represented the onset of this migration based on the conditions created by the beginnings of the county's economic boom—so too did the finish of this migration end, for all intents and purposes in 1814 with economic conditions created by the Depression of 1807-1814. During the course of subsequent years as the Depression subsided with the advent and conclusion of the War of 1812, the economy of Washington County rebounded, as it did throughout the U. S.

Consequently, people of African descent resumed their settlement in Washington County. The War had caused the U. S. to transform itself into a more self-sufficient economy whereby, the production of goods formerly imported from Europe were now being grown and manufactured in the U. S. out of necessity—"Necessity being the mother of Invention."

As this new economy developed, African descendants in Washington County who had remained during the Depression, and newly arrived African descendants who sought to take advantage of this growing economy, began to settle permanently in Washington County. Unlike during the early 1800s, when people of African descent were not economically solvent enough to purchase and own land, having just recently been manumitted from enslavement; they now began to pursue landownership on a higher scale. The New York State Census of 1825 documents an important development in the upward mobility of persons of African descent in Washington County. Specifically, the county experienced a major increase in the number of residents of African descent who purchased and owned their own land.

## LANDOWNERS OF AFRICAN DESCENT IN WASHINGTON COUNTY

The consequential availability of surplus land as a function of the state forfeiture laws of the late 1700s did not immediately result in a significant number of individuals of African descent purchasing land in Washington County. Preliminary findings establish a very small number of individuals of African descent actually owning property within the county, even considering the fact that, this available land had been divided into smaller lots and parcels. During the initial migration of people of African descent to Washington County from 1800-1820, very few were capable of undertaking this expense. In fact, of the some twenty-seven hundred (2,700) persons of African descent who comprised this initial migration only four families including nineteen individuals of African descent actually purchased any of this available land. These families included: Jim Schuyler and his family of five, who purchased a quarter acre of land in Easton in 1800 and Abiather Palmer and his family of ten purchased one hundred acres of land, also in Easton in 1800. Quack Boston and his family of four purchased one acre of land in Salem in 1810 and, John Weeks or *Wicks*, also purchased one acre of land in Greenwich in 1810.

Although these numbers may be minimal with respect to the landownership of families of African descent during this period, there unfortunately does not now remain any official record of individuals and families of African descent who may have rented or leased property in Washington County. This lack of information (which has continued to be the bane of research into the history of Washington County) does not negate the possibility that such transactions did actually occur.

The decline in the population of persons of African descent between 1810 and 1814 would lead one to conclude that the economic development aspects of this overall migration and the accompanying economic boom that developed in the county had little, if any, impact on the actual wealth development of African descendants, who migrated there, other than day to day subsistence.

And yet, the reality of this period is even more perplexing when we survey the family settlement records of families of African descent actually taking root in the various towns and villages of the county. Landownership records of persons of African descent from New York State's first official Census in 1825 details a significant rise in the number of individuals of African descent owning land. [142]

Chart 12—AFRICAN DESCENDANT LANDOWNERS IN WASHINGTON COUNTY, 1825 highlights the 1825 New York State Census, which documents the residence of some forty-four (44) families of African descent comprised of two hundred and sixteen (216) individuals throughout the county.[143] It also verifies the fact that of these forty-four families, sixteen families were landowners representing one hundred and five individuals. These individuals specifically included members of the "Migration of 1800-1820." These individuals and families remained in Washington County and pursued their dream of a stable and economically viable environment, in which they could raise their children and prosper after the chaos and degradation of enslavement.

It should also be noted that these sixteen landowning families of African descent were indeed farmers and producers of marketable products some two years prior to the official and legal abolishment of enslavement in New York State in 1827. Granted the reality of this phenomenon is the fact that the majority of these individuals, who were landowners can best be described as subsistence farmers. Their ability to progress successfully within an economic system, that was initially established solely to exploit them as free laborers and also to subjugate them as second-class citizens, is an accomplishment of major proportions.

This Landownership Chart 12 lists the individual families of African descent, who resided in Washington County in 1825. It further chronicles those of African descent who actually owned or did not own property during this period. This Chart also explicitly demonstrates the contributions to the economic sustainability of these families by representing the production of home-manufactured products such as linen, wool and cotton cloth. In fact, these individuals and families of African descent produced a total of: 149 yards of fulled cloth; 298 yards of flannel/woolen cloth; and, 250 yards of linen/cotton cloth for their personal or retail sales use according to census records.

# CHART 12

## AFRICAN DESCENDANT LANDOWNERS
## IN WASHINGTON COUNTY
## 1825

# AFRICAN DESCENDANT LANDOWNERS
## WASHINGTON COUNTY
### 1825

| TOWN / SALEM SURNAME | # FAMILY MEMBERS | ARCES OWNED | VOTER | CATTLE | SHEEP | HOGS | HOME MANUFACTURING YARDS CLOTH FULLED | YARDS FLANNEL/ WOLLEN | YARDS LINEN/ COTTON |
|---|---|---|---|---|---|---|---|---|---|
| VAN VRANK JOHN | 10 | 60 | 0 | 1 | 6 | 6 | 6 | 0 | 14 |
| DAILEY JACK | 4 | 0 | 0 | 1 | 0 | 1 | 0 | 0 | 0 |
| BOSTON QUACK | 3 | 0 | 0 | 0 | 0 | 0 | 0 | 0 | 0 |
| EPPS JOHN | 6 | 0 | 0 | 0 | 0 | 0 | 0 | 0 | 0 |
| BROWN PRINCE | 4 | 0 | 0 | 0 | 0 | 0 | 0 | 0 | 0 |
| JACKSON RICHARD | 2 | 0 | 0 | 0 | 0 | 0 | 0 | 0 | 0 |
| VAN DENBURG POMPEY | 2 | 0 | 0 | 0 | 0 | 0 | 0 | 0 | 0 |
| STILLWELL JEREMIAH | 6 | 30 | 4 | 2 | 0 | 0 | 0 | 0 | 0 |
| POWEN WILLIAM | 6 | 0 | 0 | 0 | 0 | 0 | 0 | 0 | 0 |
| PALMER JOHN | 9 | 2 1/2 | 1 | 2 | 0 | 3 | 30 | 40 | 40 |
| BABCOCK AUGUSTUS | 5 | 1 3/4 | 1 | 0 | 0 | 0 | 0 | 0 | 0 |
| **WHITEHALL** | | | | | | | | | |
| ADAMS ROBERT | 5 | 4 | 2 | 6 | 19 | 7 | 0 | 25 | 30 |
| POST THEODORE | 3 | 0 | 0 | 0 | 0 | 0 | 7 | 5 | 0 |
| **ARGYLE** | | | | | | | | | |
| SMITH CATALINA | 7 | 0 | N/A | N/A | N/A | N/A | N/A | N/A | N/A |
| VAN TUYH | 5 | 120 | 1 | 9 | 40 | 9 | 20 | 26 | 0 |
| DAGGART JOB | 3 | 0 | 1 | 0 | 0 | 0 | 0 | 0 | 0 |
| GOODE LON | 3 | 0 | 1 | 2 | 13 | 7 | 0 | 8 | 0 |
| NELSON | 4 | 0 | 0 | 0 | 0 | 0 | 0 | 0 | 0 |
| NELSON EDWARD | 2 | 0 | 0 | 0 | 0 | 0 | 0 | 0 | 0 |

| TOWN DRESDEN SURNAME | # FAMILY MEMBERS | ARCES OWNED | VOTER | CATTLE | SHEEP | HOGS | HOME MANUFACTURING YARDS CLOTH FULLED | YARDS FLANNEL/ WOLLEN | YARDS LINEN/ COTTON |
|---|---|---|---|---|---|---|---|---|---|
| NETTIS | | | | | | | | | |
| FRANCIS | 10 | 0 | 0 | N/A | N/A | N/A | N/A | N/A | N/A |
| LOYD | | | | | | | | | |
| CHARLES | 6 | 0 | 1 | 1 | 0 | 1 | N/A | N/A | N/A |
| BARIDDEN | | | | | | | | | |
| WALTER | 10 | 50 | 0 | 6 | 28 | 11 | 12 | 20 | 0 |
| BROWNETT | | | | | | | | | |
| CORNELL | 4 | 0 | 1 | 0 | 0 | 0 | 0 | 0 | 0 |
| WINNEY | | | | | | | | | |
| PETER | 6 | 0 | 0 | 4 | 2 | 0 | 6 | 38 | 31 |
| VANBUREN | | | | | | | | | |
| HARRY | 8 | 5 | 0 | 4 | 0 | 5 | N/A | N/A | N/A |
| BOSTON | | | | | | | | | |
| ERIAH | 3 | 0 | 1 | 0 | 2 | 0 | 0 | 15 | 30 |
| **FORT ANN** | | | | | | | | | |
| PETERS | | | | | | | | | |
| AMOS | 5 | 1/2 | 0 | 3 | 4 | 17 | 47 | 13 | 13 |
| JOB | | | | | | | | | |
| ROBERT | 4 | 15 | 0 | 0 | 0 | 0 | 0 | 0 | 0 |
| **FORT EDWARD** | | | | | | | | | |
| FULLER | | | | | | | | | |
| RUBEN | 3 | 0 | 1 | 0 | 0 | 3 | 0 | 0 | 0 |
| HAMPTON | | | | | | | | | |
| WILLIAM | 6 | 12 | 0 | 5 | 0 | 3 | 0 | 0 | 0 |
| PALMER | | | | | | | | | |
| JOSEPH | 2 | 0 | N/A | N/A | N/A | N/A | N/A | N/A | N/A |
| REID | | | | | | | | | |
| WILLIAM | 2 | 0 | 0 | 0 | 0 | 0 | 0 | 0 | 0 |
| **GRANVILLE** | | | | | | | | | |
| HAINES | | | | | | | | | |
| LEMUEL | 11 | 3/4 | 0 | 1 | 0 | 2 | 2 | 35 | 10 |
| NICHOLES | | | | | | | | | |
| BLUSHIA | 3 | 1 | 0 | 0 | 0 | 2 | 0 | 0 | 0 |
| SHIPHEARD | | | | | | | | | |
| JEBULON | 7 | 30 | 1 | 2 | 4 | 200 | 1 | 0 | 20 |
| HAZZARD | | | | | | | | | |
| LEVI | 2 | 0 | 0 | 0 | 0 | 0 | 2 | 14 | 20 |
| PALMER | | | | | | | | | |
| ABIATHER | 5 | 100 | 0 | 15 | 35 | 35 | 0 | 35 | 30 |
| **GREENWICH** | | | | | | | | | |
| PRITNAM | | | | | | | | | |
| JACOB | 8 | 0 | N/A | N/A | N/A | N/A | N/A | N/A | N/A |
| **HEBRON** | | | | | | | | | |
| PORTER | | | | | | | | | |
| WILLIAM | 5 | 0 | 0 | N/A | N/A | N/A | N/A | N/A | N/A |

| TOWN JACKSON SURNAME | # FAMILY MEMBERS | ARCES OWNED | VOTER | CATTLE | SHEEP | HOGS | HOME MANUFACTURING | | |
|---|---|---|---|---|---|---|---|---|---|
| | | | | | | | YARDS CLOTH FULLED | YARDS FLANNEL/ WOLLEN | YARDS LINEN/ COTTON |
| CHASE | | | | | | | | | |
| SAMUEL | 2 | 0 | 0 | N/A | N/A | N/A | N/A | N/A | N/A |
| BASHLEY | | | | | | | | | |
| HENRY | 3 | 0 | 0 | N/A | N/A | N/A | N/A | N/A | N/A |
| KINGSBURY | | | | | | | | | |
| DIXSON | | | | | | | | | |
| WILLIAM | 3 | 3/4 | 0 | N/A | N/A | N/A | N/A | N/A | N/A |
| CARRIED | | | | | | | | | |
| JACOB | 2 | 0 | N/A | N/A | N/A | N/A | N/A | N/A | N/A |
| HOMELAND | | | | | | | | | |
| CYNTHIA | 5 | 125 | 0 | 15 | 52 | 7 | 16 | 15 | 30 |
| TOT | 44 | 553.1/4 | | | | | 149 | 298 | 750 |
| | 216 | | | | | | | | |

Those individuals who are not listed as producing home-manufactured products are more than likely individuals who were employed by white landowners and more than likely rented their residences or lived on the farms of these landowners. This is not to say that individuals of African descent who owned land were not also employed by white landowners but it demonstrates the sustainable economic mindset and the entrepreneurial spirit of these people of African descent. Here were a People that survived and sustained themselves within the economic and discriminatory chaos of enslavement and racism, which still existed all around them.

Who can speak for these extraordinarily courageous and determined people of African descent, with respect to the degree of danger and uncertainty that permeated their living environment on a daily basis? They were concentrating their major focus squarely on their survival and the survival of their families and children within the context of a society that still considered them inferior and at best second-class citizens. These families of African descent manifested their ingenuity and resourcefulness through the ownership and settlement of some five hundred and fifty-three and one quarter (553¼) total acres of land in Washington County in 1825. It is important to remember that a good number of these individuals and families remained in Washington County for generations.

As mentioned earlier, there are still descendants of Johannes and Francis Van Vranken living in Washington County to this very day. This longevity of residence, actual land ownership and the settlement of these families of African descent thoroughly belies and refutes any myths propagated by certain individuals and academics. People of African descent have been historically smeared by the racist theories that proposed that the establishment of family roots and the development of a secure foundation for the raising of their children and the stability of their families, were valued differently by people of African descent than "other" cultures or races.

## Reference Notes

111 "A Statement of the ARTS AND MANUFACTURES OF the United States of America, for the year 1810: Digested and Prepared by: Tench Coxe, Esquire, of Philadelphia, Philadelphia, Printed by A. Cornman, June, 1814, Bureau of the Census Library

# A STATEMENT OF THE UNITED STATES OF AMERICA, EXHIBITING

I.   A collection of facts, evincing their benefactions to agriculture, commerce, navigation and the fisheries, and their subserviency to the public defence, with an indication of certain existing modes of conducting them, 'peculiarly important to the United States:

II.  A collection of additional facts, tending to show the practical foundation, actual progress, condition and establishment of the American arts and manufactures, and their connexion with the wealth and strength of the United States.

## TOGETHER WITH

^    One series of tables of the several branches of American manufactures, exhibiting thcm by states, territories and districts, so far as they were returned in the reports of the marshals and of the secretaries of the territories, and their respective assistants, in the autumn of the year 1810; together with similar returns of certain doubtful goods, productions of the soil, and agricultural stock, so far as they have been reported:

## AND ANOTHER

•    Series of tables of the several branches of American manufactures, exhibiting them in every eounty in the Unionise—far as they were returned in the reports of the marshals, and of the secretaries of the territories and weir respective assistants, in the autumn of the year 1810: which tables were

Prepared in Execution of an instruction of
ALBERT GALLATINT, esquire,
*Secretary qfthe Treasury,*
GIVEN BY HIM
IN OBEDIENCE TO A RESOLUTION OF CONGRESS
OF 'THE
19th day of March, 1812

## NOTICE TO THE BEADEBS.

The two series of tables, which form the third and fourth parts of this volume, were digested and published under the authority of Congress and an instruction of the Treasury. With these tables, the communication of the eighth of December, 1812, from Mr, C'oxe, (who was engaged by the government to prepare a statement of the ARTS and MANUFACTURES of the USITED STATES,) was addressed to the secretary of the Treasury. It comprised parts I. and II. of this book, and is to be considered as the work of an individual, occasioned by his desire to be useful to his country.

To the copy furnished for this publication, some recent notes have been added, to extend the exposition of the condition of our manufactures, in some degree, to the state of things in the current year. It may be proper to remark that some alterations, containing, with part of the notes, matter, which would not have been inserted in an official paper, are now introduced from considerations of public utility. Jane 30, 1814.

[112] "A Series of Tables of the Several Branches of AMERICAN MANUFACTURES, Exhibiting Them in every County of the Union, So Far As THEY ARE RETURNED IN THE REPORTS OF THE MARSHALLS, AND OF THE SECRETARIES OF THE TERRITORIES AND OF THEIR RESPECTIVE ASSISTANTS, IN THE AUTUMN OF THE YEAR 1810: Together with Returns of certain doubtful Goods, Productions of the Soil and agricultural Stock, so far as they have been received. Bureau of the Census Library

[113] Stone, pg. 300

[114] Crisfield Johnson, "History of Washington County, New York"

[115] IBID

[116] IBID

[117] IBID

[118] IBID

[119] IBID

[120] CHAPTER XXIV OF THE LAWS OF THE STATE OF NEW YORK, PASSED IN THE THIRD SESSION OF THE LEGISLATURE, HELD AT KINGSTON, IN ULSTER COUNTY; *An Act for the Forfeiture and Sale of the Estates of Persons who have adhered to the Enemies of this State, and for declaring the Sovereignty of the People of this State, in respect to all Property within the same.—Passed 22d October, 1779*

[121] A Series of Tables of the Several Branches of AMERICAN MANUFACTURES, Exhibiting Them in every County of the Union, U. S. Bureau of the Census Library (See Table 3)

[122] IBID

NOTE: Flax has been cultivated for its remarkable fiber, linen, for at least five millennia. The spinning and weaving of linen is depicted on wall paintings of ancient Egypt. As early as 3,000 B.C., the fiber was processed into fine white fabric (540 threads to the inch—finer than anything woven today) and wrapped around the mummies of the ancient Egyptian pharaohs. Mentioned several times in the Bible, it has been used as a cool, comfortable fiber in the Middle East for centuries as well.

[123]  Johnson, IBID; Stone, pg. 326

[124]  IBID

[125]  IBID

[126]  IBID

[127]  IBID

[128]  Dr. Asa Fitch, "Survey of Washington County,"

[129]  William Cormier, **Salem's Forgotten African Americans**, The Journal of the Washington County Historical Society, 2008, pg. 36

[130]  IBID

[131]  IBID

[132]  "A Series of Tables of the Several Branches of AMERICAN MANUFACTURES, Exhibiting Them in every County of the Union, U. S. Bureau of the Census Library

[133]  IBID

[134]  [111] www.fromfullingtofustainopolis.co.uk

[135]  IBID

[136]  "A Series of Tables of the Several Branches of AMERICAN MANUFACTURES, Exhibiting Them in every County of the Union, U. S. Bureau of the Census Library

[137]  The Encyclopedia of New York State, editor in Chief: Peter Eisenstadt, Managing Editor: Laura-Eve Moss, 2005, Syracuse University Press, pg. 1661

[138]  As a function of Apartheid, the African and "colored" populations were so severely discriminated against in South Africa that they were physically relegated to townships that were intentionally developed to separate this population from the ruling white population. The result of these policies culminated in the creation of a systematic institution of segregation that essentially and purposely relegated the native population of South Africa to a level of second-class citizenship. The history and implementation of this system resulted in a massive displacement of South Africa's African population to areas of the country that were soon ripe with poverty, disease and overpopulation, in an effort to provide the ruling class of white citizens with a ready and available workforce.

[139] IBID, pg. 325

[140] 1810 US Federal Census and 1814 New York State Census

[141] IBID

[142] NOTE: New York State produced its first State census in 1825 and every 10 years after that year until 1855.

[143] 1825 New York State Census for Washington County

# CHAPTER IV

## FINAL ABOLITION

# FINAL ABOLITION[144]

*"Final Abolition" presented former slaves with a myriad of proscriptive statutes and discriminatory practices, as white lawmakers limited the legal rights of former slaves, and as white employers created new forms of subordination that kept African descendants dependent."* [145]

Regarding the actual abolition of enslavement in New York, the New York State Legislature passed in 1817 "An Act relative to slaves and servants." This law was New York State's emancipation statute. It became effective on 4 July 1827.[146] Essentially, it extended emancipation to those "slaves" born before July 4, 1799 who were not included under the provisions of the Gradual Abolition Law of 1799, and it stipulated that these "slaves" were to become free as of July 4, 1827. It should be noted that the effective date of this final abolition legislation in New York State, July 4, 1827, was exactly twenty-eight years after the passage of the Gradual Abolition Act of 1799. This occurrence was not a coincidence. The effective date of this law guaranteed that slaveholders would receive a full twenty-eight years of service from male slave children who were born in the year 1799 under Gradual Abolition.[147]

Enslavement, however, was still not entirely repealed in New York State. This new emancipation law allowed at least two exceptions to the total abolition of enslavement in New York State. First, it allowed nonresidents to continue their slaveholding practices for up to nine months. Secondly, it allowed part-time residents to maintain their slaves in the state temporarily. This provision remained in state law until it was repealed in 1841.

Notwithstanding the final abolition of enslavement in New York after 200 years of unrestricted practice, African descendants in New York demonstrated a remarkable sense of political acumen by choosing not to celebrate "their emancipation" on the 4th of July in conjunction with the celebration of American Independence. After the first few years of emancipation, African descendants chose this course of action in a conscious effort to demonstrate their conflict with "the disparity between rhetoric and reality, between their country's high professions of liberty and equality and the existence of enslavement [in the South] and the high wall of color [that persisted in the United States as a whole]."[148] African descendants had also become acutely aware of the potential dangers inherent in participating in or celebrating near white crowds during the 4th of July. Since numerous instances of violence towards African descendants were reported on that date. Instead, these newly freed African descendants chose to celebrate either the 5th of July or August 1st, the anniversary of the unconditional freedom of "slaves" in the British West Indies, as their "Emancipation Day."[149]

---

William Steward in his narrative, tells us of the reaction of newly freed African descendants in Rochester, New York.

> "... the Emancipation Bill had been passed, and the colored people felt it to be a time fit for rejoicing. They met in different places and determined to evince their gratitude by a general celebration. In Rochester, they convened in large numbers, and resolved to celebrate the glorious day of freedom at Johnson's Square, on the fifth day of July. This arrangement was made so as not to interfere with the white population who were everywhere celebrating the day of their independence—" the Glorious Fourth,"—for amid the general and joyous shout of liberty—prejudice had sneeringly raised the finger of scorn at the poor African, whose iron bands were loosed, not only from English oppression, but the more cruel and oppressive power of Slavery."[150]

# THE JIM CROW STATUS OF "FREED" AFRICAN DESCENDANTS AFTER EMANCIPATION

*"Free Negroes were brutalized by ruffians and excluded from skilled employment by the hostility of white workers. Indeed, free Negroes in the nineteenth century remained as much a class apart as in the days of slavery."* [151]

## BACKGROUND

With the abolition of enslavement in 1827, whites began to establish a societal barrier that legally, economically, and socially designated people of African descent as a separate, dependent, and unequal group within the New York State community. Of greater significance was the fact that the passage of this law abolishing enslavement was accompanied by the emergence of a virulent form of racial hatred. The status of "free" African descendants in New York State was epitomized by their relegation to second-class even third class citizenship. This can be attributed to the fact that under the institution of enslavement they were "trained to pursue a great variety of crafts and occupations, while under the status of freedom they were virtually abandoned and systematically pauperized."[152] Consequently, the difference between being enslaved and being "free" was largely one of perception rather than one of practice. As an example, an account kept by Ann Bevier of Marbletown, New York shows that freed slave laborers "were given just enough compensation to cover their room and board expenses." [153]

In this manner, enslavement existed in practice longer than it did in legislation. Many more freed African descendants found themselves in county poorhouses and almshouses all across the state. These locally managed houses for paupers, indigents, travelers and abandoned "statutory slaves" offered nothing but sickness, death, and misery for most of their inhabitants. As an example, the Poorhouse, which had been constructed in New Paltz in the late 1820s to deal with the growing destitute population, offered its inhabitants only impoverished living conditions, with minimal provisions of food and water, inadequate medical attention, and ill treatment by overseers.[154]

*"New York's emancipation laws were defined to free slaves carefully and thus control and contain free blacks."* [155]

Discrimination policies relegated the status of "free" African descendants in New York State to the lowest rung of society. This reduction in status was also directly related to the massive influx of white immigrants into New York State during the nineteenth century. Alexis De Tocqueville wrote that "anti-Negro feelings were greatest in those states where slavery has never been known."[156] Historian Edgar J. Mc Manus also speaks to the issue of white resentment of these third—and sometimes fourth-generation African descendants when he states, "as the working class grew and the wage rate fell, **negrophobia,** became the anodyne of lower class [white] frustration."[157]

A classic example of this second—and third-class citizenship transpired in New York City with the passage of the "Freemanship Laws" which required local residency and enabled citizens in New York to protect their occupations against "outsider." In New York City, outsiders included "freed" African descendants who were further excluded from the privileges of citizenship. This relegation of "free" African descendants was designed to exclude them from all but the most menial trades while white applicants easily found work.[158]

Prior to the mass emigration of whites from Ireland, Germany, French Canada and other parts of Europe, African descendants held a monopoly on jobs like: coachmen, barbers, whitewashers, washerwomen, and other generally defined domestic positions. The evidence seems to suggest that during the Revolutionary and Confederation years there was a sharp increase in the number of free African descendants in the state. Census data for 1790 shows 21,329 enslaved African descendants in the state and 4,654 free African descendants, roughly 18 percent of the overall African descendant population.[159] We can surmise that some were freeman from before the war, some were freed because of their service during the war, and some had been manumitted in other parts of the country and state and had migrated to New York City after the war. Surprisingly, few of these "free" African descendants were formerly enslaved in New York City who had been manumitted by enslavers, who caught the abolitionist spirit in the wake of the Revolutionary War.[160]

Even before the law took effect, however, the percentage of "free" African descendants in the state rose precipitously and continued to rise over the next three decades. In 1800, the number of free African descendants doubled over the previous ten years: there were 8,573 free African descendants and 15,602 enslaved in New York at that time. By 1810 the "free" African descendant population had surpassed the enslaved population, 25,333 to 15,017. On the eve of the Constitutional Convention of 1821, there were 22,332 'free' African descendants and 7,573 enslaved African descendants in the state.[161]

Thus, in the opening decades of the nineteenth century, we see the same phenomenon in New York that occurred in other Northern states that passed gradual abolition laws in the late eighteenth century—namely, that African descendants were emerging from enslavement en masse over a relatively short period of time.

And yet, while relatively few in number, an increasing 'free' African descendant population became more visible in every way, particularly in the bustle of an urban center like New York City. In the latter days of enslavement, most African descendants in New York City worked as domestics in the houses of the old (Federalist) aristocracy. As laborers, they were not in competition for jobs with whites at the lower end of the economic ladder. As "citizens," they were utterly invisible, both in the political and social sense. Most African descendants lived in white-headed households rather than in their own communities on the one hand, and all but a few were disqualified from the vote on the other. With abolition came wrenching political, social, and economic changes that brought a backlash against African descendant communities just uplifted from enslavement. Economically, African descendants were perceived by working class whites as a potential threat to jobs.

## THE POLITICS OF DISCRMINATION

Politically "free" African descendants were seen by Republicans politicians seeking office as a dangerous voting block. Anthony Gronowicz in *Race and Class Politics in New York City Before the Civil War* asserts that Irish Republican fervor contributed heavily to the development of the Democratic Republican ideology well before the War of 1812, and that New York Republicans drew upon the competition between Irish and African American labor for political support.[162] In short, Tammany Hall taught the Irish that they could climb the ladder of success by shunning any contact with African descendants while Tammany leaders rode the wave of this hostility to political power.[163]

The politics of race began to again raise its ugly head as early as 1804, when Republican newspapers such as the *American Citizen* published parodies of black speech patterns in which "Zambo" degraded himself by comparing his skin to the rough rind of a coconut.[164] In 1799, the *New York Journal and Patriotic Register* pointed out not only the Federalist detestation of the Irish, but also its enthusiasm for "the black ones of Santa Domingo."[165] Republican newspapers also never hesitated to remind their readers that "nineteenth-twentieths" of all African descendant voters voted the Federalist ticket.[166]

In the decades after the final abolition of enslavement, due to this influx of European whites into New York City and the state, whites began to move into the so-called "Negro" jobs. By the Reconstruction period, these racial labor practices resulted in a wholesale displacement of African descendants.[167] The exclusion of African descendant workers soon extended to include industrial jobs where white inclusion and the exclusion of workers of African descent became the reality of New York State's employment landscape.

Despite the level of skill African descendants possessed, they were increasingly relegated to the most menial jobs and persistently forced to the bottom rung on the economic and social ladder. White immigration to the state made matters worse, but economic downturns were another factor. President Thomas Jefferson's Embargo of 1804, the depression that followed the War of 1812, and the Panic of 1819 all hit the African descendant community the hardest, as white immigrants flooded into the domestic service industry in the 1810s and 1820s, a field predominantly African American since colonial days.

According to Herman Bloch in "The Circle of Discrimination" the number of Irish filing for employment with the New York Society for the Encouragement of Faithful Domestics in the late 1820s was more than three times that of African descendants. Even the number of other "whites" filing for employment surpassed African descendants.[168]

As a consequence of these factors, many newly freed New Yorkers of African descent had no choice but to continue to live as dependent workers in white households after emancipation. This reality forced them to continue to separate themselves from their families, as expectations born under enslavement that African descendant families would live apart survived among this first generation of freedmen. While many freedmen found it difficult to support themselves, they, either lived with whites, relied on their old owners for help, or became paupers. Others successfully established their own households and reunited their families. A population that had functioned well throughout society found sudden unemployment and job discrimination once free.[169]

"Free" African descendants in the North also faced sweeping protests from white workers, a ban on the ownership of private property, land and homes, segregation in public accommodations, segregated schools, economic discrimination, poverty, disease and horrendous living conditions,[170] as well as increasing degrees of disenfranchisement. The North had become, to resident African descendants and newly arriving fugitives from the "slavocracy" of the South, a hierarchical white supremacist world of separation and degradation.

## DISENFRANCHISEMENT

The right to vote for citizens of African descent had been established in 1777, when the first New York Constitutional Convention was held and the predominately abolitionist drafters made a conscious point of not mentioning race, creed, or previous condition of servitude as an impediment to suffrage. The suffrage qualification was offered to "every male inhabitant of full age" who met the property and residence requirements. New York State under the control of Republican politicians on a number of occasions leading up to final abolition attempted to impose conditions on African descendants that would in effect disenfranchise them of the right to vote in the state's elections. Even as early as 1785, Republicans in the New York State Legislature sought to disenfranchise African descendants with the introduction of legislation that would grant gradual abolition but eliminate the ability of newly freed African descendants to exercise their preexisting right to vote.[171] This legislation mandated a recurring theme in Northern abolition laws of the period. They allowed for the "freedom of slaves" after a period of what amounted to "statutory servitude" but denied "freed" African descendants the right to vote, hold public office, intermarry with white persons and testify against white defendants in court.

In 1811 and again in 1814, Republican politicians consolidated their gains in statewide elections and moved to destroy the impact of African descendant voters in New York City. In 1811, the state legislature passed a harsh law entitled a "Bill to Prevent Frauds at Elections, and For Other Purposes." Essentially this law sought to legalize what Republican inspectors in New York City had accomplished by force in previous elections. The main provision of the law was as follows:

> *"Whenever any person of color, or black person shall present himself to vote at any election of this state, he shall produce to the inspectors, or persons conducting such an election, a certificate of freedom under the hand and seal of one of the clerks of the counties of this state, or under the hand of a clerk of any town within this state."*[172]

The provisions of this law proved regressive and made compliance for voters of African descent exceedingly difficult. In order to receive the required certificate, a potential voter of African descent had to obtain the services of a lawyer and appear before a Supreme Court judge, at which court appearance their proof of freedom could be obtained in writing. The total cost to prospective voters of African descent attempting to certify their rights as a free citizen included attorney fees, court costs and county clerk filing fees for the certificate. In addition, each voter had to take an oath saying he was the person listed on the certificate. The Federalist-led Council of Revision of the New York State once again stepped in on the side of the voters of African descent and vetoed the legislation. In its objections, the Council offered several reasons for its rejection, ranging from the feasibility of carrying out the law, to questions dealing with the scientific basis for the law, and finally to a deep skepticism of its moral underpinnings. The Council first argued that the description of "persons of color" offered in the bill was too vague for inspectors to follow accurately considering the fact that the 'races' had been mixed since their initial encounters centuries ago. The Council questioned whether inspectors were to judge voters of African descent based on differences presented to the eye, or the "quality of the blood." It emphasized the possibility that an inspector would have difficulty determining which voters were of African descent and which were not. It would seem that the Council was suggesting that a science of racial identification was nearly impossible.

We must keep in mind that this racial identification clause in the early nineteenth century may represent the first modern attempts to construct a "scientific racism." Moreover, the emergence of a science of race that placed African descendants in a subordinate position to whites formed the basis of much of the rhetoric that justified the disenfranchisement of African descendants in the first place.

The Council of Revision relied upon a natural rights argument for most of its objections, stating that, the bill selects certain persons who, "under the constitution and laws of the state, are entitled to the elective franchise, many of whom were born free." It also stipulated the fact that this legislation violated the rights of African descendants whose ancestors have uninterruptedly enjoyed the elective franchise under the colonial as well as state government. The Council further concluded that this right to vote had been transmitted with their freeholds. The bill was not passed over the Council's veto.

With the advent of the elections of 1813, African descendants again voted the Federalist ticket in the spring elections. Consequently, in 1814, the Republican-led legislature put forth a bill similar to the one proposed in 1811, in an effort to suppress the voting power of African descendants and stymie any future Federalists gains. This later version also stipulated that African descendants were to present a certificate of freedom upon voting. Interestingly enough, however, the bill only applied to New York City where Federalist election victories had been secured by the votes of citizens of African descent.

Once again, the Council of Revision vetoed it. But this time the Republican-led legislature overrode the veto. A year later, new amendments and new restrictions were added to a bill passed on April 11, 1815.[173] This bill exempted African descendants that had obtained prior certificates from the disenfranchisement provisions of the 1814 bill. This new law, however, forced African descendants to register to vote five days prior to the election and deliver their affidavits to the mayor for inspection.[174] Finally, in 1821, with the election of the Martin Van Buren-led Bucktail Republicans, the State of New York instituted what proved to be its most successful effort to disenfranchise voters of African descent. This regressive and discriminatory law required that the State of New York impose a property qualification of $250 for voters of African descent. This racist restriction on voters of African descent was levied at the same time that the state eliminated all such requirements for white voters. The law essentially denied African descendants the right to vote unless they owned land valued at $250.

> **"Prior to this act, a single qualification for voting (owning property valued at $100) had applied equally to men of both races."** [175]

Edward S. Abdy in *"Journal of a Residence and Tour in the United States"* relates the absurdity of this newly enacted law.

> *"In New York State, colored men of the qualified age, and possessed of 250 dollars in freehold estate, are entitled to the elective franchise. It is singular, that, where no political privileges are connected with property, an exception should be made in favor of those with whom vice, not virtue, is supposed to be hereditary; and that the parchment on which the pedigree is written is the skin of the claimant. Equality of civil rights is granted where equality of social rights is denied; and the same man who is admitted to the ballot-box, is thrust out of the dining room. Let the "African" carry off the palladium of the constitution; but he must not disturb the digestion of its friends. Plutus must be highly esteemed, where his rod can change even a negro into a man. If 250 dollars will perform this miracle, what would it require to elevate a monkey to this enviable distinction?"* [176]

This action, in effect and intention, eliminated the ability of African descendants to exercise their franchise in New York State. Our curiosity as to the purposes of these legislative actions on the part of the white majority tends to become jaded after a period, especially when we discuss these outright actions of institutional racism. The State of New York had abolished enslavement in 1827 and yet, it denied the right to vote to African descendants who were enthusiastic in their effort to exercise their full rights as citizens.

One theory for the passage of this 1821 legislation suggests that in 1813 the Federalist Party obtained the majority in the legislature, by way of the free African descendant electorate in New York City. The resulting victory of the Federalist Party was more than likely the reasoning behind the Republican action in 1821 to impose property eligibility qualification on African descendants. In 1821, after the victory of the Bucktail Republicans, the Republicans represented the majority of the legislature when the new state constitution of 1821 was formed.

However, not all of the Republican politicians of the day toed the "party line" with respect to this obvious attempt at legalized racial discrimination.

Republican State Assemblyman R. Clarke was among those who came to the defense of these disenfranchised citizens. He was courageously willing to assert his dismay at the inclusion of this property requirement in the following terms:

> *"It is haughtily asked", said he, "who will stand in the ranks, shoulder to shoulder, with a negro? I answer, no one in time of peace:—no one when your musters and trainings are looked upon as mere pastimes. But when the hour of danger approaches, your 'white' militia are just as willing that the man of color should be set up as a mark to be shot at by the enemy, as to be set up themselves. In the war of the Revolution, these people helped to fight your battles by land and by sea. Some of your States were glad to turn out corps of colored men, and to stand 'shoulder to shoulder' with them. In your late war [1812], they contributed largely towards some of your most splendid victories. On Lakes Erie and Champlain, where your fleets triumphed over a foe superior in numbers, and engines of death, they were manned in large proportion with men of color."*

He further states:

> *And in this very House, in the fall of 1814, a Bill passed, receiving the approbation of all the branches of your Government, authorizing the Governor to accept the services of a corps of 2000 free people of color . . . They were not compelled to go, they were not drafted, they were volunteers—yes, Sir, volunteers to defend that very country from the inroads and ravages of a ruthless and vindictive foe, which had treated them with insult, degradation, and slavery."*

> *"I never knew a man of color that was not an anti-Jackson man. In fact, it was their respectability, and not their degradation, that was the cause of their disfranchisement. The Albany Camarilla limited the suffrage to the blacks, and opened it to the Irish;—a pretty good proof that the former were not likely to be their tools."*[77]

To a large extent, the Republican members of the legislature had finally achieved the goal they set out to accomplish as early as 1785—the disenfranchisement of people of African descent. Notwithstanding the extraordinary efforts against them, African descendants persevered. They worked diligently to meet the requirements of this law as illustrated in the Introduction of this work as well as through the individual struggles and efforts of African descendants like Solomon Northup as related in his narrative: *"Twelve Years a Slave"*. While recounting the working conditions of his "free" father Northup states,

> **"Besides giving us an education surpassing that ordinarily bestowed upon children in our condition, he acquired, by his diligence and economy, a sufficient property qualification to entitle him to the right of suffrage."**[178]

# NEW YORK STATE CONSTITUTION OF 1821

In keeping with this disenfranchisement strategy and to further limit the participation of African descendants in the privileges of full citizenship, New York State ratified a new state constitution in 1821 which significantly limited the voting rights of freed African descendants. Subsequently, proposed amendments to the constitution designed to restore the voting rights of African descendants were rejected by the voters of New York State in 1846 and again in 1860. Citizens of African descent who had suffered the traumatic centuries of enslavement and discrimination in the cities and towns of New York State continued to suffer after emancipation at the hands of a white political and social hierarchy that placed them in a fully legalized position of second or third-class citizenship. These actions mirrored in much the same way those of the southern states of America after the Civil War.

This new system of "Jim Crow" discrimination and disenfranchisement existed for another fifty years until the federal government passed the Fifteenth Amendment to the United States Constitution which was ratified in 1870. It should be noted that while citizens of African descent waited for this relief from the federal government, New York State continued on its path of "Jim Crow" by enacting laws in 1841 and again in 1864 that authorized separate public schools for children of African descent

# PERSPECTIVE ON THE POLITICS OF ENSLAVEMENT AND ABOLITION IN THE UNITED STATES

It has been the opinion of many historians including Benjamin Quarles, that the abolitionist movement of the Federalist era must be viewed as a failure. The reality is, "The Northern states had all but abandoned slavery, it is true, but the chief reason had been the availability of a free labor supply which made bonded labor unprofitable."[179]

The Northern states were beginning to prosper with the growth of diversified manufacturing as part of the worldwide Industrial Revolution. Immigrants and the institution of free labor employment boosted the North's population and economic prosperity while the South became the principal provider of raw materials. Southern farms shipped agricultural products such as cotton to northern mills, which sent finished goods back to the South and Europe.

Southern prosperity based on cotton production relied on enslaved labor. Enslaved workers were considered capital resources, used in the production of raw materials. This became a source of significant friction between the North, which paid its workers wages (normally as little as possible given the abundant supply of labor that existed) and the South, which "owned" its workers. Growing concerns among groups in the north regarding the immorality of enslavement led to political moves to outlaw enslavement. Slaveholding Southerners felt threatened by what they perceived as the destruction of their (human) capital resources. In an attempt to end enslavement peacefully, congressmen drafted many compromises that proposed compensating enslavers for their "property" (just such a proposal was included in a preliminary version of Abraham Lincoln's Emancipation Proclamation) but they encountered consistent opposition by abolitionists.

On the international front, by 1832, most of Europe and Mexico had abolished enslavement. And great international pressure was placed on the United States to follow suit. However, the South held fast to states' rights, a principle that was grounded in the maintenance of their enslaved agricultural workforce. Given the fact that they relied on their enslaved workers for their livelihoods, Southern planters elected congressional representatives who would support the right of self-determination for each state and oppose the annexation of anti-slavery territories. Due to the fact that ante-bellum industrial development was concentrated solely in the north, white Southerners maintained their political and economic control in a primarily agricultural South, unaffected by the problems of wage labor. The unwillingness of these opposing regions to reach a compromise ultimately led to the Civil War.[180]

# THE GREAT COMPROMISE

Ironically, one of the fateful compromises made at the United States Constitutional Convention of 1787 played a significant role in the issue of enslavement, its abolition and the Civil War. This compromise was directly responsible for the forthright rejection of the idea of "one man, one vote" contrary to the "vision" of American democracy. At the convention that eventually produced the document ratified by nine of the thirteen colonies in 1788, one of the last issues to be resolved was how to elect a president, according to Roger A. Burns in *A More Perfect Union: The Creation of the United States Constitution.*[181]

While Southerners opposed the enfranchisement of slaves, the Southern delegates enthusiastically supported the counting of slaves within their populations, thus increasing the region's political clout and voice in the selection of the presidency, due to their increased numbers in the Electoral College. The Northern states, of course, objected to this proposal and to the disproportionate advantage the inclusion of the Southern slave population would have in the overall outcome for representation in Congress.

Hence, the Great Compromise, the notorious "three-fifths of a man" clause, that permitted enslavement to continue in the United States and thus, struck an unhappy medium between Northern and Southern states by permitting those enslaved and people of color to be counted as three-fifths of a white person when setting the number of the seats in the House of Representatives due each state. (See Chart 11 below for New York State distribution) The compromise was instrumental in giving the southern states an advantage in their representation in Congress. In fact, between the presidencies of George Washington and Abraham Lincoln, fifty (50) years of slaveholders ruled the White House. Southern white slaveholders had become the governing force of the United States. They wrote, adjudicated, and enforced the laws of the nation. Consequently, the United States truly was a slaveholding republic.

> *"By 1850, a growing number of northerners were convinced that slavery posed an intolerable threat to free labor and civil liberties. Many believed that an aggressive Slave Power had seized control of the federal government, incited revolution in Texas and war with Mexico, and was engaged in a systematic plan to extend slavery into the western territories."[182]*

# POPULATION OF THE STATE OF NEW YORK, CA. 1800[183]

STATEMENT, Shewing the Aggregate Number of PERSONS in each of the Wards of the City of New-York, and in each of the Counties in this State, including, however, no more than three-fifths of the whole number of Slaves.

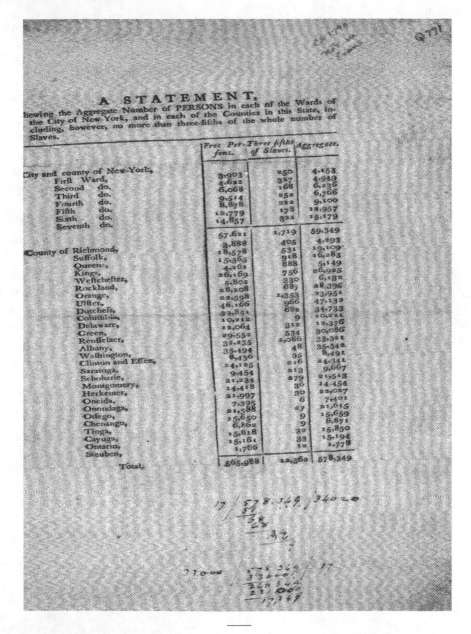

## REFERENCE NOTES

144 L. Lloyd Stewart, Reprint of Chapter 8, A Far Cry From Freedom: Gradual Abolition 1799-1827, New York State's Crime Againnst Humanity, (AuthorHouse PublishingBloomington, Il.) 2006, pg. 346

145 Berlin, 228

146 Chapter 188 of the Laws of 1817 of New York State

147 Chapter 62 of the Laws of 1799 of New York State. This law stipulated that, ". . . these same children shall be the servant of the legal "owner" of his or her mother until such child, if a male, reaches the age of twenty eight years and, if a female, the age of twenty five."

148 Quarles, 122

149 IBID

150 Austin Steward, 150

151 Williams-Myers, 139-141

152 Morris, Foreword, *A History of Negro Slavery in New York*, pg. ix; also see Thomas Archdeacon, *New York City, 1664-1710, Conquest and Change*, (Tthaca, NY: Cornell University Press, 1976)

153 Account Book, Ann Bevier, 1802-1812, *Philip Dubois Bevier Family Papers (1685-1910)*. Unpublished MSS Collection, Huguenot Historical Society of New Paltz, NY, Inc

154 Eric J. Roth, The Society of Negroes Unsettled: The History of Slavery in New Paltz, NY, May 2001, Huguenot Historical Society Library and Archives, *www.hhsnewpaltz.net/library_archives/topics_of_interest/slavery.htm*

155 Leslie M. Harris, In the Shadow of Slavery: African Americans in New York City, 1626-1863, (Chicago: University of Chicago Press, 2003) 5

156 Timothy Crumrin "Back to Africa?" The Colonization Movement in Early America, 5. Presumably, he was referring to the northern states.

157 See McManus quoted in A. J. Williams-Myers, Long Hammering, 139-141.

158 Graham Russell Hodges, 5-6

159 Census of New York State, 1855,. xi.

160 See Shane White, *Somewhat More Independent: The End of Slavery in New York City, 1770-1810* (Athens, GA: University of Georgia Press, 1991), pp.28-30. According to White, only seventy-six manumissions occurred in New York City between 1783 and 1800, not a particularly high number considering the high profile New York Manumission Society.

161 Rhoda Golden Freeman, *The Free Negro in New York City in the Era before the Civil War* (New York: Garland Publishing, 1994), 6.

162 Anthony Gronowicz, *Race and Class Politics in New York City Before the Civil War* (Boston: Northeastern University Press, 1998), 30

163  On Tammany Hall, see for instance, Gustavus Myers, *The History of Tammany Hall* (New York: Burt Franklin Press, 1917); Jabez D. Hammond, *History of Political Parties in the State of New York* (Buffalo: Phinney and Company, 1850), vol.1, ch. xvii; Alfred E. Young's *The Democratic Republicans of New York: The Origins, 1763-1797* (Chapel Hill: University of North Carolina Press, 1967)

164  Gronowicz, 32

165  *New York Journal and Patriotic Register*, March 16, 1799

166  Gronowicz, 32

167  Williams-Myers, 142-143

168  Herman D. Bloch, *The Circle of Discrimination: An Economic and Social Study of the Black Man in New York* (New York: New York University Press, 1969), 26. The numbers are as follows: 8,346 Irish, 3601 white, and 2,574 colored Americans

169  Roth, IBID

170  *Narrative of Sojourner Truth,* 1850, Boston, 14-15; Liwack, 97

171  Journal of the Assembly of New York State, 1785, 53

172  *Journal of the Senate of the State of New York*, 1811, 143

173  *New York Spectator,* April 19, 1815

174  IBID

175  Katherine Butler Jones, "They called it Timbucto", *Orion Magazine*, Winter 1998, 29

176  Edward S. Abdy, "Journal of a Residence and Tour in the United States", Vol. 2, (London, 1835)

177  IBID, INDEX

178  Solomon Northup, "*Twelve years a slave. Narrative of Solomon Northup, a citizen of New-York, 1853*", (London: Sampson Low, Son & Company, 47 Ludgate Hill., 1853) 19

179  See Quarles, *Black Abolitionists*

180  Dr. Henry McCarl, Beyond Face Value, Economic Environment, *(www.cuc.lsu.edu/economics)*

181  Roger A. Bruns, *A More Perfect Union: The Creation of the United States Constitution*, published for the National Archives Trust Fund Board.

182  See Gilder Lehrman, *The Origins and Nature of New World Slavery*, Abolition

183  GLC08893, Population of the State of New York, ca. 1800, *The "Three-Fifths Clause"*, Archive of Past Documents, The Gilder Lehrman Institute of American History, The Gilder Lehrman Institute of American History, The Collection—Newly Discovered Documents.

# CONCLUSION

# CONCLUSION

I have purposefully and with calculating intent written this work in a purely insipid historical and matter of fact manner. I've attempted this precisely due to the fact that I did not want my Family or the other individuals and families who experienced these life-altering circumstances during this period of New York State history, to be viewed or perceived by the reader as "victims." As you read this work however, you will come to the realization that only the ill-informed could interpret enslavement, discrimination and the insurmountable obstacles that were faced by the individuals in this story, as participants in a "victimless" crime.

My primary intention however, was to heighten the awareness of the reader to the difficulties and struggles that existed for this group of human beings in New York State at the turn of the 19th century. It was also designed to assist the reader in visualizing the reality that similar conditions and obstacles were experienced by millions of other unnamed and unrecorded individuals of African descent throughout America.

These courageous individuals suffered and survived in this most despicable system of subjugation in human creation. Here was a period in time when human beings were viewed by society and government as nothing more than "property"—no different than horses or swine. And yet, their ability to negotiate, bargain for and at times purchase their "freedom" is a truly heroic story that has not yet been fully vetted or told.

As I reflect on this critical period in African American history in New York State, I can unashamedly say that I feel pride and honor that I have only felt on a few occasions in my life. Imagine my Family and thousands of other African descendants tenaciously struggling to secure a life that had, heretofore, been legally denied to them. This denial was primarily the result of the color of their skin and, by manner of a vicious and unrelenting xenophobia that soured and corrupted any hopes or attempts to alter or mitigate the economic and social conditions of discrimination and racism.

For all African descendants, it was a struggle to free themselves from the vestiges of enslavement and second-class citizenship that had so viciously been thrust upon them, for no other reason than the fact that they were of African descent. Here exists a precursor for the present day terminology of "*OTHER*," as some are so inspired and prone to say in the 21st century.

During a twenty year period from 1800-1820, these individuals and families of African descent projected an example of true courage and dignity that allowed them to transition from a lifestyle embedded in the horrendous and oppressive conditions of enslavement, with all its brutal, dehumanizing and degrading mandates; to an astonishingly stable and admirable status of human achievement. This transitional period afforded them the opportunity to purchase and develop over five hundred and fifty (550) acres of land in one of the most remote and segregated counties of New York State. They had ventured to Washington County, New York with nothing more than their meager belongings, acquired during their long suffering confinement in New York State's economic generator of enslavement.

They had journeyed to Washington County, families and expectations in tow under the suggestion of a rumor of opportunity and a concomitant anticipation that a better life was possible for them at the end of this arduous and dangerous journey. Dangerous in that the precepts and ramifications of enslavement were still very much a part of the climate under which they traveled. Re-enslavement, capture, and potential sale to the south, were always a threat to their new found status of "Freedom."

In many cases, this newly acquired opportunity for social and economic advancement existed not very far from where they had most recently endured the daily humiliations of a systemic environment of racism, discrimination and inequity. Undervalued as human beings and exploited for their labor and skills, these pioneers of African American history toiled through excruciatingly difficult times. And yet, they survived and ultimately produced a legacy that cannot be challenged, discredited, discounted or denied.

Imagine the obstacles inherent in attempting to establish a new and independent life as a "free" person of African descent, when your only prior experiences were as an enslaved person—fully restricted and regulated by a system based on total and complete subjugation. Your entire life would have been monitored, restricted and scripted by individuals who had only their own best interests at heart. You and your family would serve for generations, literally, at their beck and call. The ability to think and act on your own and in your and your families' best interest was denied you because of your official status as "property". And now you were on your own, able to make your own decisions but without employment or a means to support and protect your family.

Truly their story is real and although not fully documented in official records, it occurred throughout the North, a region of a nation, where abolition or gradual abolition were being established and implemented in the late 1700s and early 1800s. It gives me great pleasure and I feel fortunate and honored to be able to assist in bringing just one of the many, as yet, undiscovered and unrecorded moments in the extraordinary history of people of African descent in New York State, to light.

Prior to my writing this work, I was fully engaged and focused intently on my own families' story. The ultimate mission was uncovering their unique and forgotten history in New York State. What I found was the bewildering reality that my families' story was not that unique when compared to the tens of thousands of other individuals and families of African descent, who preceded them and also traveled along side them on the exact same road to "Freedom."

One other binding point that inextricably unites my family with these other individuals and families of African descent, who also migrated to Washington County, is the festering wound of omission that has still not been healed or resolved—*WHERE* did they come from? I think that this is the most compelling failure that I must at the present time admit to, accept and internalize.

The inability to accurately and fully document this extraordinary journey in the middle of enslavement in New York State causes great anxiety on my part.

The answer to the question: Where did your people come from?—seems like a very simple question to answer. Especially due to the fact that we are in a period of extraordinary technological advancement with respect to digitizing library and local, state and national documents and records. Yet, when it comes to people of African descent, this lack of necessary documentation and the misappropriation and, destruction of official records would seem to border on criminal.

As helpful as the numerous local historians, local and county historical societies, county archivists, and the New York State Library and Archives have been; the fact remains that the majority of these individuals and institutions had little if any knowledge of this "Migration" within their own localities and throughout Washington County, itself.

*Notwithstanding these difficulties, let's recap what we do know about this period in African American history in New York State between the years 1800-1820.*

# THE GRADUAL ABOLITION ACT

With the enactment of the Gradual Abolition Act and its Manumission Provision in New York State in 1799, New York enslavers were given the authority to manumit under their own seal certain enslaved men and women and families that they considered to be capable of providing for themselves without any reliance on the part of localities to provide for their maintenance and support.

It is my contention that this Manumission Provision would prove to be the major impetus for the increase in the number of "free" persons of African descent in New York State between the years 1799-1827. Census records reveal the fact that between the year 1790, when New York State's "free" African descendant population totaled 4,682 individuals and 1800 when this population totaled 10,374 individuals, New York State experienced an increase in the number of "free" African descendants of 5,692 individuals, a one hundred and twenty-two percent (122%) increase. This clearly highlights the influence that the Manumission Provision of the Gradual Abolition Act may have had on New York State enslavers. Further evidence can be garnered from Census data for the years 1800 to 1810—the apex of this migration to Washington County—revealing the total population of "free" African descendants increased by 14,759 to 25,133 "free" African descendants. A four hundred and thirty-seven percent (437%) increase over the total for 1790.

It should be noted that New York may not have been the only state in this new Union that served as a source of individuals for this migration. A significant number of African descendants also migrated from Vermont and other parts of New England and surrounding states to Washington County throughout the existence of the New York Colony and State. Some of this number were recorded within the New York State Census of 1855, which for the first time, listed the places of origin for all New York residents.

# ECONOMIC BOOM IN WASHINGTON COUNTY

The massive boom of agricultural production and manufacturing that initiated this now documented migration is fully recorded in New York State and Federal publications. The new found status that the county garnered as the major agricultural and textile producer in New York State was not lost on these persons of African descent, neither was it lost on other New York citizens. We have illustrated the fact that Washington County's overall population grew by some 10,000 residents between the years 1800 and 1810 according to census reports. Of this number, some 3,000 newly arrived residents were of African descent.

The ability and skills that people of African descent acquired while confined to enslavement on the farms and plantations throughout New York State assisted Washington County landowners in addressing their ever growing demand for cheap labor. These African descendants were additionally well equipped to transition to various textile and other manufacturing opportunities that presented themselves. The fact that Washington County could lead the state in the production and processing of products such as cotton and linen, while at the same time trailing more economically sophisticated counties in the number of manufacturing plants and equipment, speaks emphatically and directly to the impact that labor intensive production and processing had on this significant economic development

As stated earlier, the major and I would suggest, the primary initiator of this mass relocation centers squarely on the changing economic realities and conditions that were fundamentally transforming the economy in Washington County during the early1800s. While these growth patterns and conditions encompassed a fifteen (15) to twenty (20) year period, particular emphasis is placed on the "boom" year of 1810, where census and economic data chronicle a noteworthy advancement in the economy of Washington County's towns and villages.

The year 1810 provides a significant window into the economic resurgence of Washington County and its various demographic populations. Replete with federal documentation, our survey of the economy of Washington County during this period further substantiates the extreme expansion and rapidly developing economic conditions that completely support the promotion of Washington County as a major economic producer in the state. At the same time, it emphatically supported and sustained all of the necessary elements for this unique "Migration" of people of African descent.

Two federal supplemental economic records, mentioned earlier, that were attached to the 1810 Federal Census[184] provide the primary source documentation necessary to track and reconstruct this seemingly transformative economic revitalization in Washington County. See Table 3—Washington County Manufacturing.

As the Manumission Provision of New York State's Gradual Abolition Law and other pre and post war "freedom initiatives" provided the impetus of what proved to be a truly significant advancement in the social, political and economic status of persons of African descent in New York State; simultaneously, in Washington County, an economic boom created an unprecedented opportunity for these newly "freed" citizens to solidify and actualize their dreams of freedom and prosperity. The prospects of "free" status would prove meaningless without the opportunity to provide for and sustain a family, by way of real and substantive employment.

183

# AGRICULTURAL AND MANUFACTURING DEVELOPMENT

Historically since its settlement; agricultural, mineral and timber-related industries had consistently made up the largest sectors of the economy of Washington County. The early 19th century however, ushered in a new economic boom and created a major shift in the fortunes and production capabilities of Washington County.

With newly acquired land from Albany County that was included in the renaming and restructuring of Charlotte County into Washington County in 1784, New York State, through negotiated land settlements with Massachusetts and Vermont, significantly restructured the boundaries of the county. In addition, the parceling of tens of thousands of acres of forfeited land acquired after the Revolution from British loyalists into smaller portions and lots for sale or rent provided a seemingly endless resource for increased production in agriculture and textile manufacturing. The "Act of Forfeiture" records details the sale of some 450-500 lots or some 62,000 acres of land to large, mid-sized and smaller farmers in Washington County.[185]

These records provide us with some insight into the economic development of Washington County during the beginning of the 19th century. The lands sold under the auspices of forfeiture legislation and documented in forfeited land records during the middle 1780s were still producing in 1810 during Washington County's "boom" period.

Chart 5—"FORFEITURE LANDOWNERS WITH PERSONS OF AFRICAN DESCENT 1810," allows us to account for the descendants of some of the families that were involved in the original sales of these forfeited lands in Washington County. It also creates a window exposing the number of "free" persons of African descent who worked these same properties in conjunction with these descendant family members.

The resulting increase in production in Washington County was focused on four primary areas (products) all considered labor intensive industries with respect to their successful enterprise. These products included the increased production of flaxen; wool; and cotton goods and the measured production of fulling mills.

Table 3 further establishes the fact that Washington County ranked number one in New York State in the production of flaxen and woolen goods (yards) and number two in the state in the production of cotton (yards) and in the production of Fulling Mills (yards produced). Washington County also ranked number three in the State of New York in the production from hatteries (hats) and tanneries (calf skins).

The key to this major augmentation in production and the heightened advancement in the economic status of Washington County in New York State can best be answered partially by the increase in the availability of land as mentioned earlier; but, even more important is Washington County's major boost in the availability of cheap labor. All of the production increases cited for the county could be attributed to labor intensive production. Without a significant labor force for production and processing, Washington County would have remained marginally successful economically. The operation of these various production apparatuses necessitated a concomitantly high number of machine workers and a significantly high number of laborers. This substantial labor force was readily available due to the major influx of individuals of African descent who migrated to Washington County in the 1800s.

As stated earlier, the labor intensive nature of the production of flax, wool, and cotton and the processing mechanism involved in the manufacturing of "fulled-cloth" required a massive labor force. Individuals of African descent satisfied this requirement and also began to develop the means of enhancing their own individual and family economies through farm labor production and the home-manufacturing of cloth.

## DEPRESSION IN WASHINGTON COUNTY IN 1807

Following this boom within the economy of Washington County—a depression ensued that devastated the economy of the United States *and* Washington County, respectively. The most likely reason for the Depression of 1807-1814 was the trade embargo imposed by President Thomas Jefferson in an attempt to keep the United States from becoming involved in the war raging in Europe.

A major result of the Embargo was the disappearance of export demand which closed down many important industries in the United States. The trade embargo also significantly disrupted and consequently reduced American imports. In principle, the loss of foreign markets for U.S. business could have been compensated for by a shift to production for domestic markets, however, such a shift would have taken time and, the resulting economic recession created by the Embargo reduced domestic demand throughout the Nation.

The War of 1812 between the United States and England, which followed the Embargo, coincidentally, gave a dramatic boost to the manufacturing capabilities of the United States. The British blockade of the American coast created a shortage of cotton cloth in the United States, leading to the creation of a revived cotton-manufacturing industry. The war also spurred construction of the Erie Canal project in New York State, which was built initially to promote commercial links yet, was also perceived as having military uses should the need ever arise.

The War of 1812-1815, declared between the United States and Great Britain found Washington County struggling under the same depression which affected the agricultural and textile industries throughout the nation. The war caused the price of flax, Washington County's major crop and the product that represented the county's major economic generator, to plummet. Beginning in the 1820s, the wool market started a recovery that once again prompted hill country farmers bordering the Hudson Valley to turn to wool and tallow as surplus crops. Seven years after the marked beginning of this recession in 1814, the economy was considered by most economic scholars to be recovered.

## ECONOMIC RECOVERY

We learn however, that this depression period in Washington County caused tremendous turmoil throughout the county to the point that by 1814 the population of the county had decreased by some seven thousand five hundred (7500) due to the effects of the economic upheaval. It can be surmised that this reduction in population was caused by these depression related conditions and the need on the part of individuals and their families to seek employment opportunities in other parts of the state and in the newly developing western regions of the U. S.

The consequences of the 1807-1814 Depression also had an incredible impact on the plight of communities of African descent in Washington County. African descendants began to develop a more "migrant worker" mentality due to the financial realities associated with their transition from a system of enslavement to a more capitalistic approach to production. Families of African descent were now being faced for the first time with the reality of searching for survival employment opportunities, wherever possible.

Those that had not been able to develop a sustainable environment of subsistence farming or in securing manufacturing labor in Washington County were now in constant search of temporary and/or subsistence employment. This dramatic change caused great hardships within the African descendant community. The specter of being relegated to the most menial of jobs and the constant competition for employment with newly arriving European immigrants forced African descendants further to the bottom of the social and economic ladder. This consequence precipitated a standard, where African descendants were often forced to accept wages below those of their European immigrant counterparts.

As this Depression progressed, it became imperative for survival purposes that individuals and families of African descent leave Washington County, in an effort to preserve their economic independence. It became clear that the reality of these depressive conditions had a harsher economic impact on the African descendant population than the county population, as a whole.

The effects of this Depression literally decimated the population of African descent in the county. In 1810, the total "free" population of African descent amounted to 2,815 residents, as mentioned earlier, this figure was the high point of the population and migration of individuals and families of African descent at the turn of the century. It was soon reduced in 1814 to a total population of three hundred and one (301) individuals, a reduction in the population of African descent of some eighty-nine percent (89%) over the four year period of 1810-1814.[186]

The ending of this "Migration Period" for people of African descent in Washington County created by the Depression of 1807-1814 was predictable given the economy based incentive that had instigated it in the first instance.

As the economy began to improve in Washington County during and after the War, African descendants sought to take advantage of this new growing economy. As the New York State Census of 1825 highlights Washington County experienced a major increase in the number of residents of African descent, who purchased and owned their own land. Many of these families remained in the county for generations—growing and contributing to the economic stability of the county and flourishing as independent and "free" citizens of both Washington County and New York State.

As we end this amazingly yet heretofore, hidden story of the survival and prosperity of a people who struggled through seemingly insurmountable obstacles to establish a "new" life in the ever changing landscape of a new nation. We are obligated to acknowledge a courageous and determined people willing to sacrifice and suffer the most extraordinary hardships of life, in an effort to provide a positive environment for themselves and their children. They chose to live and prosper in the United States of America and New York State as fully actualized, entitled and sufficiently equipped citizens in an often hostile and violent homeland.

### *THE VAN VRANKENS WERE ONE OF THESE FAMILIES!*

## REFERENCE NOTES

[184] "A Series of Tables of the Several Branches of AMERICAN MANUFACTURES, Exhibiting Them in every County of the Union, So Far As THEY ARE RETURNED IN THE REPORTS OF THE MARSHALLS, AND OF THE SECRETARIES OF THE TERRITORIES AND OF THEIR RESPECTIVE ASSISTANTS, IN THE AUTUMN OF THE YEAR 1810: Together with Returns of certain doubtful Goods, Productions of the Soil and agricultural Stock, so far as they have been received. Bureau of the Census Library

[185] CHAPTER XXIV OF THE LAWS OF THE STATE OF NEW YORK, PASSED IN THE THIRD SESSION OF THE LEGISLATURE, HELD AT KINGSTON, IN ULSTER COUNTY; *An Act for the Forfeiture and Sale of the Estates of Persons who have adhered to the Enemies of this State, and for declaring the Sovereignty of the People of this State, in respect to all Property within the same.—Passed 22d October, 1779*

[186] 1810 US Federal Census and 1814 New York State Census

# PART II

## THE VAN VRANKEN FAMILY

# CHAPTER V

## THE HISTORY OF MY VAN VRANKEN FAMILY

# MY VAN VRANKEN FAMILY HISTORY

The values and love that our families have given to us as sustenance and nourishment over these past 400 some years on this continent still shines with the brilliance of a thousand heavenly bodies in the faces and expressions of Love that define and reflect the beauty and righteousness of our children.

## INTRODUCTION

People of African descent in America have had an almost insurmountable struggle to maintain, grow and nourish positive family circles. Every aspect of the early laws, customs and values of this country were developed, orchestrated and designed to diminish, denigrate and even destroy the ties that bind family circles of African descent. In fact, the privileged and elitist economic and social foundation of this nation depended upon it! And yet, we as a People have survived in these inhuman and life debilitating conditions. In fact, we have flourished and thrived. We have served the world as a living embodiment of the **true** nature of human beings: "*MAAT*" (Truth, Justice, Righteousness, Balance, Order, Harmony and Reciprocity).

It was during my initial genealogical research period that I was able to trace my Ancestors back to the middle 1700s in New York State. Thus, began the laborious effort of identifying and documenting both the life of my Great-Great-Great-Great-Great Grandfather Johannes Van Vranken (1777-1865) and the lives of his family members to the present day. Johannes, (John Van Bronk) as he is referenced in most official documents of the period and his son, Samuel Van Vranken are recorded on Samuel's death certificate as having been born in Schagticoke, New York.[187] *I AM PRESENTLY IN SEARCH OF THEIR AND MY ANCESTORS!*

Notwithstanding the feelings of accomplishment, excitement and joy, that this initial research gave me; I felt and still feel that the primary purpose of this effort had not been fully realized. I search my subconscious for the reasons for these feelings of futility each day when I stare incessantly at the few pictures of my Ancestors that I have in my living room but, more profoundly when I talk to, visit with, or play with my grandchildren.

At this writing, they number thirteen (ten biological and three blended)—with two on the way. They are the most curious, intelligent and loving creatures that the Creator has ever made. To me they represent: *The Lights of our lives, the Reflections of our past and the Brilliance of our future.* The fact, that the Creator has allowed me a small role in this ever growing drama of life. It has caused me to want to take on the responsibility of gifting them with the full sustenance and knowledge of who they are and who/where they have come from. All human beings require, long for and are entitled to a "sense of the immortal" in their lives—be it through the oral renditions of surviving grandparents or great grandparents or by way of the joy and fulfillment of family gatherings and reunions. How does one survive and flourish without such intimate details and knowledge of their past? Telling as much of the story of how we got here and how we have survived has now become the defining purpose for my life. For, I am now the eldest living member of my immediate Family. I take this responsibility willingly and with solemn and enthusiastic dedication.

It is safe to say that Johannes and his family were *enslaved* in New York during the time of his birth. In fact, New York State was in the middle of its long and sordid history of enslavement during this period. I have not yet been able to document our family's history prior to his birth, so I am unable to identify the persons and/or families to whom my Ancestors in New York were enslaved. However, undoubtedly the various Van Vranken family members of Albany, Rensselaer, Schenectady, and Saratoga Counties played some role in their bondage and/or emancipation.

## THE VAN VRANKEN FAMILY CHRONOLOGY

What I do know is that Johannes and his brother, Francis, were long surviving members of the Washington County, New York State community of African descent. The fact that their descendants reside in Washington County to the present day impacts greatly on our ability to trace and record the genealogical history of our Van Vranken family. You are about to learn about my Van Vranken family, particularly with respect to Washington County and, more importantly, you will learn that what we do not know about our family is in direct correlation to what we do not know about the other 2,700 individuals of African descent who also migrated to Washington County at the beginning of the 19th century.

Genealogy is the reconstruction of a lineage using family records that can be found in family collections, as well as in the many archives and other facilities all across the country that house historical records. Genealogical research is usually approached one generation at a time, starting with your own individual generation and working back as far as you can, until all possible records have been researched. Genealogy also requires that you use family and historical records to prove or disprove that an individual or group of individuals are connected through kinship or by "blood."

For people of African descent, it is often more difficult to perform this research than for their white counterparts. African descendant researchers often need to include other unrelated families to document and establish their ancestral past. From 1619-1869, often the only records of a person of African descent's existence were the notes of his/her enslaver. According to RootsWeb, a well known genealogical website, only one out of every 19 persons of African descent was free in 1861, when the Civil War began. Since those enslaved held non-citizen status, extant early vital records seldom included data on them.

Due to this unfortunate circumstance, quite often researchers and family members are unable to prove or disprove a significant family event, like your great-grandparents' birth, origination/location in this country or even their marriage using these records alone. You are forced then to rely on "surmise." If John and Jane Smith were listed in many records as husband and wife, but you can't find a marriage record stating that they were married on a specific date in a specific place; then you can still conclude that John and Jane Smith were probably married. Even though, an actual marriage or birth record cannot be located.

You are therefore, forced to give the reasons for *not* being able to locate or produce these records:

1- They may have been born or married in a different state, but you can't identify which state;
2- The county was not recording births or marriages at that time;
3- They were born or married during enslavement, and were not recorded; or,
4- The records were burned in a courthouse fire (of which there were many or they were destroyed in some other natural disaster) and you, therefore, are unaware as to whether these records ever existed at all.

These are not all the reasons, but some of the most likely ones that you could give for not finding a record of the birth or marriage of John and Jane Smith.

African-American historical research is scattered through a variety of correspondence of private citizens and government agency reports. One's success in researching African-American ancestry in the years prior to the Civil War depends largely on what one's status was, enslaved or free, particularly in the southern portion of this country. (Enslavement records are difficult to locate and are rarely found, even in the North).

In census records, from 1790-1840 in the south and from 1790 to 1830 in the north, only names of the head of the household were provided, along with the number of those enslaved. In 1850 and 1860, the Federal government undertook a supplemental enslavement census (slave schedules), giving the enslaver's name, and the number of enslaved by gender and age, and with a designation of Black or mulatto.

During enslavement, enslaved persons were considered "property", thus "slave schedules" included the names of enslavers and a description of those enslaved. However, the enslaved were rarely listed by name, due to the racist viewpoint that these persons who were enslaved were not human but "property". Therefore, your only options for tracing your family members of African descent is to look for wills, probate records, plantation records, family inventories, bills of sale, land deeds and even runaway slave advertisements in newspapers. The names of all free persons of African descent were included in the 1850 and 1860 census and beginning in 1870, the census listed the names of all persons of African descent.

*GIVEN THE BACKDROP AND CONSTRAINT OF THESE HISTORICAL REALITIES, WE WILL NONETHELESS ATTEMPT TO DOCUMENT THE HISTORICAL AND GEOGRAPHICAL RECORD OF MY VAN VRANKEN FAMILY.*

The Van Vranken family name for people of African descent in the latter half of the nineteenth and early twentieth century to the present day in New York State has been primarily associated with Ft. Edward and Hudson Flatts in Washington County, New York.[188] They made their first documented appearance in Washington County according to various census reports in the early 1800s. Early official records inform us that John Van Vrank (Johannes Van Vranken) is listed in the 1825 New York State Census of Salem, Washington County, New York, as living on a sixty acre farm with his family. His family was comprised of ten members, (seven males and three females) with one male in the family recorded as having died in 1824. This tragedy is further reflected in the 1830 Federal Census for Salem, Washington County, New York, where the composition of Johannes' (John Van Bronk) family is reduced from ten members to nine members. They are listed in these census reports as a family of "Free Colored(s)."

The family is also recorded in the 1825 census as owning, "a cow, two horses, six sheep, six hogs and having domestically manufactured fourteen yards of cotton, linen or other cloth."[189] Johannes Van Vranken, listed as John Van Bronk, Van Vrank, Van Vronk, and Van Rankin, in several later state and federal censuses, continues to reside in Washington County for another forty years in the towns of Salem and Argyle. He raises his children into adulthood and probably was accused of spoiling his 13+ grand and numerous great-grandchildren. His life could best be described as that of a subsistence farmer. Johannes' brother, Francis Van Vranken is an even earlier recorded resident of Washington County having been documented in the 1820 Census for Jackson, Washington County, New York, as Francis Van Woak with nine family members living in the same residence.

As is usually the case in remote and/or rural areas of this country, where small numbers of African descendant families choose to settle for economic or other reasons, they often "band" together. They become very dependent on this unity for protection and survival and to enhance the abilities of both the individuals and families themselves to grow and prosper. In our story, this unification of protection and survival is illustrated in the fact that one of Johannes' daughters, Catherine, marries a member of the Hazzard family and Johannes' oldest son, Samuel's daughter, Ellen, marries a member of the Latimer family. The Hazzards and Latimers were two families of African descent who migrated to Washington County in the early 1800s along with the Van Vrankens.

The point here is that Johannes and Francis Van Vranken and their family were typical of the families of African descent who lived and worked in the numerous farming communities throughout upstate New York. These "free" families labored tirelessly on the farms and small plantations of upstate New York. In some instances, they were even able to purchase and work their own farms as illustrated by the 1825 record of John Van Bronk and his family.

In the New York State Census of 1835, John Van Vrank ( Van Vranken) is listed with 9 members (6 males and 3 females). By the Federal Census of 1840, the households of John Van Bronk (Van Vranken) in Argyle and his eldest son Samuel Van Vronk's (Van Vranken) family in Salem comprised a total of sixteen persons (five males and eleven females). These documented large numbers of persons within this family would lead one to surmise that they were living together as an extended family unit.

Interestingly enough, just this small sampling illustrates the various manipulations of the surname of "Van Vranken" and the difficulty that exists when tracing African descendant families within official records of the period. However, the most consistent usage and form of the surname was and is Van Vranken:

> *"Every person having the name of van Frank, Van Vranken, Van Vrankin or Van Vrancken is a direct descendant of Claes Gerritsen. It is exclusively an American name never used in any other country and only used by this family. No other immigrants came to America who used or were called by this name."*[190]

The earliest history of this potential African descendant branch of the Van Vranken family (there are several) documents one of the many disturbing and dehumanizing aspects of enslavement in New York during the 17th and 18th centuries. The inability of present day families of African descent to trace their family genealogies and histories directly to their arrival in the "New

World," is directly related to the unavailability of cogent and well-documented governmental record-keeping. Although this phenomenon of the absence of individualized documentation and record-keeping is normally associated with the enslaved populations in the southern region of the United States; its origin is firmly implanted in the earliest explorations and settlements of America. For it was in the northern region of America that enslavement began to perfect its gruesome litany of the lost, stolen and often ignored history of African enslavement and its enslaved; as well as its' dehumanizing practices of racial discrimination, inequality and segregation.

Given the primary precept of this work—to tell the story of my Van Vranken family within the context of the history of people of African descent migrating to upstate New York—this reality of history presents an indelible and imposing barrier to any attempts to seek the true representation of history itself. A 'Wall' is erected that excludes true historical scholarship, while at the same time it serves to protect and ensure the anonymity of the dehumanizing and sordid practices undertaken by persons, families and communities in this country. A nation reputed to be founded on the principles of "freedom, justice and equality" for *ALL* men!

As best can be surmised, my Van Vrankens arrived in Washington County from the surrounding area of Albany, Schenectady, Saratoga or Rensselaer counties. Most likely they migrated from present day Halfmoon, Saratoga County. Half Moon has a well documented history of enslavement and numerous records speak to the issue of the white Van Vranken hierarchy's participation and profiteering from the practices of human enslavement.

As was the case in the southern states of America, families of African descent were often labeled with the last names of their enslavers, either by practice or by choice. Assuming that my Van Vranken ancestors were willing or unwilling participants in a similar "naming custom" in New York State, then the Van Vrankens of Half Moon could easily be the family whose surname was adopted by my family. It would also suggest that they were indeed the family who enslaved them.

# THE HISTORY OF THE TOWN OF HALF MOON, SARATOGA COUNTY, NEW YORK

If we accept the premise that my Van Vranken family came to Washington County from one or more of its surrounding counties, the most plausible county of choice would be Saratoga and potentially, the Town of Half Moon. According to the earliest census records, we can be confident in the knowledge that the enslaved population of Half Moon decreased rapidly after 1800, primarily due to the results of New York State's Gradual Abolition Law's Manumission Provision.[191] We are also aware of the fact that Half Moon's enslaver families were well represented by the Van Vrankens, formerly of the City of Albany, New York.

## EARLY SETTLEMENT

In the early 1600's, the site of a cluster of islands located where the Hudson and Mohawk River meet, along with the surrounding area became known as Half-Moon Point. The area had been an Native American trading site for some years controlled by the Mohawks, who bartered among themselves and with other nations. Passage across the river at Half-Moon was facilitated by the low waters, which ran from the Point to Haver (Peebles) Island. The initial settlement of Half-Moon Point centered in present-day Waterford, where Dutch traders, trappers and homesteaders who had traveled up the river from Albany made their homes. As settlement in Waterford took hold, the more pioneering Albany Dutch went north from Waterford and entered the wilderness that is now part of the Town of Halfmoon.[192]

The Albany Dutch settlement extended up the Hudson River, as more families came to the area. A group of Schenectady Dutch, mostly farmers, traveling from the southeast also settled in the Town of Half Moon.[193] Records indicate that the land in Half Moon was purchased and developed in 1667. The majority of lands comprising Half Moon were once a part of the Van Schaick Patent of 1674. The early settlers of Half-Moon were under the jurisdiction of Albany County from 1683 until 1791, when Saratoga County was made a separate governing body. Half-Moon at that time also extended across the Mohawk River to include the Boght and Niskayuna to the north boundary of the manor of Rensselaerwyck. One of the four "mother towns" of newly created Saratoga County, Half Moon included the present area of Waterford until 1816, Clifton Park until 1828, and Mechanicville which was separated in 1910. When its boundaries were finally fixed, the Town of Halfmoon emerged somewhat irregularly shaped and without a central focus of settlement. For a short time, from 1816 to 1820, Halfmoon was known as Orange. Few people were comfortable with the name change and the original name of Halfmoon was restored.[194]

As early as the 4th of March 1669, only seven years after the settlement of Schenectady by Arendt Van Curler and his associates, at the great flats on the Mohawk; it is recorded that Pieter Danieke Van Olinda sells "his certain great island" in the Mohawk at Niskayuna—to three persons, viz., Jan Verbeck, Philip Pieter Schuyler, and Pieter Van Olinda. We also learn that on the 31st of October 1677, Claes Janse Van Boeckhoven bought land *over the river'* at Niskayuna. The parties selling were Harman Vedder and Barent Reyndertse Smit. Boeckhoven was united in the purchase with Ryck Claes Van Vranken. This shows the settlement of these four families (and undoubtedly, there were others with them) to have been in Halfmoon, in the vicinity of Vischer's Ferry, more than three hundred years ago.[195] When Ryck Claes Van Vranken died about the year 1713, the property passed to his wife, and after her death in 1717, it passed to their children.

"The Mohawk Valley attracted settlers, and there is evidence that even before 1667 an opening had been made in the forests of this town. Families, daring the dangers of frontier warfare, pushed away from Albany and Schenectady to find homes for themselves and their children. Unfortunately, we learn that very little can be obtained with respect to competent information about this earliest settlement in the wilderness of upstate New York. From the old maps, it appears that the Niskayuna of earlier times was mostly on the north side of the Mohawk, and within the present limits of Clifton Park, perhaps including the western portion of Half-Moon. The points of settlement were undoubtedly Vischer's Ferry, and down the river, including Fort's Ferry. The old name for Niskayuna was Canastigione upon an old map of 1773. This name appears just north of the southerly bend of the Mohawk, enclosing the present lower portion of Halfmoon. Saratoga, Half-Moon, and Niskayuna are the three points occupied by white men before 1700 in the soon to be County of Saratoga".[196]

The Census of Albany County for 1723 gives the following names of the residents of Canastigione. This is a list of all the residents at Niskayuna some three hundred years ago. There are twenty names, but several may have belonged to the same family, leaving it probable that there were thirteen or more families living there. Of these, some were no doubt on the south side of the river. Families residing in this section of the county were: John Quacumbus, John Foort, Jacob Pearse, Derrick Brat, Maes Rycksen, Evert Rycksen, Gerrit Rycksen, Nicholas Van Vranken, Lapion Canfort, Cornelius Christianse, Eldert Timonze, John Quackenboss, Jr., Peter Ouderkirk, Jacob Cluit, John Cluit, Frederick Cluit, Samuel Creeger, Derrick Takelsen, Mattias Boose Snor,

Johannis Christianse.[197] "The name Rycksen is said by some to be the same as Van Vranken, yet they both appear upon the census roll."[198]

Clifton Park was separated from the Town of Halfmoon in 1828, the last town to be formed in Saratoga County. However, the roots of the town go back 340 years to the year 1672, when two Dutch settlers from Albany, Ryckert Claase Van Vranken and Claes Janse Van Boeckhoven contracted to buy land over the Mohawk River at Canastagione on 17 May 1672. The price was 550 skipples (wicker baskets) of wheat, and the final papers were issued on 31 October 1677, when it was paid in full. "Canastagione", a native American word meaning corn flats, referred to the lands along the north shore of the Mohawk River. Ryckert Claase Van Vranken sold his house and lot on North Pearl Street in Albany, and moved to his land at Canastagione in 1684.[199] He resided there until his death in 1713. Upon his death, his land was divided between his three sons, Gerrit, Maas and Evert. These three brothers established farms east of present day Vischers Ferry.[200]

Ryckert Claase Van Vranken's children were Maas, Gerrit, Evert and Margaret. Both Maas and his brother Gerrit owned farms on the north side of the Mohawk, in what is now Halfmoon, but then a part of Niskayuna, (to which an additional one mile was added to the farm, extending north, made by patent of date April 22, 1708.) It is recorded that in 1704, Maas Ryckse built a fort at Niskayuna, probably on or near his own farm for the sum of 12 pounds.[201]

## ENSLAVEMENT IN HALF MOON

Canastagione referred to the lands along the north shore of the Mohawk River. It was here that Ryckert Claase Van Vranken relocated in 1684. As one of the oldest, and most firmly established of the Dutch families in the Town of Half Moon, later separated into Half Moon and Clifton Park in 1828, the Van Vrankens were also among the most extensive enslavers in the early history of this area. In 1684, when Ryckert Van Vranken moved from Albany to his farm along the Mohawk River, "he brought a number of enslaved persons with him. They are the ones who made it possible for him to develop his property".[202]

## THE ENSLAVED LABOR FORCE

Enslaved persons and families of African descent in the various cities, towns and villages of New York State very often worked as: coopers, tailors, sailors, bakers, tanners, goldsmiths, naval carpenters, blacksmiths, spinners, weavers, bolters, sail makers, millers, masons, candle makers, tobacconists, caulkers, carpenters, shoemakers, brush makers, glaziers, wheelwrights, tailors, butchers, metal workers, silversmiths and the construction of frame houses. Their skills and experience in these trades matched in all areas those of white artisans. On the larger plantations throughout the state, Africans and their descendants were concentrated in agriculture. Their ability to keep "plantations" in the north operating fully and efficiently was well documented.[203]

From the earliest days of its establishment, enslaved and free Africans and their descendants were part of the upstate New York community. The enslavers of the area like the Van Vrankens utilized "slaves much as the Southern planters did, as farm workers, house servants and in the many trades necessary to a self-sufficient manor."[204] They were also used to meet the tremendously laborious requirements of an agrarian economy. Females of African descent were also utilized as domestics and personal servants to the aristocratic hierarchy of the community.

They were also engaged as nursemaids, companions, shop assistants, tradesmen, scouts and woodsmen, as well as laborers.

The first enslaved persons to be used extensively in Saratoga County were those of Johannes Schuyler who developed his lands in the 1720s at Old Saratoga. The Schuyler family compound called the Flatts was three miles north of Albany. Conditions at the Flatts were very similar to those further north in Saratoga County. While few families like the Schuylers numbered their enslaved persons in double figures, most had only one or two enslaved persons working their farms. In upstate Saratoga County, "most households had neither the acreage nor the range of duties particularly in winter to support more than a few enslaved persons. For example, the two African matrons in the Flatts' household of Saratoga had children, but were husbandless and could expect their children to be sold. Most married women of African descent lived in separate households from their husbands, depending upon their spouses' visits to sustain expectations of family life."[205]

The kitchen was the domain of the enslaved, where women of African descent served as cooks, seamstresses and laundresses. Men of African descent were skilled in caring for livestock, cutting wood, and serving as field hands. There was a seasonal house to the outdoors, sometimes in a permanent structure as at the Schuyler House in Old Saratoga, but often in a temporary wooden hut where the enslaved lived until the weather became cold. Wheat cultivation required field hands during spring planting and summer harvesting. The other seasons were devoted to cutting trees for lumber or barrel staves and the transport of produce to market. Persons enslaved in upstate New York, performed a variety of tasks, rather than the steady field labor of their southern counterparts.

Even in the areas where African descendants were not the largest demographic element, they tended to be well placed in upper class residences. In North America, for example, the enslaved were most likely to be found in the largest estates and wealthiest households. For example, William Byrd, living in Virginia in the 1680s on land occupied by his estate and the smaller farms of former indentured servants, still felt that he was living in a "great family of Negro's [sic]."[206] Byrd's enslaved labor not only worked the fields but also provided domestic service in close proximity to their European enslavers.[207] This same situation prevailed in New Netherland and New York as well. The wealthiest had large estates of enslaved persons, where everywhere else European indentured servants prevailed. Thus, only the Dutch West India Company officials and the governors had as many as forty enslaved persons in New Netherland. Those enslaved also provided most of the domestic service in the homes of the elite, even though some visitors to their homes may have preferred Europeans believing that "Angolan slave women are thievish, lazy and useless trash."[208] But whatever the overall Dutch opinion of them, Africans and their descendants were virtually ubiquitous in domestic service among the "better" households.

Enslavers could also engage "in large-scale nonagricultural enterprises without the problems contingent upon using indentured servants, especially in some skilled tasks, where the loss of a trained servant might be hard to make up."[209] In technical skill and versatility African and African descendant workers spanned the entire range of free labor and were a vital component in transforming an unstable Dutch outpost into a rich and powerful state.[210]

## STATUS OF ENSLAVEMENT

According to the 1790 Federal Census, there were one hundred and thirty-five enslaved persons in the Town of Half Moon, "which amounted to 3.7% of the town's total population. This African descendant population designated Half Moon as the largest enslaver town in Saratoga County. These one hundred and thirty-five enslaved persons were divided among fifty-five of the families residing in Half Moon. Ballston, Stillwater, and Saratoga (then the only towns) followed with sixty-nine, sixty-one, and fifty-three enslaved persons respectively, for a total of three hundred and eleven."[211]

Overall the number of enslaver households was divided thus: Half Moon-fifty-five, Ballston-thirty-four, Stillwater-twenty-six, and Saratoga-nineteen. While Half Moon led in the number of enslaved persons and enslavers, they must have been equally dispensed because it possessed only one of the largest enslavers. This elite group consisted of John Bradstreet Schuyler of Saratoga with fourteen, Cornelius Van Vechten of Saratoga with ten, Dirck Swart of Stillwater with eight, James Gordon of Ballston with seven.[212]

*"The largest enslaver in Half Moon was Janatie Van Vranken, who lived on a farm near Vischer Ferry. She was the widow of Nicholas Van Vranken and she possessed seven (7) ENSLAVED PERSONS."[213]*

## VAN VRANKEN ENSLAVEMENT RECORD, 1790 CENSUS, HALF MOON, SARATOGA COUNTY, NY

# TABLE 4

|  | GIVEN | MALE | OV16 | U16 | FEM | OTH | SLAVES | TOWN |
|---|---|---|---|---|---|---|---|---|
| V: Vranken | Gertrude | 1 | 0 | 8 | 0 |  | 0 | Halfmoon |
| V: Vranken | Adam | 2 | 0 | 0 | 0 |  | 6 | Halfmoon |
| V: Vranken | Adam, Jr. | 1 | 0 | 2 | 0 |  | 2 | Halfmoon |
| V: Vranken | Gerrit | 1 | 0 | 3 | 0 |  | 1 | Halfmoon |
| V: Vranken | Jacob | 1 | 1 | 5 | 0 |  | 1 | Halfmoon |
| V: Vranken | Ryart | 1 | 2 | 4 | 0 |  | 1 | Halfmoon |
| V: Vranken | Maria | 1 | 0 | 5 | 0 |  | 0 | Halfmoon |
| V: Vranken | John G | 1 | 4 | 3 | 0 |  | 1 | Halfmoon |
| V: Vranken | Johannis | 2 | 1 | 2 | 0 |  | 0 | Halfmoon |
| V. Vranken | Janatie | 2 | 0 | 2 | 1 |  | 7 | Halfmoon |

*According to the 1800 Federal Census for Saratoga County, "its population of enslaved persons was 358 the largest number it would ever have. While this was well behind other Hudson Valley counties, it was considerably ahead of Washington and Warren Counties or other newly settled counties in the state's north or west"[211]*

After Ryckert Van vranken died in 1713, his Half Moon farm and those enslaved on his property were divided between his three sons, Gerrit, Maus, and Everet. (Janatie's husband, Nicholas, was Everet's son). Since those who were enslaved in America were considered by their enslavers to be "property", they were often mentioned in wills. One of Ryckert Van Vranken's sons, Maus, wrote a will in 1759, which gave and bequeathed to his "dear and loving wife Anneka Van Vranken "the choice out of all my slaves, the one she chooses shall be at her free disposal."[215] The rest of his estate he left to his wife until her death, at which time it was to be divided among his children.

Additionally, one of Maus Van Vranken's sons, Adam inherited his father's Half Moon farm, and probably a number of those enslaved on his property. Adam's will of 1793 gives the farm to his eldest son, Maus and additionally his "old wench named Deane." However, it was to be understood that any children produced afterwards by Deane would be "owned" in common by all his children equally, and that Deane's living children would also remain in common with all Adam's children unless bequeathed otherwise. Maus was to divide twenty-five (25) pounds between his brothers and sister as compensation for Deane. Adam also bequeathed Maus "one negro boy named "Mink." Adam Van Vranken also willed enslaved persons who worked on his farm to his other children; Jacob was willed a "negro wench named Kate;" Ryckert, a "negro wench named Jarr;" Adam, a "negro boy named Jack;" and Gertruy, a "negro wench named Sarrn."[216]

The Van Vranken's were not the only enslavers in Half Moon. The 1790 census informs us that Nathan Garnsey who lived in the Rexford area possessed one enslaved individual, as did Peter Groom of the Groom Corners area. Both Nicholas and Eldert Vischer, both of Vischer Ferry, each possessed one enslaved individual. James Pearse of Fort's Ferry, a neighbor of the Van Vrankens possessed four enslaved persons, while his neighbor, Nicholas Fort possessed three enslaved persons.[217]

As the enslaved population of Half Moon increased between 1790 and 1800, Eldert Vischer is now listed with three enslaved persons, and his brother, Nanning, has acquired two enslaved persons since 1790. By far the largest population of those enslaved in Half Moon in 1800 was located on the farm lands of: Nicholas Fort, three enslaved; Derick Bradt, three enslaved; Jacob Pearse, three enslaved; Daniel Fort, two enslaved; Maus Van Vranken, five enslaved; John Pearse, one enslaved; Adam Van Vranken, three enslaved; Ryckert Van Vranken, one enslaved; Derick Volwieder, one enslaved; and Everit Van Vranken, four enslaved."[218]

A neighbor of Eldert Vischer of Vischer Ferry in 1800 was Christopher Miller who possessed three enslaved persons. An extant bill of sale dated June 24, 1786 indicates that Miller purchased a "negro wench about twenty six years of age named Nann together with a male child about eleven months old named Yap" from Derrickje Van Vranken of Albany for forty-five (45) pounds. Derrickje was probably the widow of Abraham Van Vranken and they lived in Niskayuna. Perhaps Nann had another child which would account for the 3 enslaved persons that Miller possessed in 1800.[219]

Likewise, Maus Van Vranken made provisions for those enslaved that he received from his father, Adam, in 1793. In his will of 1822, twenty-three years after the enactment of the Gradual Abolition Act of 1799, Maus, who was childless, requests that his "old and faithful servant Deane be comfortably and decently maintained and supported"[220] by his brothers Jacob, Richard and Adam. Deane would "have her choice to reside with which of the three brothers she pleases during her natural life." Remarkably, Maus granted to his faithful servant Mink one hundred acres of land situated along the line of the Kayadarosseros Patent.[221]

> *Maus Van Vranken's brother, Adam, possessed a negro boy named Jack (willed to him by his father), and is listed as having three enslaved persons in the 1800 census. "His son also named Adam (1798-1880) inherited the family farm east of Vischer Ferry, but he was among the first in the family not to inherit any slaves." [222]*

## MANUMISSIONS

Only two early Saratoga County records of Van Vranken Wills contain references to those that they enslaved: Adam Van Vranken (Saratoga Co. Wills, 7/45; recorded Feb. 27,1790 and Maus Van Vranken (Saratoga Co. Wills, 5/444; recorded c. 1822). Two other early Van Vranken Wills appear in Albany County; Maus (1/ 340) and ykert *(2/*79) Van Vranken.

**Ryckert (c. 1642-1713)**
Gerrit (c. 1670-1749)
Maus (c. 1672-1759)

**Adam (1717-1793)**
Maus (1745-1822)—willed wench, Deane & boy, Mink
Jacob—willed wench, Kate
Ryckert—willed wench, Jarr
Adam—willed boy, Jack
Gertruy—willed wench, Sarrn

**Everet (c. 1681-1748)**
Nicholas, m. Janatie "[223]

**(Note: Fathers in Bold)**

# HISTORICAL PREMISE FOR PLACING MY VAN VRANKEN FAMILY IN HALF MOON

As we pursue the historical path of my Van Vranken Family, we must be ever cognizant of the reality of the "lost, stolen or strayed" history of people of African descent in New York State. In particular, our historical correctness will always be influenced in one degree or another by the actual documented fact of not only—what we do know and do not know but more importantly on the reality of what we can prove and what we cannot prove. This reality is extremely profound, especially when we analyze the facts of the preceding census records and documents of families and persons of African descent mentioned in Halfmoon, Saratoga County. The reality is that these records did not specifically refer to or document any of my actual Van Vranken family members by name living there during this period (1790-1810).

A comprehensive search of official town and county records and documents for the towns and cities of Half Moon, Clifton Park, Niskayuna, Canastigione, Schagticoke, and Albany have also proven fruitless with respect to the reference or a named individual within my Van Vranken family circle. This lack of information unfortunately is the result of the loss or misappropriation of vital records due to the constant change during this period of newly formed and reconstructed county boundaries and the subsequent reshuffling of these towns and cities into new county configurations. Another major deterrent to the acquisition of these important records could be attributed to a rash of fires and floods that destroyed various town records and minutes, gradual abolition documentation and, various family documents. In particular, records and other forms of documentation for the original Van Vranken family itself are virtually non-existent in these municipalities. Given the fact that this family played such a significant role in the settlement and development of this region of New York State, the lack of these resources borders on criminal with respect to historical scholarship.

My Van Vranken family however, does settle in Washington County in the early 1800s for a continuous period that extends to the present day and yet we are limited, due to the aforementioned "Wall of Enslavement" that considerably restricts our ability to represent the true and accurate presence of my family in any actual county of upstate New York prior to 1810. My initial premise for the placement of my Van Vranken family in Half Moon is based on the documented census information of the period which informs us that the enslaved population of Half Moon decreased rapidly after 1800 and the fact that this decrease was due primarily to the passage of the Gradual Abolition Act and its manumission provisions.[224]

It should be noted that we chose Half Moon for the initial placement of my Van Vranken family, even though this placement is not presently historically documented or indisputable, one way or the other. There is statistical evidence that would support the premise that my Van Vranken family was indeed located in the Half Moon, Saratoga County area. The fact that Half Moon's major enslaver families were well represented by the Van Vrankens, formerly of the City of Albany would also support the contention that my Van Vranken family may have been enslaved by these Van Vrankens. And, as was mentioned earlier, my Van Vranken family may have chosen or were given the Van Vranken surname as a customary practice during the period of enslavement in America both north and south.

The 1800 and 1810 Census for Half Moon does provide documentation that illustrates a reduction of the town's enslaved population; as well as, similar documentation for an increase in its "free" population of African descent during this period. In the 1800 census, Half Moon recorded a total enslaved population of one hundred and sixty-three persons living in the homes and on the farms of its local residents. In addition, these same records reflect a "free" population of African descent of fourteen persons also living in the homes and on the farms of these local residents.[225] However, in the 1810 census for Half Moon the number of enslaved and "free" African descendants is changed dramatically.

The 1810 census for Half Moon now documents a total enslaved population of just twenty-eight persons, a decrease of some eighty-two percent (82%) over the data in the 1800 census.[226] Astonishingly however, the "free" population of African descent has increased some twelve hundred and sixty-four percent (1264%) to one hundred and ninety-one "free" persons during this same period. (Note: What we will learn later in this work is that the year 1810 represented a significant date in the ever increasing population of people of African descent in upstate New York counties.) Both of these statistics would lend additional support to the argument that the Manumission Provision of the Gradual Abolition Act of 1799 played a significant role in increasing the "free" population of people of African descent in Half Moon.

How is it that these statistics and data relate to my Van Vranken family? If we focus specifically on the Van Vranken family of Half Moon during this period and incorporate within our analysis the assumption that our Van Vranken family was enslaved on their numerous family farms. We can visualize a similar pattern in the decreasing numbers of enslaved persons and the increasing numbers of "free" persons of African descent living and working with the Van Vranken family. According to the 1800 Half Moon census, the various Van Vranken family members held a total of fifteen enslaved persons and zero "free" African descendants on their farms and estates. However, by the 1810 census for Half Moon, the various Van Vranken family members now record just two enslaved persons and fourteen "free" persons of African descent working their lands.[227]

These documented figures for the Van Vrankens could easily be projected to illustrate the fate of my Van Vranken family: 1—If in fact our Van Vranken family was represented in the fifteen enslaved persons held by the Van Vranken family in 1800; and, 2—if our Van Vranken family was represented in the fourteen "free" persons of African descent that were *now working* with the Van Vrankens in 1810. Fortunately, the next phase of the journey with our Van Vranken family to Washington County is replete with documented facts and official historical records in order to better satisfy our scholarly intent.

Chart 14 lists persons of African descent living in Saratoga County with white Van Vranken families. Note: The Albany listing represents the family of Andreis (Andrew) Van Vranken, the Grandson of Ryckert Claase Van Vranken, the original member of the Van Vranken family, who purchased the Van Vranken land/farm in Canastiglione, Saratoga County, New York. Andreis (Andrew) Van Vranken's four (4) children recorded in this Chart in actuality represented an African American branch of the Van Vranken family. However, *the mother or mothers of these children is not recorded anywhere!*[228]

Additionally, the Van Vranken family headed by David Van Vranken and including his wife and three (3) children living in Half Moon, Saratoga County in 1820 also represents an African descendant branch of the original Van Vranken family.[229]

# CHART 14

## AFICAN DESCENDANTS
## WITH VAN VRANKEN FAMILIES
## 1800-1820

| YEAR | CITY | NY COUNTY | SURNAME/GIVEN NAME | # FREE | SEX/AGE | # SLAVES | SEX/AGE |
|---|---|---|---|---|---|---|---|
| 1800 | Half Moon | Saratoga | Van Vranken | | | | |
| | | | Anneka | 0 | | 0 | |
| | | | Gerrit | 0 | | 0 | |
| | | | Maus | 0 | | 5 | |
| | | | Adam | 0 | | 3 | |
| | | | Ryckert | 0 | | 1 | |
| | | | Getruy | 0 | | 0 | |
| | | | Maria | 0 | | 0 | |
| | | | Evert | 0 | | 4 | |
| | | | Jacob | 0 | | 1 | |
| | | | John G. | 0 | | 1 | |
| | | | | 0 | | 15 | |
| 1810 | Half Moon | Saratoga | Van Vranken | | | | |
| | | | Jacob | 0 | | 0 | |
| | | | Ryckert | 3 | | 1 | |
| | | | Maus | 4 | | 0 | |
| | | | Adam | 4 | | 0 | |
| | | | Getty | 0 | | 0 | |
| | | | Evert | 3 | | 1 | |
| | | | John | 0 | | 0 | |
| | | | Gerrit | 0 | | 0 | |
| | | | | 14 | | 2 | |
| 1820 | Princetown | Saratoga | Van Vranken Henry | | | | |
| | | | | 0 | | 0 | |
| 1820 | Half Moon | Saratoga | Van Vranken | | | | |
| | | | David | 5 | F/26-45 2F/under 14 M/45+ M/ 14-26 | | |
| | | | Adam R. | 0 | | 0 | |
| | | | Adam | 2 | F/14-26 M/26-45 | 1 | F/14-26 |
| | | | Evert | 2 | F/14-26 M/Under 14 | 0 | |
| | | | Maus | 2 | F/under 14 M/under 14 | 2 | F/45+ F/14-26 |
| | | | | 11 | | 3 | |
| 1820 | Albany | Albany | Van Vranken | | | | |
| | | | Andrew | 6 | F/45+ F/26-45 2F/under 14 M/26-45 M/under 14 | 0 | |

## MY VAN VRANKEN FAMILIES' ARRIVAL IN WASHINGTON COUNTY

Based on the earliest information available in official documents and records, the first official recording of my Van Vranken family originates with Francis Van Woak (Van Vranken) in the Town of Jackson, Washington County in the 1820 census. This census record occurs just a few years after the passage of the New York State Gradual Abolition Act of 1799. It is this author's opinion that this Law played a very significant and profound role in the history of my Van Vranken family and that of an incalculable number of other families of African descent during the end of the 18th and the beginning of the 19th centuries in New York State. As we detailed earlier in this work, the Manumission Provision of the Gradual Abolition Act may have had a tremendous impact on the underlining causes for the migration of thousands of people of African descent to Washington County between the years of 1800 and 1820. My Van Vranken family constituted a small portion of this migration and yet they are symbolic of the courage, fortitude and exceptionalism that characterized this major event in the history of people of African descent in New York State. The passage of the Gradual Abolition Act of 1799 could indeed provide the rationale and gateway for the relocation of our Van Vranken family members and others of African descent to the tranquil and sedate rural communities of Washington County.

## MY VAN VRANKEN FAMILY SETTLEMENT

However relevant the Gradual Abolition Law may be with respect to the "free" status of my Van Vranken family and their first documented residence in Washington County in 1820, there now exist recently discovered records that establish the arrival of our Van Vrankens in Washington County at an earlier date than that recorded in the 1820 Federal Census.

## THE FIRST UNITED PRESBYTERIAN CONGREGATION CHURCH

The records of The First United Presbyterian Congregation in Cambridge in the village of Cambridge, Washington County, N. Y., transcribed by The New York Genealogical and Biographical Society inform us that: "John Van Vronk (Van Vranken) and his wife Hannah/Elizabeth were baptized together in the church on 9 February 1812. Additionally, five of their children were also baptized in the same church: Samuel and Hannah on the 25th of July 1812,

Robert on the 13th of November 1814, Margaret on the 11th of May 1817 and Elizabeth on the 9th of August 1818."[230]

Several of these baptisms are footnoted in these church records as follows:

> *Footnote 34: "In the original list the words "black people" appear above these three Van Vrancan names (Hannah, John and Elizabeth Van Vrancan); they are not designated as colored people in the Session Records; Cf. Session Records, pp. 13 and 218."* [231]

These church records would establish the residence of my Van Vranken family in Washington County prior to 1820 as recorded in the federal census of that year for Francis Van Woak (Van Vranken) or in the first New York State Census of 1825, with John Van Vrank (Van Vranken). And yet, we have been unable to document their presence in Washington County prior to either of these dates in either the Census of 1800 or 1810. Of even greater interest is the fact that these church records as with the various census reports of the period, lists several different surnames for John Van Vranken and his family: Van Vronk, Vanvronk, and Van Vrancan. Other similarities with the inaccuracies and nuances highlighted in the various censuses are the names of John Van Vranken's wife, Hannah/Elizabeth/Roseanna. In these church records Samuel is born on 13th February 1804, Samuel Vanvronk's mother is listed as Hannah; however, Hannah Vanvronk born on the 1st of July 1812 and also baptized on the 25th of July 1812 has Elizabeth Vanvronk listed as her mother. Robert and Margaret have John and Hannah Van Vrancan listed as their parents, when they are baptized on 14 November 1814 and 11 May 1817, respectively. And finally, Elizabeth Van Vrancan is baptized on the 9th of August 1818.[232]

Although these "official" church records clearly support and establish the presence of my Van Vranken family in Washington County some eight years prior to the aforementioned Federal Census of 1820 and only thirteen years after the passage of the New York State Gradual Abolition Act in 1799; they do not completely answer the primary question of: From *WHERE* did my Van Vranken family migrate to Washington County? To resolve this primary mystery, it will require a more comprehensive search of the surrounding counties, cities and towns of upstate and downstate New York. It would also seem to require us to make certain assumptions as to their possible place of origin and location, as we have attempted to present earlier in the Section on Half Moon.

Among the families of African descent who settled in Washington County during the early 1800s, the Van Vrankens had probably worked the farms and small plantations of the white Van Vranken families of either: Saratoga, Rensselaer, Schenectady or Albany Counties.

As mentioned earlier, in 1825 John Van Vronk (Johannes Van Vranken) and his family settled on sixty acres (60) of improved land in Salem, Washington County, New York.[233] This amount of acreage would seem to have qualified Johannes to vote, however, he is not listed in the census record as "eligible". The franchise for qualifying to vote during this period in New York State history was based on residency and ownership of land valued at $100 for all voters. This requirement was later changed by New York State in its Second Constitution of 1821 to $250 in land value for African descendants *only*.[234]

> *". . . but no man of colour, unless he shall have been for three years a citizen of this state, and for one year next preceding any election, shall be seized and possessed of a freehold estate of the value of two hundred and fifty dollars, over and above all debts and incumbrances charged thereon; and shall have been actually rated, and paid a tax thereon, shall be entitled to vote at any such election. And no person of colour shall be subject to direct taxation unless he shall be seized and possessed of such real estate as aforesaid."*[235]

As we begin the process of delineating and examining the individual histories of my Van Vranken family members, it is essential that we establish the genealogical connections that we have discovered linking individual Van Vranken family members. This narrative will trace my Van Vranken family from the "Unknown" Van Vranken mother of Johannes and Francis through a forty-five year period culminating in the death of Johannes in 1865 in Argyle, Washington County, New York. The majority of the resources for this genealogical research focus primarily on official governmental records such as: census reports, probate records, land records and deeds, birth and death certificates, marriage licenses and obituaries; additionally we use church records, some newspaper articles and other documents and photos.

What we will not be able to present at this particular point in time are more personalized records of my Van Vranken family's history such as letters, diaries, journals, etc. One exception to this scarcity of personal records or documents is a letter written by one Harry Cole of Salem, NY in 1937.[236] This letter represents our only true personal record linking my Van Vranken family with the broader Washington County community of residents. Its significance in telling the story of my Van Vranken family is extraordinary and truly fortuitous. Its importance to our story lies in the fact that it firmly establishes my Van Vranken family as a fully functioning and interactive human contingent within the everyday life of Washington County and in particular in the Town and Village of Salem, NY in the beginning of the 19th century.[237]

The following is an excerpt from this letter written on 1 Mar 1937, Salem, Washington, NY, by Mr. Harry Cole which states:

> *"I have today gone to the Old Cemetery (Evergreen Cemetery of Salem) where I found four grave stones . . . the first was that of "Sally," wife of Samuel Van Vranken, d. 22 Apr 1861, 69y; Mary Matilda, wife of James Burk, d. 10 Apr 1861, 29y; Samuel, son of James & Matilda Burk, d. 2 Nov 1868, 17y. It is my belief that Mary Matilda, the wife of James Burk, was the daughter of Samuel Van Vranken & his wife Sally. Three or four years ago an old lady past 80 years told me that she had gone to school in this village with two Van Vranken girls; that they were very bright scholars and well thought of by the village people."* [238]

He continues:

> *"I well remember when I was a youth of ten years (abt.1870), my father introducing me to Mr. Samuel Van Vranken, a man of 60 years, I should say, a good-looking man, and I recall later on of seeing this same person in Albany. Back in the 1850's I believe there were several of the Van Vranken name residing in this village; one of whom was "Den" Van Vranken [Dennis Van Vranken, Samuel's son], a barber; well thought of here. The James Burk whose name appears above was a very popular barber in this village and had a local reputation as a musician. He died suddenly about 1876, leaving no children that I know of."*

> *The 1840 Salem, Washington, NY census shows Samuel VAN VRONK, free colored persons, 2 males aged 10-24, 1 male 35-55 (Samuel), 2 females under 10, 3 females 10-24, 1 female 36-55."* [239]

Chart 15—"VAN VRANKENS OF AFRICAN DESCENT IN WASHINGTON COUNTY, 1820-1870" further documents the presence and residency of our Van Vranken family in Washington County, New York for the period beginning in 1820 and extending forty-five (45) years to 1865. This Chart represents an extended period of sustainability and growth for the Van Vranken family in New York State.

# CHART 15

## AFRICAN DESCENDANT VAN VRANKENS
## IN WASHINGTON COUNTY
## 1820-1865

# AFRICAN DESCENDANT VAN VRANKENS
## WASHINGTON COUNTY
### 1820 -1870

| YEAR TOWN Family Name, Given | Relationship | SEX | AGE | Place of Birth | Occup | REMARKS |
|---|---|---|---|---|---|---|
| 1820 Jackson Van Wonk Francis | Head | M | 45+ | | | |
| | | F | 45+ | | | |
| | | 3/M | 26-34 | | | |
| | | M | 14-25 | | | |
| | | M | Under 14 | | | |
| | | 2/F | Under 14 | | | |
| 1825 Salem Van Vrank John | Head | M | | | | Owned 60 arres, cow, 2 horses |
| | | 7 males | | | | 6 sheep, 6 hogs, 14 yds. Linen |
| | | 3 Females | | | | cloth |
| | Child | F | Under 16 | | | |
| | | M | | | | Died 1824 |
| 1830 Argyle Van Bronk John | Head | M | | | | |
| | | 4 males | | | | |
| | | 5 females | | | | |
| 1835 Argyle Van Vrank John | Head | M | | | | |
| | | 9 Members | | | | |
| | | 6 males | | | | |
| | | 3 femal | 2/ Under 16 | | | Married 1834 |
| | | | 1/F | | | 2 cows, 1 hog |
| 1835 Salem Van Vronk Samuel | Head | M | | | | |
| | | 2 Females | | | | |
| | | 6 males | | | | |
| 1840 Argyle Van Bronk John | Head | M | 36-55 yrs. | | | |
| | | M | 10-24 yrs. | | | |
| | | 2/F | Under 10 | | | |
| | | 2/F | 10-24 yrs. | | | |
| | | F | 36-55 yrs. | | | |
| 1840 Salem Van Vronk Samuel | Head | M | 36-55 yrs. | | Farmer | |
| | | 2/M | 10-24 yrs | | | |
| | | F | 36-55 yrs. | | | |
| | | 3/F | 20-24 yrs. | | | |
| | | 2/F | Under 10 | | | |
| 1850 Salem Van Vanking Samuel | Head | M | 55 | NY | Laborer | |
| | Sally | wife | F | 45 | NY | |
| | Margaret | child | F | 27 | NY | |
| | Andrew | child | M | 23 | NY | |
| | Matilda | child | F | 18 | NY | |
| | Elise | child | F | 20 | NY | |
| | Susanna | child | F | 17 | NY | |
| 1850 Argyle Van Rankin John | Head | M | 73 | NY | Laborer | 2 Years older then in 1855 |
| | Rosanna | wife | F | 63 | NY | | 5Years older then in 1855 |
| | Mary Jane | child | F | 13 | NY | | |
| Hagas Delia A. | child | F | 3 | NY | | |
| George W | child | M | 2 | NY | | |

| Year/Place | Surname | Given | Relation | Sex | Age | Birthplace | Occupation | Notes |
|---|---|---|---|---|---|---|---|---|
| 1850 Kingsbury | Hazzard | Eli | Head | M | 23 | NY | Laborer | $100 value of Real Estate |
| | | Catherine | wife | F | 23 | NY | | |
| | | | | | | | | |
| 1855 Argyle | Van Vronk | John | Head | M | 71 | Rensselaer Co. | Farmer | 25 years in Argyle |
| | | Rose Ann | Wife | F | 58 | Washington Co. | | 25 years in Argyle |
| | | Mary Jane | Child | F | 17 | Washington Co. | | 17 years in Argyle |
| | Palmer | William | Grandchild | M | 30 | Washington Co | Boatman | 25 years in Argyle |
| | | Mary | Wife | F | 29 | England | | 1 year in Argyle |
| | Hazzard | Adelia A. | Grandchild | F | 8 | Washington Co. | | 5 years in Argyle |
| | | George W | Grandchild | M | 6 | Washington Co. | | 5 years in Argyle |
| | | Catherine | Grandchild | F | 8 | Washington Co. | | 3 years in Argyle |
| | | | | | | | | |
| 1855 Saratoga Springs | Van Vranken | Samuel | Head | M | 50 | Washington | Teamster | $800 value property |
| | | Sally | wife | F | 57 | Albany | | |
| | | Susannah | daughter | F | 22 | Washington | | |
| | | Catherine | sister | F | 27 | Washington | | |
| | | Andrew | son | M | 29 | Washington | Waiter | |
| | | Anna | dau-in-law | F | 20 | Washington | | |
| | | Margaret | daughter | F | 26 | Washington | | |
| | | | | | | | | |
| 1860 Salem | Vrankin | Samuel | Head | M | 56 | | Farm L | 400 value property, 250 personal |
| | | Sarah | wife | F | 64 | | Cook | |
| | | Dennis | son | M | 39 | | Barber | |
| | | Charles | Grandson | M | 6 | | | |
| | | | | | | | | |
| 1860 Argyle | Van Bronk | John | Head | M | 76 | NY | Farmer | $120 value of Real Estate |
| | | Susanna | wife | F | 63 | NY | | |
| | Hazzard | George W | Grandson | M | 11 | NY | | |
| | | | | | | | | |
| 1860 Cambridge | Van Vranken | Andrew | Head | M | 32 | NY | Barber | $400 value of Real Estate |
| | | Ann | wife | F | 23 | NY | | |
| | | | | | | | | |
| 1860 Kingsbury | Van Vranken | Frank | Head | M | 34 | NY | Barber | |
| | | Loretti | wife | F | 22 | NY | | |
| | | George V. | child | M | 8 | NY | | |
| | | Frank | child | M | 4 | NY | | |
| | | | | | | | | |
| 1865 Argyle | Van Bronk | John | DIED | M | 82 | NY | | Died April 10, 1865 |
| | | | | | | | | Wash. Co. Poor House |
| | | Frank | servant | M | 10 | Washington Co | servant | |
| 1865 Greenwich | Hazzard | Eli | Head | M | 40 | Washington Co | Laborer | |
| | | Catherine | wife | F | 40 | Washington Co. | | Mother of 7 children |
| | | Emery | child | M | 8 | Washington Co. | | |
| | | Charles | child | M | 6 | Washington Co. | | |
| | | Eliza J. | child | F | 2 | Washington Co. | | |
| | | Tilden (?) | child | F | 2 mos | Washington Co. | | |
| | Van Bronk | Roseanna | Mother in Law | F | 70 | Washington Co. | | Mother of 10 children |
| | | | | | | | | Discharged Poor House |
| | | | | | | | | 12 April 1865 |
| | | | | | | | | Readmitted 1868 |

## REFERENCE NOTES

[187] Listed on the Death Certificate of Samuel Van Vranken, 14 March 1891, Lansingburgh, NY, Certificate # 101214

[188] Perry, Kenneth, IBID

[189] 1825 New York State Census

[190] George Curry quoted in "The Van Vranken Van Frank Genealogy" compiled by Roberta (bobbi) Dodge, 2005; pg. 349

[191] *A BIT OF HISTORY:* Slavery in Halfmoon by John L. Scherer, pg. 4

[192] Ellen Kennedy, "History of the Town of Half Moon," www.townofhalfmoon.org/history

[193] IBID

[194] IBID

[195] Nathaniel Bartlett Sylvester, History of Saratoga county, New York, 1878, pg. 1; G.B. Anderson, Our County and its People, The Saratogian, The Boston History Company, Publishers, 1899, pg. 46

[196] Sylvester, pg. 2-3

[197] IBID, pg. 3

[198] G. B. Anderson, Our County and Its People, pg. 46; Kennedy, "History of the Town of Half Moon," www.townofhalfmoon.org/history

[199] Dodge, Roberta, Van Vranken, Van Frank Genealogy, 2005, pg. 2:2

[200] Scherer, John L., *A BIT OF HISTORY*: **Halfmoon's First Family**, pg. 1

[201] *Contributions for the Genealogies of the Descendants of the First Settlers of the Patent and City of Schenectady, from 1662 to 1800* by Jonathan Pearson (Albany, NY: J. Munsell, 1873

[202] Ibid

[203] **Workforce population**: See Peter Charles Hoffer, *Law and People in Colonial America,* (Baltimore, MD: The John Hopkins University Press, 1998) 124; **Slave skills and experience**: See Elkins, 94-95; Phillips, 98-114, McManus, 47-48; also see New York Gazette and Weekly Post Boy, March 26, 1749 and July 20, 1747; White, 10-12, A. J. Williams-Myers, *Long Hammering,* (Trenton, NJ: Black World Press, 1994) 7, Goodfriend, 118-119

[204] Charles B. Swain, "Black's roots in Albany: Old as Fort Orange", Viewpoint, Times Union Newspaper, Feb. 19, 1983; Theodore Corbett, Saratoga County Blacks, 1720-1870, *The GRIST MILL*, Quarterly Journal of the Saratoga County Historical Society, vol. XX, no. 3, 1986, 2;

[205] IBID

[206] Thornton, 148-149

[207] IBID

[208] IBID

[209] Northrup, Judd, Slavery In new York, State Library Bulletin—History No. 4, Albany, University of the State of New York, 1900, pg. 247

[210] **Concerning skills of Africans**: See McManus, xi-xii; Ulrich B. Phillips, *American Negro Slavery, (New York*, 1918,) 98-114; **For Transformation role**: See Arthur Zilversmit, *The First Emancipation: The Abolition of Slavery in the North*, (Chicago: The University of Chicago Press, 1967) 34

[211] John Sherer, Community News, "Several Local Families Once Thrived Using Slave Labor," pg.3, Fri. 12 March 1999

[212] IBID

[213] "Several Local Families Once Thrived Using Slave Labor," Friday, March 12,1999 and *A BIT OF HISTORY:* Slavery in Halfmoon by John L. Scherer

[214] Theodore Corbett, pg. 3

[215] "Some Notes Towards History and Genealogy Of the African American Population of Washington County, New York,"—Compiled and Edited by Kenneth Perry, February 2005, pgs. 237-238

[216] IBID

[217] IBID

[218] IBID

[219] IBID

[220] IBID

[221] IBID

[222] IBID

[223] **NOTE**: In this Section on Enslavement, we are relying heavily on the work of John Scherer, the present-day historian of Clifton Park, from his articles: "Several Local Families Once Thrived Using Slave Labor" and *"A BIT OF HISTORY:* Slavery in Clifton Park" that recount the practices of enslavement undertaken by the Van Vranken family and other families of Half Moon/Clifton Park.

[224] "Several Local Families Once Thrived Using Slave Labor," Friday, March 12,1999 and *A BIT OF HISTORY:* Slavery in Halfmoon by John L. Scherer

[225] 1800 US Federal Census, Halfmoon, NY

[226] 1810 US Federal Census, Halfmoon, NY

[227] 1800 US Federal Census, Halfmoon, NY

[228] 1820 US Federal Census, Albany, NY

[229] 1820 US Federal Census, Halfmoon, NY

[230] *"Records of the First United Presbyterian Congregation in the Village of Cambridge, Washington County, N.Y"* Transcribed by: The new York Genealogical and Biographical Society; Edited by: Royden Woodward Vosburgh, New York City, March 1917, pgs. 50, 54, 60, and 231. (Records of the Congregational Church of Sangate, Vermont, bound in this volume, back of page 141) Also see History of Washington County, New York by Crisfield Johnson for a history of the 1st United Presbyterian Congregation in Cambridge, NY, pg. 265

[231] IBID, Pg. 231, Footnote 34: In the original list the words "black people" appear above these three Van Vrancan names (Hannah, John and Elizabeth Van Vrancan); they are not designated as colored people in the Session Records. Cf. Session Records, pp. 13 and 218.

[232] IBID, pgs. 50, 54, 60 and 231

[233] NOTE: In 1785, Forfeited Land of 60 to 80 acres in Washington County was sold for approximately $30.

[234] **THE SECOND CONSTITUTION OF NEW YORK STATE, 1821, ARTICLE II.**

[235] New York (State). Secretary of State. Article II, Second Constitution of the State of New York, 1821, Series A1804-78, New York State Archives

[236] Dodge, "The Van Vranken Van Frank Genealogy": FAMILY, pg. 133

[237] **NOTE: With Johannes' birth date being documented at 1777 and given the fact that he had a mother that we can only best identify as "Unknown" Van Vranken; we can safely declare that my Van Vranken Family has resided on this continent for a period preceding the establishment of the United States of America (1776).**

[238] NOTE: Cole is actually referring to the Old Revolutionary War Cemetery in Salem.

[239] Dodge, pg. 133

# CHAPTER VI

---

# THE VAN VRANKEN FAMILY GENEALOGY

# GENEALOGY OF MY VAN VRANKEN ANCESTORS

## *GENERATION 1*

**1. UNKNOWN VAN VRANKEN**[240]

Unknown Van Vranken had the following children:

i. FRANCIS VAN BRONK (VAN WOAK), Birth: c. 1775 and Death Unknown
ii. JOHANNES VAN BRONK (VAN VRANKEN) Birth: 1777, Schaghticoke, Albany County, N.Y. Died: 10 April 1865, Argyle, Washington County, NY. (Washington County Poorhouse)

## *GENERATION 2*

**1. FRANCIS VAN BRONK (VAN WOAK)**

The Van Vranken family first made their official appearance in Jackson, Washington County, NY in 1820, with Francis Van Woak, and a household of nine. Francis purchased land with his brother John Van Bronk, 22 Sept. 1847, Argyle, Washington, New York:

An Indenture was entered into, 22 Sept. 1847, between Mary Carle, widow of Thomas Carle, late of Argyle (Wash. Co. Deeds, 17/ 30) and the other heirs of Thomas Carle (Abraham Carle & his wife Eve, of Geneva, Genesee Co.; Duncan Carle & his wife Elizabeth, of Queensbury, Warren Co., and James Carle & his wife Abigail, Lemuel Carle & his wife Mary, John Snyder & his wife Ann, Neal McConelle & his wife Eleanor, and Maria Carle, all of Argyle) and, on the second part, John Van Bronk and Francis Van Bronk of Argyle, for a part of lot no. 106 of the farm lots in Argyle Patent.

The lot in question was bounded beginning at the northwest corner of the lot, running south to a public road or highway, and then northeast along the road to the intersection of the north line of lot no. 106, and then west to the point of beginning.

It was a triangularly shaped lot, containing 2 acre Lot no. 106 of the farm lots of the Argyle Patent lies in the north range of "The Street" as it was laid out in the Patent map.

Superimposing its boundaries upon the 1866 Atlas map of Argyle, the very northwest corner of lot no. 106 is intersected by Coach Road, which runs northward from S. Argyle roughly parallel to modern day Rt. 40 until it converges with Rt. 40 in the Town of Hartford. In the northeast corner of lot no. 107 was John S. McDougall, and directly opposite the boundary line between lots no. 106 & 107, was the triangular piece described in the County Record of Deeds. A stream also runs through this corner of lot no. 107 and into the larger town lot no. 109, where a gristmill is marked on the south side of the stream.

On the current county road map, this location appears to be near the intersection of Rt. 47 (Roland McDougall Rd.) with the Coach Road, and is almost directly east of the southeast limits of the Village of Argyle, and about a mile distant.

No other records exist for Francis hence we have no birth or death records, other than census records of age 45+ in 1820. Which would place his birth date at the latest 1775.

## 2. JOHANNES (JOHN VAN BRONK) VAN VRANKEN

Johannes/John was born in 1777 in Schaghticoke, NY. He died on 10 Apr 1865 in Argyle, NY (Washington County Poor House). He married ROSEANA/HANNAH SYLVESTER. She was born in 1787 in Salem, Washington, New York.

In 1825, John Van Vrank (Van Vranken) and a household of ten are identified in the 1825 New York State Census as Van Vronk. It included ten (10) members (non taxed). Seven members were male and three were females, with one male child being born during the year. Of the 3 women in the family—one was married and under the age of 45 (Roseanna/Hannah) and one female under the age of sixteen. The record fails to identify the age of the third female member of the family.

The Van Vranks (Van Vrankens) settled on sixty acres (60) of improved land in Salem, NY. This acreage would qualify Johannes to vote, however, he is not listed as eligible. They had one cattle, sheep (6), and hogs (6) on their farm and domestically manufactured fourteen yards of cotton, linen or other cloth.

The Federal Census of 1830 lists John Van Vronk's (Van Vranken) family as now living in Argyle (Washington County) NY. The family is now composed of four men and five women. Unlike the NYS Census, in this census no records are recorded with respect to land ownership or property. Also in 1830, this family has a household of nine, and is later recorded as Van Vankin in 1835. By 1840, the two households of John Van Bronk in Argyle and his son Samuel Van Vronk in Salem, contained a total of 16 individuals, five males and eleven females.

By 1850, he appeared as John Van Rankin, b. 1777, N. Y.; laborer, resides Argyle, with his wife, Rosanna, b. 1787, N. Y., and children Elizabeth, b. 1835, N. Y., and Mary Jane, born in 1837 in Washington County, N. Y. Their grandchildren, Delia A. Haggard [sic], b. 1847, and George H. Haggard, 1 year old born in 1848, also resided with them. (They are the children of Catherine (Van Vranken) and Eli Hazard.

In 1855, the name was entered as Van Vronk, John, b. 1784, Rensselaer. Co., farmer, resident since 1830, residing in a frame house valued at $300.00. His wife, Rose Ann is born in 1797, Washington Co. with their daughter Mary Jane. The following Hazzard children also lived with them: Adelia A., b. 1847; George W., b. 1849; and Catharine, b.1852. Also included in the household was William Palmer, b. 1825, Washington Co.; a boatman, listed as a son of Rose Van Vronk, a resident since 1830. His wife was Mary, born in 1826 in England, a resident for one year. John and Susanna were residing in Argyle in1860, with their real estate valued at $120.00, and their grandson, George H. Hazzard, residing with them.

According to Washington County Deeds, Book #25, Pages 3, Year 1851: Hanna & Frances (John) VanVronk of Kingsbury sell 2 acres of land in Argyle to William Palmer of Argyle. In 1865 according to Book 53, page 571 of Washington County Deeds, just before they enter the Washington County Poorhouse: Hanna & Francies (John) VanVronk of Kingsbury sell an additional 2 acres of land in Argyle to William Palmer of Argyle.

On 3 Jan. 1865, John Van Bronk and his wife, Susanna (Roseanna) are admitted to the Washington County Poor House for palsied and old age, respectively. John Van Bronk (Van Vranken) dies on 10 April 1865 at the age of 82 years old of apoplexy and his wife, Roseanna Van Bronk (Van Vranken), 70, moves in with her daughter Catherine Hazzard and her husband, Eli and their children: Emery, 8; Charles, 6; Eliza J., 2; and Tilden, 2 months old.

### ROSEANA /HANNAH (SYLVESTER) VAN BRONK

Hanna Sylvester was born in 1787 in Salem, Washington, New York. She is recorded in the 1620 Federal Census as (single) living in Salem, Washington County, NY.

Children of JOHANNES VAN VRANKEN and ROSEANNA are:

i. SAMUEL VAN VRANKEN, b. February 13, 1804, Schagticoke, Rensselaer Co., NY; d. March 14, 1891, Lansingburg, NY.
ii. HANNAH VAN VRANKEN, b. July 01, 1812.
iii. ROBERT VAN VRANKEN, b. August 14, 1814
iv. CATHARINE VAN VRANKEN, b. November 1823.
v. MARGARET VAN VRANKEN, b. 1817
vi. ELIZABETH2 VAN VRANKEN, b. 1835.
vii. MARY J. VAN VRANKEN, b. 1837.

"Johannes VAN VRONK and Roseanna/Hannah VAN VRONK are both baptized as adults on the 9th of Feb 1812 in 1st United Presbyterian Congregation Church in Cambridge, Washington, NY. The following children were all baptized in this same church and Johannes is listed as the father. However, in one instance Elizabeth is listed as the mother.

CHILDREN: *

i.   Samuel J. VAN VRONK b. 13 Feb 1804, bp. 25 Jul 1812. (mother: Hannah)
ii.  Hannah VAN VRONK b. 1 Jul 1812, bp. 25 Jul 1812. (mother: Elizabeth)
iii. Robert VAN VRANCAN b. 14 Aug 1814, bp. 13 Nov 1814. (mother: Hannah)
iv.  Margaret VAN VRANCAN bp. 7 April 1817. (mother: Hannah)
v.   Elizabeth Van Vrancan bp. 9 Aug. 1818

*Records of The First United Presbyterian Congregation in The Village of Cambridge, Washington County, N.Y. Transcribed by: The New York Genealogical and Biographical Society; Edited by: Royden Woodward Vosburgh, New York City, March 1917 Pg. 231.

FOOTNOTE 34: In the original Records of the Church, it includes the words "black people" above these three Van Vrancan names (Hannah, Robert and Elizabeth Van Vrancan); they are not designated as colored people in the Session Records. Cf. Session Records, pp. 13 and 218.

Roseanna (Susanna) Van Vranken, is discharged from the Washington County Almshouse in Argyle, NY on 12 April 1865 after the death of John on 10 April 1865 and moves in with her daughter Catherine (Van Vranken) Hazzard in Greenwich, Washington Co., NY. She is re-admitted into the Washington County Poorhouse in 1868.

## GENERATION 3

## CATHERINE VAN VRANKEN

**CATHERINE** was born in 1826 in Argyle, Washington, New York, USA. She married (1) ELI HAZZARD, son of Levi Hazzard [241] on 19 Sept. 1848 in Argyle, Washington, New York. He was born in 1826 in New York. He died in Sep 1870 in Washington, New York

According to the Marriage Records of Argyle, Washington County, NY (dated: 15 March 1848), Catharine Van Vranken (Van Bronk) married Eli Hazard of Kingsbury, Washington County, NY on 19 September 1848.

Children of CATHARINE VAN VRANKEN and ELI HAZARD are:

    i.    **ADELIA A. HAZARD,** b. 1847.
    ii.   **CATHERINE ELLEN HAZARD,** b. 1847.
    iii.  **GEORGE W. HAZARD,** b. 1848.

George Hazard was born within Washington County though his exact birthplace and ancestry is hard to pin down. County Clerk's records for 1847[242] note the marriage on September 19, 1847, of Eli Hazzard of Kingsbury and Catherine Van Bronk of Argyle, in the latter town. This same source also records the birth of their daughter Catherine. At the time of the 1850 census, Catherine Van Bronk Hazard's parents, John and Rosanna "Van Rankin" of Argyle, had two children residing with them, Delia A. and George Haggard (Hazzard). On the 1855 census the grandparents reappear under their proper surname, "Van Bronk," with a third Hazard grandchild, Catherine, also in their household. In 1860 George was still living with his grandparents in Argyle, though the old couple would enter the Argyle Poor House not long afterwards, and by 1864, George Hazard, Company E, 3 1 st New York Colored Regiment, had enlisted at Ft. Edward. Under the "Remarks" section of his muster roll sheet, we find the information: "Killed 30 July 1864 . . . in action at Petersburg Va." (The 31st USCT was among those ill-fated Union regiments involved in the debacle of the above date known as "The Crater.")

By 1865 Rosanna Van Bronk was residing with her daughter, Catherine Hazzard, on John Street in Greenwich. The 1 865 Census notes Catherine as the mother of seven children; four of whom are later mentioned in "Letters of Guardianship" given to Catherine on the same date (not until July 9, 1879! [18]) as she was granted an "Administration of the Estate" of her husband, Eli, who had died in the state on September 22, 1 864. By the time of the 1865 census, Rosanna's husband, John Van Bronk, had died in the Poor House in Argyle.[243]

    iv.  **EMERY HAZARD,** b. 1857.
    v.   **CHARLES HAZARD,** b. 1859

CHARLES HAZZARD married an unknown spouse in 1892.

    vii. **TILDEN HAZARD,** b.1865.
    viii.**ELIZA HAZARD,** b. 1863.

Eliza was born in 1863 in New York. She married GEORGE W. MORRIS. He was born in 1861.

**EDWIN H. PALMER AND CATHERINE VAN VRANKEN** had the following child:

i. WILLIAM PALMER was born in Dec 1859 in New York. He married (1) LILLIAN PALMER in 1882 in Saratoga County, New York, USA. She was born in Apr 1865 in New York. He later married KATHERINE RICE. She was born in 1874 in Ireland.

William Palmer and Katherine Rice they had the following children:

i. DANIEL RICE was born about 1897 in New York.
ii. EDWARD RICE was born in 1900 in New York.
iii. MARY RICE was born in 1902 in New York.
iv. KATHERINE RICE was born in 1904 in New York.
v. MARGARET RICE was born in 1907 in New York.

## SAMUEL VAN VRANKEN

Samuel was born on 13 Feb 1804 in Schaghticoke, NY. He died on 14 Mar 1891 in Lansingburg, NY. He married Sally (Unknown) Van Vranken of Albany, NY in Washington County, NY.

The 1835 New York State Census lists this Van Vronk family as living in Salem, NY. with Samuel Van Vronk (Van Vranken) listed as the head of the family. Samuel is the third generation descendent of the Van Vranken branch of our Family and the son of John Van Bronk (Van Vranken). The family is comprised of two men and six women (1 married under the age of 45 and 5 unmarried under the age of 16 with one being born in the preceding year), this newborn daughter was Susanna. All family members untaxed with one meat cattle and one hog. The entire Family is identified as "persons of colour, not taxed".

The 1840 Census again lists Samuel Van Vronk, between the ages of 36 and 55, as living in Salem, NY. His wife is between the ages of 36 and 55; he has three daughters between the ages of 10 and 24 years old and one daughter, Susanna, under 10 years old. His two sons are also between the ages of 10 and 24 years old. (No cattle or hogs) It further identifies one member of the Family as employed in agriculture and another in manufactures and trades.

The 1850 Federal Census is the first to list the names of family members and gives us a clearer picture of the composition of the Family. Now known as the Van Vrunks, the family consists of Samuel, age 55 and a Laborer, Sally, age

45, Margaret, age 27, Andrew, age 23 and a Laborer, Matilda, age 18, Ellen, age 20, and Susanna, age 17. The two youngest daughters attended school during 1850. The Family is now identified as Mulatto.

Susanna and Matilda are listed a second time in the 1850 Census as Van Bronk. This time Susanna is 15 and Matilda still 17 years old. It would seem that the two young ladies are listed this time as workers on the farm of John Williams, a well to do Salem resident.

The Family next appears in the 1855 New York Census as living in Saratoga Springs (Saratoga County), NY. The family is comprised of Samuel, 50; Sally, 57; Susanna, 22; Catharine, 27 (Samuel's sister); Andrew, 29 and his wife, Anne, 20; and Margaret, 26 years old.

Samuel is employed as a Teamster, owns his own Frame house ($800) and is listed as a voter for the first time. Sally is listed as having been born in Albany and the rest of the family including Samuel are listed as born in Washington County, NY. They are all listed as having been residents of Saratoga Springs for 2 months, which would mean since April, 1855; with the exception of Catharine, who has been a resident for 1 month.

Samuel Van Vranken's death certificate states that he was born in Schaghticoke (Rensselaer County), New York. His parents, are (J) illegible and Hannah Van Vranken. His father, Johannes/John Van Vranken was also shown to have been born in Schaghticoke, NY. The certificate further informs us that Samuel was 81 years old when he died in 1891.

## SALLY VAN VRANKEN

Sally was born in 1805 in Albany, NY. She died on 22 Apr 1861 in Salem, Washington, New York

We have so far been unable to identify Sally Van Vranken's family due to the fact that we lack her maiden name. However, just as importantly, we have through the use of mitochondrial DNA (mtDNA) sequencing identified the maternal genetic ancestry of our Family with Africa, using Sally Van Vranken as the first recorded link in America. This mtDNA sequencing has determined that we share our ancestry with the Tikar people of Cameroon, West Africa.

The Tikar had a large population, sophistication in war, government, industry and the arts, the old Tikar dynasties dominated Central and West Africa for at least three centuries before their decline in the nineteenth century. It is estimated that there were more than one million Tikar people. Today there are less than 100,000 in the French-speaking zone and 300,000 in the English speaking zone (Banso). They obviously met the criteria for "good slaves."

They were attractive, learned quickly and had a tradition of enslavement within their own society. As the Tikar people attempted to abandon their traditional grassy savannahs and the plains where they were easy "slave trade" targets with no natural protection, they were forced to leave their villages, with enslavers on the one side and four hostile tribes on the other side, seeking revenge.

One of the strategies the Tikar applied to fight off the enemy was to dig moats around their villages; these skills exist in at least five kingdoms. However this strategy failed and the survivors found refuge in the forest. The "slave trade" during this period drained their brightest and most physically fit young people.

Having been weakened by war and the "slave trade", the Tikar became vulnerable to neighboring tribes who had been subjected by the Tikar for several centuries. While much more could be known about the Tikar; very little scholarship has been invested to recount their history. Only that their ceramic techniques, architecture and kon smelting kilns were very advanced.

## DEATH NOTICES from WASHINGTON COUNTY, NEW YORK NEWSPAPERS, 1799-1880 WASHINGTON COUNTY PEOPLE'S JOURNAL January 5, 1854—December 30, 1879 (Pg. 206)

"Sally, d. Apr. 22, 1861, at about 68 yrs. old, Salem, N.Y. "after a long and painful illness" according to her death notice, Apr. 30, 1861.

## DEATH NOTICES FROM SALEM PRESS

VAN VRANKEN Sally abt 68y wife of Samuel in Salem, NY April 22, 1861 Buried in the Revolutionary War Cemetery (Salem, NY) located by William A. Cormier (Historian Salem, NY).

Stone inscribed: "Sally wife of Samuel Van Vranken, died April 22, 1861, age 69 years"

## SAMUEL AND SALLY VAN VRANKEN HAD THE FOLLOWING CHILDREN:

**DENNIS VAN VRANKEN** was born in 1821 in Washington Co., NY. He was an accomplished Barber in Salem, NY for several years.

**MARGARET VAN VRANKEN** was born in 1823 in Salem, NY.

**CHARLES VAN VRANKEN** was born in 1854 in Salem, Washington, New York. He died on 21 Feb 1874 in Salem, Washington, New York, and is buried in the "African Grounds of the Evergreen Cemetery.

**ANDREW VAN VRANKEN** was born on 02 Feb 1825 in Salem, NY. He died on 02 Jun 1870 in Cambridge, NY and is buried in the AFRICAN GROUNDS of EVERGREEN CEMETERY Salem, Washington County, New York.

"Andrew Van Vranken, born Feb. 6, 1825 in Salem; parent Samuel; resided in Cambridge "Village; spouse, Leonora; place of death, Cambridge; died, Feb. 23, 1870; age, 45 y., 17days,)."

Andrew also married ANNA VAN VRANKEN. She was born in 1841.

The 1865 New York State Census shows Andrew Van Vranken, 36 years of age, living in Cambridge (Washington County), NY. Andrew, a barber, is married to Anna Van Vranken.

**ELLEN VAN VRANKEN** was born in 1830 in Salem, Washington County, New York. She died in the 1870s in Troy, Rensselaer, New York. She married Benjamin T. Latimer on 15 Jan 1852 in Salem, NY He was born about 1835 in Troy, New York.

**MARRIAGE NOTICES from WASHINGTON COUNTY, NEW YORK NEWSPAPERS, 1799-1880 SANDY HILL HERALD May 12, 1829—December 28, 1876 (Pg. 54)**

VAN VRANKEN Ellen of Salem, NY & LATIMER Benjamin T. of Troy, NY January 15, 1852). He was born about 1835 in Troy, New York.

Benjamin T. Latimer and Ellen Van Vranken had the following children:

i.   HELENA A. LATIMER was born in 1854.
ii.  ROBERT B. LATIMER was born in 1857.
iii. MARY E. LATIMER was born in 1859.
iv.  ELLEN LATIMER was born in 1852 in Troy, NY.
v.   ALLICE F. LATIMORE was born about 1860 in New York.

**MARY MATILDA VAN VRANKEN** was born in 1832 in Salem, NY. She died on 10 Apr 1861 in Salem, Washington, New York. She married JAMES BURK. He was born in 1829. He died on 18 Apr 1881 in Salem, Washington, NY (Heart Disease).

Matilda (Van Vranken), 23, is listed in the 1855 New York State Census as living in Salem, NY (Van Vranken), living with her husband, James Burk, a 26 year old Laborer from Virginia and two children: Samuel Burk, aged 3, and Haty Burk, a year old. Living with the Burks is Dennis Van Vranken, 35, who is listed as Matilda's brother.

Matilda dies (yellow fever (?)) on 10 April 1861 within 2 weeks of her mother, Sally Van Vranken, and is buried next to Sally in the Old Revolutionary War Cemetery in Salem, NY.

James Burk and Matilda Van Vranken had the following children:

i.   HATY BURK was born in 1854 in Salem, NY.
ii.  SAMUEL BURK was born in 1852 in Salem, Washington, NY. He died on 02 Nov 1868 in Salem, Washington, New York (Old

Revolutionary Cemetery). and is buried next to Matilda at the Old Revolutionary War Cemetery in Salem, NY;

iii. KATHERINE BURK was born in 1853 in Salem, Washington, New York. She died on 30 Aug 1857 in Salem, Washington, New York and is also buried along side Matilda in the Old Revolutionary War Cemetery in Salem, NY.

JAMES BURK was a Barber in Salem, NY. He was born enslaved in the South and came to Salem with the late Abram (Brommie) Lansing, as a coachman. Burk is mentioned by former Salem resident James Shields in his street-by-street description of the Village of Salem as it looked in 1868. Shields notes that Burk, a barber ran his own business next to the Salem National Bank in the heart of commercial Main Street.[244]

**SUSANNAH VAN VRANKEN** was born in 1835 in Salem, NY. She married James E. Peterman, son of Henry Peterman and Annie Mulvany about 1854 in Washington Co., NY. He was born in 1824 in Petersburg, NY. He died on 11 Jun 1903 in Cambridge, NY.

The 1860 Census shows James, 30, and Susannah, 25, married and living in Cambridge, NY with two children: Charles, 5 years old and Anna Mary, 1 year old. (Interestingly enough, after being identified as colored and Black in previous censuses, James and his family are now Mulatto.)

By 1870, James and his Family reside in the Town of Stillwater (Saratoga) New York. James, now thirty-eight (38) and Susannah, now 35, have five (5) children living with them. They are: Anna Mary, 12; Estella, 8; Ida May, 5; Annetta Amelia, 3; and Frederick Douglas, 1 year old.

Anna Mary, Estella and Ida May are listed as being in school and they all can read. Also living in the house, at this time, is Alice Latimer, age 10. Susannah's sister, Ellen Latimer's daughter.

It was during this time that Anna Mary met and soon married Joseph Epps, also of Stillwater. Joseph had escaped enslavement in Petersburg, VA., and traveled to NY by way of the Underground Railroad.

The 1875 NY State Census finds the Peterman Family living in their own home in Lansingburg, (Rensselaer) NY. The house they are living in is valued at $1000. James, now 44, and Susannah, now 43, live with Estella, 13; Ida M, 11; Nettie (Annetta), 9; Fred D., 6; and a new daughter, Jessie L., 2 years old. Also living in the House were two other Mulatto/Black families: the Morgans and their son and the Huttons and their son and daughter. Henry Morgan is also a Barber like James; they may even have worked together.

In 1880, the Peterman's are again living in Lansingburg at 525 Whipple Ave. James and Susannah live with their five (5) children and James now works in an Oil Cloth Factory and Stella, 18 and Nettie, 13, both work as domestic servants.

In 1883 things seem to change; Susannah is now listed as the head of the household in the Troy City and Lansingburg Directory. The Family has now moved to 620 John St. in Lansingburg. From this point onward, James is no longer listed with the Family. Oral History tells us that James, at some point in time, wanted to go back to the Reservation but Susannah refused. It seems that Susannah was not happy with Reservation life and chose to stay in the city.

In 1888, both Estelle and Nettie are married to Walter F. Wilson of Albany and William Loyd Garrison of Boston, respectively. Nettie and William have a child, William Lloyd, in 1892, who unfortunately dies during a visit to Lansingburg at the age of eight (8) months.

By 1890, Susannah Peterman is residing at 513 Fourth Ave. in Lansingburg, NY with her father, Samuel Van Vranken of Salem, NY. He is 81 years old at the time of his death in 1891 in Lansingburg. Frederick Douglas Peterman dies on 24 March 1895 in Lansingburg at the age of 26 years old.

In 1890, Susanna Peterman is working as a live-in domestic servant for the Van Schomburg Family on Third St. in Lansingburg, NY.

## JAMES E. PETERMAN

James Peterman, Henry Peterman's only son, had moved to Hoosick, NY. prior to 1850, ostensibly, to find work or because of a job. He lived there with Mr. Ransom Thompson and his family according to the 1850 Census for Hoosick (Rensselaer County) NY.

Rensselaer County Vital Records for Birth 1846-1850 list James Peterman as having had a daughter, Frances M., by a Betsey Van Buren. This would represent James'; first marriage or at least his first offspring. No other records exist as yet documenting either Betsey or Frances.

James Peterman pursues a living as a Barber working in a Hair Salon in Cambridge, (Washington) New York.

James Peterman reappears, having entered the Washington County Poorhouse in 1903. He dies two months later on 11 June 1903 at the age of 79 years old, from organic heart disease, debility and old age. He is buried in the Washington County Poorhouse Cemetery, stone # 87.

## WASHINGTON COUNTY (NY) POORHOUSE CEMETERY NUMBERED STONES—K-R

| STONE #<br>CERT # | LAST NAME | FIRST NAME | AGE | DOD | CAUSE of DEATH |
|---|---|---|---|---|---|
| 87 | PETERMAN | JAMES | 79 | 6/11/ 1903 | DEBILITY & OLD<br>AGE |

James E. Peterman and Susannah Van Vranken had the following children: i. CHARLES PETERMAN was born in 1855 in Cambridge, NY. ii. ANNA MARY PETERMAN was born on 25 Nov 1857 in Cambridge, NY. She died on 28 Mar 1911 in Waterford, NY. She married Joseph Epps in 1874 in Waterford, NY. He was born in Sep 1847 in Petersburg, VA. He died on 15 Oct 1908 in Waterford, NY. iii. ESTELLA PETERMAN was born in 1862 in New York. She married Walter F. Wilson on 06 Jun 1888 in Lansingburg, NY. He was born in 1864 in Albany, NY. iv. IDA M. PETERMAN was born in 1864 in New York. v. FREDERICK DOUGLASS PETERMAN was born in 1869 in Lansingburg, NY. He died on 24 Mar 1895 in Lansingburg, NY. vi. JESSIE PETERMAN was born in 1873 in Lansingburg, NY.

## ANNA MARY PETERMAN

Anna Mary was born on 25 Nov 1857 in Cambridge, NY. She died on 28 Mar 1911 in Waterford, NY. She married Joseph Epps in 1874 in Waterford, NY. He was born on Sept. 1847 in Petersburg, VA. He died on 15 Oct 1908 in Waterford, NY.

## THE EPPS FAMILY HISTORY

According to Oral Family Tradition and existing documented record, the patriarch of the Epps Family, Joseph Epps, was born into enslavement in Petersburg, VA. and escaped at an early age, by way of the Underground Railroad. So far, the earliest record that we have, of Joseph, is that he settled in Stillwater, NY around 1870. The 1870 census records a Joseph Epps, Black and 18 years of age, working on the farm of Thomas J. Clement of Stillwater, NY. The data also notes that he was unable to read or write. This same census lists the Peterman family, a Black family, as residents of Stillwater, New York.

The significance of the proximity of these two families lies in the fact that James E and Susannah Peterman had five children living with them in Stillwater. Their oldest daughter, Anna Marry, then listed as 12 years old, would soon become Joseph Epps' wife. Joseph and Anna Mary met, courted and were later married while living in Stillwater, NY. (It should be noted that age discrepancies for individuals are common within census records from one census to another.) The Petermans are listed in the census as the 100th Dwelling House numbered in order of visitation, while the Clements, where Joseph resided, are listed as the 187* Dwelling House.

Joseph and his wife, Anna Mary, appear next in the 1880 census. At this point they lived in Waterford, NY on First Street, the actual address, as documented in later censuses, was 1 Front St., an alley behind First Street. Joseph is now twenty-six (26) years of age His occupation, unfortunately, is illegible while Anna Mary is listed as a housewife. Their lives have changed by this time. They have two children, Bella Davis, five years old and Edward, aged three.

Waterford is where much of the history and tradition of the Epps Family takes place. It is where the other children to come are born, baptized, married and in the case of my Grandmother, Anabel Puels and the other grandchildren are born. It is also where the majority of the Epps Family dies and is buried.

The Waterford Censuses for 1890 and 1900 show the Epps Family continues to live in Waterford, NY at 1 Front St. Their residence, at this address is also documented in the Troy and Lansingburg City Directories of 1890 and 1896. Between 1880 and 1886, the Epps Family continues to grow with the births of: Albert in 1879, Estella Frances in 1881, Ida May in 1886, Alice in 1886 and Raymond in 1890. Another child, Joseph, Jr. was born sometime during this period, however, records are presently incomplete.

An excerpt from:

## "A HISTORY OF WATERFORD, NEW YORK"
### By Sydney Ernest Hammersley

"SLAVERY existed in Waterford, even as our first churches were being organized. These unfortunates first came to our shores in the West India Company's slave ship in 1647. They were sold for peas and pork. Holland's statesmen tried in vain to stop this practice. But New York State looked easily upon it, and had upon its books a law providing the death penalty for runaway slaves found forty miles north of Albany. Some of Waterford's larger homes, including the General Samuel Stewart place at Broad and First Streets, had slave quarters in the basement with bricked ovens for cooking. The daughter of one of these slaves is described as being all that was excellent in an old family servant of the past. An old paper says that her father worked overtime for Jacobus Van Schoonhoven and with the money thus earned, purchased the freedom of the slave's mother. Twenty-eight years before the Civil War broke out, Waterford hated slavery."[245]

*"In August of 1833 Waterford's Young Men's Anti-Slavery Society appeared, taking the formal name of the American Colonization Society The society was engaged in wiping out slavery and its slogan said that $30.00 would send a Negro back to his land of African freedom. Kindness or even good intentions were dimmed as we read of the separation of Negro mothers and children, such as the advertisement "For Sale: an active, lively, Negro wench: a female child will be sold with her or not as suits the purchaser."*

*"The final atonement for this violation was cited by Lincoln, ". . . until every drop of blood, drawn by the lash (of slavery) shall be paid by another, drawn by the sword. The end of New York's slavery in 1827 was due more to our uncongenial climate and the wrong kind of work, rather than to any phase of our theology or humanity. New York took a step in the right direction in 1799 when a bill was passed freeing all children born in slavery. Waterford once had a number of Negroes and we remember them as being among our best citizens and an integral part of our town fellowship."*[246]

It is also during this period that Joseph, Sr. begins working for the Breslin Family in Waterford as a Coachman and Groom. The Breslin family is and was an influential and politically powerful Family in then Saratoga, Rensselaer, and Albany Counties. Since the 1990's, their family legacy included three brothers of political note: an Albany County Court Judge, an Albany County Executive and a New York State Senator, representing Albany County; and all serving during the same period.

My Grandmother was fond of telling the story of Joseph, Sr. racing horses on the frozen Hudson River. It seems that this sport was a major source of recreation and entertainment during the winter months in Waterford.

It also seems that Edward and Albert, Joseph's sons were also exceptional athletes in Football during the 1900's. The book "The History of Waterford, New York" also makes several references to the Epps boys—Albert (Bert) and Edward—as stars of Waterford's "Rough Riders" Football team. This team composed of Waterford Y.M.C.A. men and included "the noted Epps (Negro) boys whom their team mates defended valiantly when the former were rough play victims." [247]

Joseph Epps and Anna Mary Peterman had the following children:

i.  RAYMOND EPPS was born in Waterford, NY. He died in 1890 in Waterford, NY.

ii. JOSEPH EPPS JR. was born in Waterford, NY. He died on 29 February 1900 in Waterford, NY.

iii. FREDERICK EDWARD EPPS was born in Feb 1877 in Waterford, NY. He died on 29 Jun 1900 in Waterford, NY.

iv. IDA MAE EPPS was born on 12 Mar 1883 in Waterford, NY. She died on 04 Nov 1939 in Troy, Rensselaer, New York. She married GERALD ALBERT JACKSON. He was born on 05 Dec 1883 in Albany, Albany, New York. He died on 12 Feb 1949 in Troy, Rensselaer, New York.

v.  CHARLES ALBERT EPPS was born on 11 Apr 1879 in Waterford, NY. He married (1) ANNA EPPS in 1889. She was born in Jun 1866 in Virginia. He also married MARY M EPPS. She was born about 1882 in New York.

vi. BELLA (BAMA) DAVIS EPPS was born on 28 Sep 1875 in Waterford, NY. She died on 14 Jan 1959 in Albany, NY. She married Alfred Clarence Smith, son of Jeremiah R.B. Smith and Rachel Murphy on 10 Oct 1906 in Grace Episcopal Church, Waterford, NY. He was born on 02 Mar 1874 in Bath, NY. He died on 16 Nov 1911 in Troy, NY.

vii. ALICE EPPS was born in Waterford, NY (U). Alice died in 1886 in Waterford, NY.

Waterford, in particular, The Waterford Rural Cemetery became the sacred Burial Ground of the descendents of Joseph and Anna Mary Epps. The Waterford Rural Cemetery lists as buried on its grounds, the following members of the Epps Family: Alice, 1886; Raymond, 1890; Joseph, Jr., 1900; Edward, 1900; Joseph, Sr., 1908; Anna Mary, 1911; and Bella Davis, 1959.

## GENERATION 6

## IDA MAE EPPS

Ida Mae was born on 12 Mar 1883 in Waterford, NY. She died on 04 Nov 1939 in Troy, Rensselaer, New York. She married Gerald Albert Jackson He was born on 05 Dec 1883 in Albany, Albany, New York. He died on 12 Feb 1949 in Troy, Rensselaer, New York.

Gerald Albert Jackson and Ida Mae Epps had the following child:

i.    Albaet Bloss Jackson, Sr.. was born on 21 Feb 1910 in Troy, Rensselaer, New York. He died on 02 Dec 1978 in Kinderhook, Columbia, New York, USA. He married HENRIETTA ANN AMBROSE. She was born in 1922 in Charlestown, Boston, Mass. She died in 1954 in Troy, Rensselaer, NY.

## CHARLES ALBERT EPPS

Charles was born on 11 Apr 1879 in Waterford, NY. He married (1) ANNA EPPS in 1889. She was born in Jun 1866 in Virginia. He married MARY M EPPS. She was born about 1882 in New York.

Charles Albert Epps and Anna Epps had the following child:

i.    ROBERT EPPS was born in Sep 1889 in Virginia.
ii.   ESTELLE M. EPPS was born about 1904 in New York.
iii.  HAROLD A. EPPS was born about 1908 in New York.
iv.   FLORENCE M. EPPS was born about 1914 in New York.
v.    GEORGE G. EPPS was born about 1916 in New York.
vi.   ETHEL L. EPPS was born on 17 Oct 1905 in New York. She died on 18 Oct 1994 in Albany, New York.
vii.  CHARLES EPPS was born about 1919 in New York.

## BELLA (BAMA) DAVIS EPPS

Bella was born on 28 Sep 1875 in Waterford, NY. She died on 14 Jan 1959 in Albany, NY. She married Alfred Clarence Smith, son of Jeremiah R.B. Smith and Rachel Murphy on 10 Oct 1906 in Grace Episcopal Church, Waterford, NY. He was born on 02 Mar 1874 in Bath, NY. He died on 16 Nov 1911 in Troy, NY.

Bella Davis Epps was my Great Grandmother, Bama, as we called her, was the oldest of Joseph and Anna Mary's children. Bama was baptized in the Grace Episcopal Church in Waterford on 14 May 1905. She, as well as her mother (who taught her) and her sisters, were accomplished seamstresses. It seems that this skill was more a family profession then a hobby for the Epps women, because it was passed down from one generation to the next—from Anna to Bama and her sisters to Mamoo and probably from Anna's mother, Susannah Peterman, to her. The passing of family skills and trades from one generation to the next is very much an African tradition.

On 10 October 1906, Bama was married to Alfred Clarence Smith, the second youngest of the five (5) children of Rev. Jeremiah R.B. Smith, pastor of Troy, NY's 7th AVE. AME Zion Church, and Rachel (Murphy) Smith. They were married at the Epps residence in Waterford, by Rev. Sleight, Pastor of the Grace Episcopal Church of Waterford. They probably met in Troy/Lansingburg where Anna Mary's parents were living at the time.

The community of people of African descent was relatively small in this part of the country, so there was socializing between the people of African descent in the three cities of Albany, Schenectady and Troy. At any rate, they met and were married.

While still on their honeymoon, Bama had a stroke and was paralyzed on one side of her body. She was also pregnant, incredibly, she carried full-term and blessed the world with a daughter, baptized Anna Belle Smith and later confirmed as Anabel Elizabeth Smith, fondly known as "Mamoo" to her family and friends. Bama lived with her devoted daughter until her death in 1959 at the age of eighty-four (84) years old.

Alfred Clarence Smith and Bella (Bama) Davis Epps had the following child:

i.   **ANABEL SMITH** was born on 27 Jun 1907 in Waterford, NY. She died on 01 Nov 2002 in Albany, NY. She married (1) WILLIAM EARL HEATH, son of G. Leroy Heath and Nettie Hart on 05 Aug 1924 in Lansingburg, NY. He was born on 17 Dec 1902 in Warrenton, GA. He died on 04 Aug 1974 in New York, NY. She married (2) RICHARD CONRAD PUELS, son of Peter C Puela and Agnes

Puela on 10 Jan 1966 in New York (Cathedral of All Saints). He was born on 20 Jul 1900 in Brooklyn, Kings, New York. He died on 30 Apr 1995 in Albany, Albany, New York

## GENERATION 7

# ANABEL "MAMOO" SMITH

Anabel born Anna Belle Smith, on 27 June 1907 in Waterford, New York to Bella Davis Epps and Alfred Clarence Smith. was born on 27 Jun 1907 in Waterford, NY. She died on 01 Nov 2002 in Albany, NY.

She was baptized at the Grace Episcopal Church in Waterford on 29 April 1908. Her Family moved to Troy and then to Lansingburg, N.Y. in her early years. At 9 years old, she and her mother moved to Cambridge, MA. to live with her maternal aunt, Stella Garrison and her Uncle William Lloyd Garrison. While in Cambridge, she was confirmed as Anabel Elizabeth Smith on 24 April 1921. At the age of 14, she and her mother returned to Lansingburg, where she attended Lansingburgh High School and Troy Business College. Anabel worked after high school taking care of children in the community. Anabel had three (3) Brothers from a previous marriage of her Father, Alfred C. Smith. These Brothers, now deceased, were Warren Morris, Edward Morris and Francis Morris Smith.

She married (1) WILLIAM EARL HEATH, son of G. Leroy Heath and Nettie Hart on 05 Aug 1924 in Lansingburg, NY. He was born on 17 Dec 1902 in Warrenton, GA. He died on 04 Aug 1974 in New York, NY.

She married (2) RICHARD CONRAD PUELS, son of Peter C Puela and Agnes Puela on 10 Jan 1966 in Albany, New York (Cathedral of All Saints). He was born on 20 Jul 1900 in Brooklyn, Kings, New York. He died on 30 Apr 1995 in Albany, Albany, New York.

# FAMILY

Anabel married William E. Heath on August 5, 1924 and moved to Albany. While in Albany, Anabel and Bill Heath lived with the Dorsey Family on Second Street before moving to a house at 229 Clinton Ave. While at this residence, Anabel worked as a housewife and did some catering and Bill Heath worked as a Red Cap at the Railroad Station. It was while on Clinton Ave. that the newlyweds were blessed with the birth of their daughter, Elizabeth Mary Louise Heath on 28 December 1925. Soon after the birth of Elizabeth, the new family moved back to Lansingburg, where Anabel worked as a live-in housekeeper (with her family) for George Biddle Kelly, who while at Cornel University in 1906, was one of the SEVEN (7) JEWELS (Founding Members) of the Alpha Phi Alpha Fraternity, Inc. Anabel and family including her mother, moved back to Albany in 1928 where Anabel, a lifetime Episcopalian, joined the Cathedral of All Saints in 1928. On, 10 January 1966, she married longtime friend, Richard Conrad Puels.

Mamoo had one daughter, Elizabeth Mary Louise Heath who married Louis Stewart on 27 August 1947. Mamoo has six grandchildren:: Louis Lloyd, Timothy Alan, and Arthur-David Heath, (three grandchildren: Gary Edward, Judith-Ann and Steven Douglas Stewart) are now deceased).

The ironic part of this expanding family is that Mamoo told us that her Mother told her "never to have more Children then you can afford." So, she had one Child. It was during this population explosion that Anabel was given the title—"MAMOO". The story goes that Judith-Ann, her first Grandchild, unable to pronounce GrandMa, chose instead Mamoo. (It should be noted that Judy was 3 years old at the time.) The name stuck!

Anabel was known as Mamoo by most everyone, in the Tri-City area, who loved and cherished this special and unique lady, not just by her Family.

## CAREER

Mamoo began her volunteer work in 1940, as a sewing and crafts instructor working with young girls at the Booker T. Washington Center and the YWCA. Many women learned how to knit, sew and embroider under her tutelage at these after-school programs.

## ACTIVITIES IN MIDDLE YEARS

Mamoo's extensive volunteer and community involvements include the Neighborhood House where she has served in many leadership roles. She has been a member of the Board of Directors of Family and Children Services, Child Guidance, the Council of Community Services, Planned Parenthood, the YWCA, the YMCA, the United Way and the Arbor Hill Community Center.

She also has held leadership roles in Episcopal Church Women, the Church Periodical Club, Trinity Institute and the Church Counseling Service.

## ACTIVITIES IN SENIOR YEARS

She has served as a member of the Outreach Committee for the Cathedral of All Saints and received the Century Club Award from the YMCA for her support, help and enthusiasm in making the Albany YWCA's programs and activities a success. In recent years, she also has received the Clarence Parker Memorial Award from the Albany Girls Club for her outstanding support of the Club and has been honored by the Albany District Links for her contributions to the community over the years. She was most recently an active member of the Board of Directors of Parsons Children and Families Center. Parsons Children and Family Center describes Mamoo as "an intelligent woman, devoted to church and family. She has a pleasant personality and is loved by all who know her. As a mother, grandmother, great-grandmother, and great-great-grandmother, she has inspired her "Children" to be caring, committed and contributing members of the community."

William Earl Heath and Anabel "MAMOO" Smith had the following child:

i. **ELIZABETH MARY LOUISE HEATH** was born on 28 Dec 1925 in Albany, NY. She died on 27 Dec 1977 in Albany, NY. She married Louis Stewart, son of Charles Hughes and Estelle Stewart on 27 Aug 1947 in Albany, NY. He was born on 03 Aug 1925 in Philadelphia, Montgomery, Pennsylvania. He died on 06 Aug 1994 in Albany, NY.

# THE VAN VRANKEN FAMILY TREES

# MY VAN VRANKEN
# DESCENDANT'S FAMILY TREE

## OUTLINE FAMILY TREE FOR UNKNOWN VAN VRANKEN

1  Unknown Van Vranken (Female)

. . . . 2  Francis Van Bronk (Van Woak)

. . . . 2  John (Van Vranken) Van Bronk b: 1773 in Schaghticoke, NY, d: 10 Apr 1865 in Argyle, NY; Washington County Poor House

. . . . +  Roseana (Hannah) Sylvester b: 1787 in Salem, Washington, New York

. . . . . . 3  Robert Van Vranken b: 14 Aug 1814 in Washington County, NY

. . . . . . 3  Hannah Van Vranken b: 01 Jul 1812 in Washington County, NY

. . . . . . 3  Margaret Van Vranken b: Abt. 1829 in New York

. . . . . . 3  Elizabeth Van Vranken b: 1835 in New York

. . . . . . 3  Mary Jane Van Vranken b: 1837 in New York

. . . . . . 3  Samuel Van Vranken b: 13 Feb 1804 in Schaghticoke, NY, d: 14 Mar 1891 in Lansingburg, NY

. . . . . . +  Sally Van Vranken b: 1805 in Albany, NY, m: Washington County, NY, d: 22 Apr 1861 in Salem, Washington, New York;

. . . . . . . . 4  Margaret Van Vranken b: 1823 in Salem, NY

. . . . . . . . 4  Charles Van Vranken b: 1854 in Salem, Washington, New York, United States, d: 21 Feb 1874 in Salem, Washington, New York, United States

. . . . . . . . 4  Dennis Van Vranken b: 1821 in Washington Co., NY

. . . . . . . . 4  Andrew Van Vranken b: 02 Feb 1825 in Salem, NY, d: 02 Jun 1870 in Cambridge, NY;

. . . . . . . . +  Leonora Van Vranken

. . . . . . . . +  Anna Van Vranken b: 1841

. . . . . . . . 4  Ellen Van Vranken b: 1830 in Salem, Washington, New York, United States, d: 1870s in Troy, Rensselaer, New York

. . . . . . . . +  Benjamin T. Latimer b: Abt. 1835 in New York, m: 15 Jan 1852 in Salem, NY; MARRIAGE

. . . . . . . . . . 5  Helena A. Latimer b: 1854

. . . . . . . . . . 5  Robert B. Latimer b: 1857

. . . . . . . . . . 5  Mary E. Latimer b: 1859

. . . . . . . . . . 5  Ellen Latimer b: 1852 in Troy, NY

. . . . . . . . . . 5  Allice F. Latimore b: Abt. 1860 in New York

. . . . . . . . 4  Matilda Van Vranken b: 1832 in Salem, NY, d: 10 Apr 1861 in Salem, Washington, New York

. . . . . . . . +  James Burk b: 1829, d: 18 Apr 1881 in Salem, Washington, NY; Heart Disease

. . . . . . . . . . 5  Haty Burk b: 1854 in Salem, NY

.......... 5 Katherine Burk b: 1853 in Salem, Washington, New York, d: 30 Aug 1857 in Salem, Washington, NY

.......... 5 Samuel Burk b: 1852 in Salem, Washington, NY, d: 02 Nov 1868 in Salem, Washington, New York;

........ 4 Susannah Van Vranken b: 1835 in Salem, NY, d: 11 Apr 1888

........ + James E. Peterman b: 1824 in Petersburg, NY, m: Abt. 1854 in Washington Co., NY, d: 11 Jun 1903 in Cambridge, NY

.......... 5 Charles Peterman b: 1855 in Cambridge, NY

.......... 5 Anna Mary Peterman b: 25 Nov 1857 in Cambridge, NY, d: 28 Mar 1911 in Waterford, NY

.......... + Joseph Epps b: Sep 1847 in Petersburg, VA, m: 1874 in Waterford, NY, d: 15 Oct 1908 in Waterford, NY

............ 6 Raymond Epps b: Waterford, NY, d: 1890 in Waterford, NY

............ 6 Joseph Epps Jr. b: Waterford, NY, d: 29 February 1900 in Waterford, NY

............ 6 Frederick Edward Epps b: Feb 1877 in Waterford, NY, d: 29 Jun 1900 in Waterford, NY

............ 6 Ida Mae Epps b: 12 Mar 1883 in Waterford, NY, d: 04 Nov 1939 in Troy, Rensselaer, NY

............ + Gerald Albert Jackson b: 05 Dec 1883 in Albany, Albany, New York, d: 12 Feb 1949 in Troy, Rensselaer, New York

.............. 7 Albert Bloss Jackson Sr. b: 21 Feb 1910 in Troy, Rensselaer, New York, d: 02 Dec 1978 in Kinderhook, Columbia, New York, USA

.............. + Henrietta Ann Ambrose b: 1922 in Charlestown, Boston, Mass, usa, d: 1954 in Troy, NY,

............ 6 Charles Albert Epps b: 11 Apr 1879 in Waterford, NY

............ + Anna Epps b: Jun 1866 in Virginia, m: 1889

.............. 7 Robert Epps b: Sep 1889 in Virginia

............ + Mary M Epps b: Abt. 1882 in New York

.............. 7 Estelle M Epps b: Abt. 1904 in New York

.............. 7 Harold A Epps b: Abt. 1908 in New York

.............. 7 Florence M Epps b: Abt. 1914 in New York

.............. 7 George G Epps b: Abt. 1916 in New York

.............. 7 Ethel L. Epps b: 17 Oct 1905 in New York, d: 18 Oct 1994 in Albany, Albany, New York

.............. 7 Charles Epps b: Abt. 1919 in New York

.......... 6 Bella (Bama) Davis Epps b: 28 Sep 1875 in Waterford, NY, d: 14 Jan 1959 in Albany, NY

. . . . . . . . . . . . + Alfred Clarence Smith b: 02 Mar 1874 in Bath, NY, m: 10 Oct 1906 in Grace Episcopal Church, Waterford, NY, d: 16 Nov 1911 in Troy, NY

. . . . . . . . . . . . . 7 Anabel "MAMOO" Smith b: 27 Jun 1907 in Waterford, NY, d: 01 Nov 2002 in Albany, NY

. . . . . . . . . . . . . + William Earl Heath b: 17 Dec 1902 in Warrenton, GA, m: 05 Aug 1924 in Lansingburg, NY, d: 04 Aug 1974 in New York, NY

. . . . . . . . . . . . . + Richard Conrad Puels b: 20 Jul 1900 in Brooklyn, Kings, New York, m: 10 Jan 1966 in NY; Cathedral of All Saints, d: 30 Apr 1995 in Albany, Albany, New York

. . . . . . . . . . . 6 Alice Epps b: Waterford, NY; U, d: 1886 in Waterford, NY

. . . . . . . . . . 5 Estella Peterman b: 1862 in New York

. . . . . . . . . . + Walter F. Wilson b: 1864 in Albany, NY, m: 06 Jun 1888 in Lansingburg, NY

. . . . . . . . . . 5 Ida M. Peterman b: 1864 in New York

. . . . . . . . . . 5 Frederick Douglass Peterman b: 1869 in Lansingburg, NY, d: 24 Mar 1895 in Lansingburg, NY

. . . . . . . . . . 5 Jessie Peterman b: 1873 in Lansingburg, NY

. . . . . . 3 Catherine Van Vranken b: 1826 in Argyle, Washington, New York, USA

. . . . . . + Eli Hazzard b: 1826 in New York, m: 19 Sep 1848 in Argyle, Washington, New York, d: Sep. 1870 in Washington County, New York

. . . . . . . . 4 Delia H. Hazard b: 1847

. . . . . . . . 4 George H. Hazzard b: 1848

. . . . . . . . 4 Ellen Hazzard b: 1847

. . . . . . . . 4 Lillie Hazzard b: 1865

. . . . . . . . 4 Emily Hazzard b: 1857

. . . . . . . . 4 Eliza Hazzard b: 1863 in New York

. . . . . . . . + George W. Morris b: 1861

. . . . . . . . . . 5 George W. Morris b: 1895

. . . . . . . . 4 Charles Hazzard b: 1861 in New York

. . . . . . + Edwin H. Palmer b: 1831, d: 1911

. . . . . . . . 4 William Palmer b: Dec 1859 in New York

. . . . . . . . + Lillian Palmer b: Apr 1865 in New York, m: 1882 in Saratoga County, New York, USA

. . . . . . . . + Katherine Rice b: 1874 in Ireland

. . . . . . . . . . 5 Daniel Rice b: Abt. 1897 in New York

. . . . . . . . . . 5 Edward Rice b: 1900 in New York

. . . . . . . . . . 5 Mary Rice b: 1902 in New York

. . . . . . . . . . 5 Katherine Rice b: 1904 in New York

# CHART 16

## LIST OF
## AFRICAN DESCENDANT VAN VRANKENS
## IN UPSTATE NEW YORK

| SURNAME | GIVEN NAME | RACE | DOB | RELATIONSHIP | SEX | PLACE OF BIRTH | DATE/DEATH | REMARKS |
|---|---|---|---|---|---|---|---|---|
| VAN VRANKEN | | | | | | | | |
| | Ryckert Claase | W | 1645 | HEAD | M | Beverwyck N.N. | 13 April 1713 | Bought land Canastiglione |
| | Hillegonda | | | WIFE | F | Beverwyck N.N. | | 17 May 1672 |
| | Maas Ryckse | W | 1672 | SON | M | Albany N.N. | | |
| WINNE | | | | | | | | |
| | Annake | W | 15 Oct 1677 | WIFE | F | Albany N.N. | Mar 1778 | |
| | Adam | W | 8-Dec 1717 | SON | M | Albany N.N. | 1793 | |
| CLUTE | | | | | | | | |
| | Ariaantje | W | 1715 | WIFE | F | Albany N.N. | | |
| | Rykhart | W | 1750 | SON | M | Schenectady | 15 Aug 1833 | |
| GROOT | | | | | | | | |
| | Barbara | W | 1757 | WIFE | F | | | |
| | Andries/Andrew | W | 5-May 1789 | SON | M | Schenectady,NY | 26 Feb 1862 | |
| CRAGIER | | | | | | | | |
| | Dorcas | W | 15-Sep 1800 | WIFE | F | | 21 Jun 1883 | Not the Mother of Children |
| | | A | 26 - 45 | | F | | | 1820 CENSUS/ Albany |
| | | A | Under 14 | | F | | | |
| | | A | Under 14 | | F | | | |
| | | A | 26 - 45 | | M | | | |
| | Francis | A | 7-Feb 1814 | SON | M | Salem NY | 29 Dec 1876 | Alb. Rural Cemetery |
| HARDEN | | | | | | | | |
| | Abbigail | A | 5-Jun 1825 | WIFE | F | Albany NY | 1 Apr 1890 | Alb. Rural Cemetery |
| | Anna E. | A | Jan. 1845 | DAUG | F | Albany NY | 20-Jun-05 | Alb. Rural Cemetery |
| | Frances M. | A | 30-Jun 1846 | DAUG | F | Albany NY | 15 Apr 1857 | Alb. Rural Cemetery |
| | Howard E. | A | 14-Mar 1848 | SON | M | Albany NY | 3 Dec 1848 | Alb. Rural Cemetery |
| | Charles Howard | A | 15-May 1849 | SON | M | Albany NY | | |
| | Mary D. | A | 7-Jan 1851 | DAUG | F | Albany NY | 20 Apr 1853 | Alb. Rural Cemetery |
| | Abbigail S. | A | 1852 | DAUG | F | Albany NY | | |
| SINCLAIR | | | | | | | | |
| | William T. | A | | SON-IN-LAW | M | Buffalo NY | 10-Sep-34 | |
| | Edgar | A | 24-Apr 1854 | SON | M | Albany NY | | |
| | Hattie G. | A | 1854 | WIFE | F | Pittsfield MA | 20 May 1886 | Alb. Rural Cemetery |
| | Francis Jr. | A | Jul 1857 | SON | M | Albany NY | 7-Jul-35 | |
| | Fredezick A. | A | 30-Apr 1859 | SON | M | Albany NY | 6-Sep-13 | Died Bright's disease |
| VAN VRANKEN | | | | | | | | |
| | Francis | A | | BROTHER | M | | | |
| | Johannes/ John | A | 1777 | HEAD | M | Schagticoke, NY | 10 April 1865 | |
| SYLVESTER | | | | | | | | |
| | Roseana/ Hannal | A | 1775 | WIFE | F | | | |
| | Samuel | A | 13 Feb 1804 | SON | M | Schagticoke, NY | 14 March 1891 | |
| | Hannah | A | 1-Jul 1812 | DAUG | F | Wash.. Co. NY | | |
| | Catherine | A | Nov. 1823 | DAUG. | F | Wash. Co. NY | | |
| HAZZARD | | | | | | | | |
| | Eli | A | 1825 | SON-IN-LAW | M | Wash. Co. NY | | |
| | Elizabeth | A | 1835 | DAUG | F | Wash. Co. NY | | |
| | Mary Jane | A | 1837 | DAUG. | F | Wash. Co. NY | | |
| VAN VRANKEN | | | | | | | | |
| | Samuel | A | 13 Feb. 1804 | HEAD | M | Schagticoke, NY | 14 March 1891 | |
| | Sally | A | 1805 | WIFE | F | Albany NY | 22 April 1861 | |
| | Dennis | A | 1820 | SON | M | Salem NY | | |
| | Margaret | A | 1823 | DAUG | F | Salem NY | | |
| | Andrew | A | 6-Feb 1825 | SON | M | Salem NY | 23 Feb 1870 | |
| | Anna | W | | WIFE | F | England | | |
| | Ellen | A | 1830 | DAUG | F | Salem NY | | |
| LATIMER | | | | | | | | |
| | Benjamin | A | | SON-IN-LAW | M | Troy NY | | |
| | Mary Matilda | A | 1832 | DAUG | F | Salem NY | 10 April 1861 | |
| BURK | | | | | | | | |
| | James | A | 1829 | SON-IN-LAW | M | Salem NY | 18 April 1881 | |
| | Susanna | A | 1834 | DAUG. | F | Salem NY | 11 April 1888 | |
| PETERMAN | | | | | | | | |
| | James | A | 1823 | SON-IN-LAW | M | Petersburgh NY | 11-Jun-03 | |
| | Charles | A | 1854 | SON | M | Salem NY | 21 Feb 1874 | |

| SURNAME | GIVEN NAME | RACE | DOB | RELATIONSHIP | SEX | PLACE OF BIRTH | DATE/DEATH | REMARKS |
|---|---|---|---|---|---|---|---|---|
| VAN VRANKEN | | | | | | | | |
| | Margaret | A | 1781 | | F | NY | | |
| | Catherine | A | 1785 | | F | NY | 1871 | |
| | David | A | 1789 | HEAD | M | NY | 22 April 1874 | Alb. Rural, Lot 14, Sec 49 |
| | Hagar | A | | WIFE | F | NY | 28 Feb 1844 | |
| | Robert | A | 1829 | SON | M | Albany NY | | |
| | Adelaide | A | 1831 | WIFE | F | NY | | |
| | David H. | A | 1852 | GR. SON | M | Albany NY | | |
| | Robert A. | A | 1853 | GR. SON | M | Albany NY | | |
| | Walter A. | A | 1855 | GR. SON | M | Albany NY | | |
| | Anna L. | A | 1859 | GR. DAUG. | F | Albany NY | | |
| VAN VRANKEN | | | | | | | | |
| | David | A | 1836 | SON | M | Albany NY | | Alb. Rural, Lot 41 |
| | VAN BUREN | | | | | | | |
| | Margaret | A | Nov. 1831 | WIFE | F | Albany NY | 20-May-07 | Alb. Rural  Lot 41 Sec. 99 |
| | Elizabeth | A | 1852 | GR. DAUG. | F | Albany NY | | |
| | David | A | 1857 | GR. SON | M | Albany NY | 17 Feb 1891 | Alb. Rural, Lot 41 |
| | Bertha | A | | GR. DAUG | F | Albany NY | 7 Aug. 1908 | Alb. Rural, Lot 41 |
| VAN VRANKEN | | | | | | | | |
| | Thomas | A | 36-55 | HEAD | M | Pittstown NY | | 1830 Census Pittstown, NY |
| | | A | 24-36 | WIFE | F | | | |
| | | A | Un/10 | DAUG. | F | Pittstown NY | | |
| | | A | Un/10 | SON | M | Pittstown NY | | |
| VAN VRANKEN | | | | | | | | |
| | Frank | A | 1826 | HEAD | M | NY | | |
| | Lorette | A | 1838 | WIFE | F | NY | | |
| | George | A | 1852 | SON | M | Kingsbury NY | | |
| | Frank | A | 1856 | SON | M | Kingsbury NY | | |
| VAN VRANKEN | | | | | | | | |
| | Peter (Prov) | A | Un/44 | | F | Troy NY | | G. A. Cem. 8 April 1819 |

# REFERENCE NOTES

[240] This "Unknown" Van Vranken represents Francis and Johannes' mother. Since it was the law and custom during this period of enslavement that the social status of children followed the condition of their mother (enslaved or free), we are beginning our Family history by designating these brothers' mother as the initial Family Ancestor.

[241] Another African-American veteran of the Revolutionary War (not noted in this publication) also resided in Washington County, remaining unknown at least partially due to lack of a burial site and marker. This was Levi Hazzard of Granville, who appeared in open court, August 29, 1 820, to declare his oath and apply for a Revolutionary War Pension.

He based his claim upon services in "Capt. Jeremiah Miller's Co., Col. Joseph Vose's 1$^{st}$ Massachusetts Regt.," from summer 1781 until summer 1784.[2] The records of his enlistment and an accompanying descriptive list[3] identify Hazzard as an African American. Levi Hazzard, veteran of the Revolutionary War, forms a good starting point for any account of black veterans of the Civil War. Hazzard's 1820 pension declaration mentions two sons, Levi and Avery, young men of Granville described by their father as "working out." Descendants of Levi, Jr., remained in the Kingsbury, Ft. Edward, and Argyle area, while sons of Avery eventually settled in the Town of Greenwich (via Salem and Jackson). Both of these lines produced Civil War soldiers. Reference: Levi Hazzard, "Revolutionary War Pension Application, filed 29 Aug.1820," Court of Common Pleas, Polder 6, p. 36, Washington Co. Archives, Ft. Edward, NY. Interestingly, this county record contains no indicationHazzard was an African American, and *Massachusetts Soldiers and Sailors of the Revolutionary War*, Vol. 7, pp. 643, 650 (available online at www.mass.gov).

[242] "Washington County Town Clerks' Records of Births, Deaths, and s. 1X47 1849," Keel 289, Wash. Co. Archives

[243] William Cormier, *Salem's Forgotten African Americans*, The Journal of the Washington County Historical Society, 2008, pg. 31 and 36. The "Van Rankins" and "Van **Bronks**" of early census and other records (of this area) became **in** more modern times the "Van Vrankens." **IX.**—'Guardianships," Folder 170 (1870), Washington Co. Archives

[244] IBID

[245] Hammersley, Sydney Ernest, The History of Waterford, New York", 1957; pgs. 195-196

[246] IBID

[247] IBID

# CHAPTER VII

# THE VAN VRANKEN BURIALS IN WASHINGTON COUNTY, NY

# THE VAN VRANKEN BURIALS IN WASHINGTON COUNTY

## HISTORICAL BACKGROUND

The cemeteries and burial grounds of people of African descent are significant historical, archeological, religious, and cultural sites. In these sacred places of mourning, remembrance and celebration are many clues to the history of those buried there and the communities that surrounded them in both life and death. Through the markers, stones, monuments, landscapes, enclosures, and epitaphs, the burial grounds of generations of people of African descent are not only a commentary on religious beliefs, customs, culture and ancient traditions but also on the lifestyle, society, and heritage of a people and a race.

The significance of these sacred places extends far beyond the seemingly simplistic variety of artifacts or bareness found there. A complex system of belief and social practice, shaped by centuries of interaction between African and European cultures, has produced a landscape of multiple layers. While recent scholarship has begun to focus more attention on the presence of people of African descent, cemeteries and burial grounds remain largely unexplored for their potential as valuable and informative windows into the past.

As Africans and their descendents encountered the New World, parallels between Christianity and the traditional spiritual practices of various African cultures created an experience that represented a combining of philosophies and beliefs. This amalgamation of cultural values allowed for the survival of certain African ideas, symbols and beliefs. Traditional beliefs, such as the distinction between the body and spirit, and the existence of a separate world for the deceased, transferred easily to life in America. An African Worldview persisted in customs such as the use of ornamental plantings—reflecting an African belief in the living spirit, or the placement of "offerings" on top of the gravesites.

While such practices remained most prevalent in the coastal areas of America, where a greater proportion of the African population descended directly from Africa; hey are also evident to some degree in communities of African descent all across the United States.

Throughout much of the eighteenth and nineteenth centuries, economic adversity fostered many innovative burial practices within African American communities. Simple wooden coffins were common, while the use of grave vaults, a technique frequently used in white cemeteries to maintain an even surface for mowing and walking, remained rare. As a result, their uneven terrain easily identifies many cemeteries and burial grounds of African descent, even those without markers.

## NON-TRADITIONAL LANDSCAPES

Historic African American cemeteries and burial grounds are sometimes difficult to identify and can be easily overlooked by the uninformed observer. Many are situated in remote locations, often on what was once the poorest or least developed land in a community. In rural areas, these cemeteries and burial grounds can be hard to reach, if they lack large, upright monuments and difficult to spot during a survey. In more urban locations, their "segregated" status within traditional European cemeteries excludes them from "perpetual care" upkeep and thus adds to their neglect. Many of these cemeteries and burial grounds succumb to the pressures of urban development because their existence and significance to the history of a particular community goes unrecorded and therefore unrecognized.

Most cemeteries and burial grounds of people of African descent are relatively simple, displaying little or no formal landscaping. This is intended. Trees and shrubs are generally native to the area though the use of ornamental vegetation, and plantings to mark gravesites are not uncommon. This practice also hints at African origins and may stem from the African belief in the continuation of the spirit.

Gravesites often seem to be scattered or randomly placed, with little symmetrical thought given to their arrangement however, this too has an African traditional significance. More often in urban than rural settings, the prominence of the family burial plot reveals the importance of family ties as a source of strength and comfort in the community. These cemeteries and burial grounds rarely feature elaborate monuments; rather, simple monuments constructed of stone or wood predominated. Many of which are made or inscribed by hand, indicating a community's traditions of folk art and craftsmanship. Many gravesites are unmarked or are marked only with fieldstones set on end and the lack of grave vaults is typical. Deep depressions reveal the location of many otherwise unmarked graves.

## THE BURIAL GROUNDS PROJECT

In early 2002, while researching my Van Vranken family in Washington County and with the guidance of the Salem, New York historian Al Cormier and Bancroft Library (Salem) archivist, Peg Culver, a "forgotten" burial ground of African descendants was located in Salem (Washington County) New York. This

African Burial site called the "African Grounds" was located in a remote area of the Evergreen Cemetery just outside of Salem, New York. The "African Grounds", although delineated on the Evergreen Cemetery's map of its property,[248] was completely unknown to the Board of Directors of the Evergreen Cemetery and its staff, with respect to its existence, location, or individuals buried therein.

Through the expert research of Mr. Cormier and Ms. Culver the exact location of the "African Grounds" was determined and a list of the families and individuals of African descent buried on the site was compiled. However, due to the lack of knowledge of the site on the part of the Board of the Cemetery, the Cemetery had made little or no effort to maintain the "African Grounds" in a manner similar to the other burial sites located at the Cemetery. That being "perpetual care". This may have been due to the racially and geographically "segregated" nature of the "African Grounds," in an area far removed from the main burial sites of the Cemetery.

This area, highlighted on Map 6 below as the "African Grounds, now un-mowed, overgrown and littered with brush has been identified as the burial site of some fifteen (15) individuals of African descent who lived in the Town of Salem or vicinity during the middle 1800s. In its present condition, it was without question unacceptable as a sacred place, where families of African descent could come and pay their respects to their deceased relatives. In addition, the condition of the "African Grounds", was described as "neglect" by one of the Vice Presidents of the Board of the Cemetery. Its condition deprived the community of African descent still living in the area, the Town of Salem and the County of Washington, as well as the State of New York the opportunity to celebrate this significant re-discovery as a noteworthy African American historical, archeological, religious, and cultural site.

Through the intervention of the New York Department of State, Division of Cemeteries, and with the cooperation of the Board of Directors of the Evergreen Cemetery and the Salem Town Historian a plan was developed to restore the "African Grounds". By way of a grant I obtained from the New York State African American Institute, the Subsurface Informational Services was retained to conduct a ground penetration radar survey of the African Grounds, in an attempt to locate the original gravesites. This search was inconclusive. However, the Cemetery did restore the site. (See Photos # 3 and 4) This restoration involved the clean-up of the site, a survey of the gravesites within the "African Grounds", and the repair and securing of existing grave stones and markers. A thorough identification of the individuals of African descent buried at the site was conducted by Mr. Cormier, Ms. Culver and myself. We also attempted to make contact, where possible, with the relatives of the individuals buried in the "African Grounds." A marker was placed designating the area as the "African Grounds."[249]

# MAP 6

## MAP OF EVERGREEN CEMETERY
## SALEM, NY

# EVERGREEN CEMETERY

# AFRICAN GROUNDS

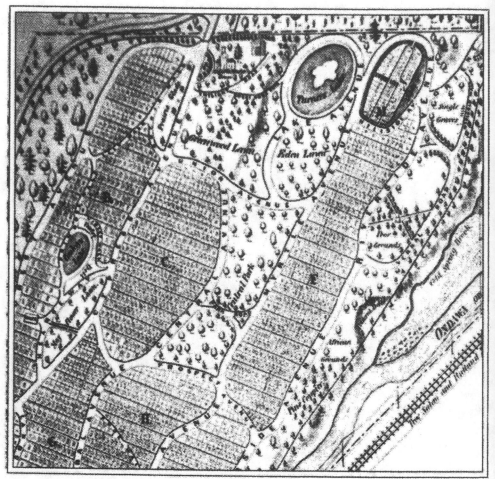

**Detail of Evergreen Cemetery, showing the "African Grounds" on the lower right.** (Courtesy Salem Town Historian)

This Project was truly a vivid representation of "the thrill of victory—the agony of defeat" in reverse. Map 7 represents the documented placement of a portion of the gravesites in the African Grounds, Section P of the Evergreen Cemetery.[250] Based on the official listing of burials at the African Grounds which was discovered in storage at the Cemetery, some fifteen (15) individuals of African descent were buried in the African Grounds between the years 1867 and 1891.[251] Among these 15 individuals was my Great-Great-Great-Great Grandfather Samuel Van Vranken who died in 1891 in Lansingburgh, New York while living with his daughter Susanna Peterman, at the age of 87 years old; and his sons: Charles who died in 1874 in Salem at the age of 20 years old and Andrew who died in 1870 in Cambridge, NY at the age of 45 years old.

Additionally, James Burk, husband to Samuel's daughter Mary Matilda, aged 52 at the time of his death; his son James H. Burk, by James' second wife Helen, age 10 years old at death are also buried in the African Grounds at the Evergreen Cemetery. These family members are buried adjacent to each other with Samuel, plot #1935, Charles, plot # 915 and Andrew, plot # 671 in one family Lot and James, plot #1345 and his son, James H., plot # 1480 in the very next Lot.

On Map 7, you can clearly delineate the gravesites (top to bottom) for: B. Freeman for most likely Elizabeth Freeman in #2 grave; a two-tier Robertson family Lot including at least three (3) grave plots—one of which is probably occupied by Susan Freeman in #1 grave. Susan was the Robertson's daughter and at least two (2) empty plots for future family burials. There is a headstone for Susan Freeman that was recovered buried underground in the vicinity of this gravesite and repaired by Cemetery staff. (Photos # 3, 4, and 5)

The next section of the African Grounds is separated by a 4-foot walkway. In this section, we have the following:

1- The Van Vranken Lot #1 (10x20) recorded at the bottom of the Map as being purchased by Samuel Van Vranken for $20.00 on June 30, 1870; about a month before his son Andrew's death. Samuel received a Deed for this plot—Deed # 358.

2- James Burk also purchased a Lot on the same day as Samuel, it is labeled Lot #2 Burk on this Map also 10x20 dimensions and also for $20.00. His Deed is #357, which may mean he purchased his Lot just before Samuel. (See Photos #12 and 13—New Van Vranken/Burk Gravesite)

The description of the location of these Lots at the bottom of this Map is what allowed us to pinpoint the exact location of the African Grounds (Section P) and the gravesites listed above.

> *"It's Northeast corner 12 feet south of the range of the line between Lots 352 and 360 of Section F."*

# MAP 7

## SECTION P
## AFRICAN GROUNDS

MAP OF OCCUPIED PART

## Section P. African Grounds.

| No. | Section. | Dimension. | Contents. | ¶816R. | PURCHASER. | REMARKS. |
|-----|----------|------------|-----------|--------|------------|----------|

*Map of the occupied part of Section P.*

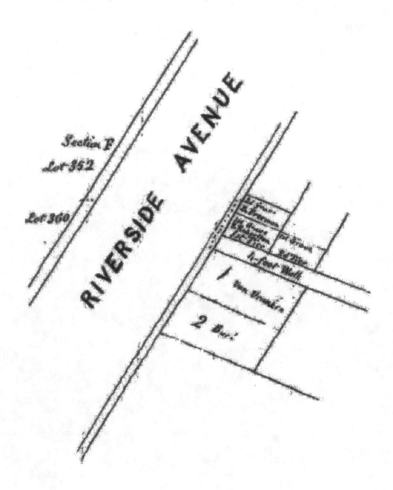

1   P   10 × 20   200   20·00   *Samuel Van Peuken*   June 30, 1850.  Deed 352.
The South-west corner in feet South of
the range of the line between Lots
352 and 360, of Section E.


2   P   10 × 20   200   20·00   *James Shack*   June 30, 1850.  Deed 353.

# EVERGREEN CEMETERY, SALEM, NY AFRICAN GROUNDS, SECTION P

## LIST OF INDIVIDUALS

Samuel Van Vranken, b. 2/13/1804, Schaghticoke;, p. Johannis & Hannah, wife Sally,d. 3/14/1891, Lansingburg African Grounds #1935

Charles Van Vranken, b. Feb. 1854, Salem Village; p. Samuel & Sally; d. Feb 21/1874, Salem, African Grounds* #915

Andrew VanVranken, d. Feb. 23; 1870, parent Samuel, wife Leonora, age 46.

James Burk, w. Helen, d. April 18, 1881, a barber by trade, African grounds, plot #1345

James H. Burk, p. James and Helen, d. Saratoga Springs, single, d. May 19, 1883, age 10, plot #1480

Eva Gansevourt, aka Elira Eveline, parents Alexander and Jane Gansevourt, d. March 18, 1870, age 1.

Jane Ann Gansevoort, parents Cuff and Rachel Simmons, born Schaghticoke, husband Alexander, d. August 11, 1870, age 62.

Elizabeth Freeman, b. Hebron, d. Salem, Nov. 2, 1870, age 87, cancer and asthma.

Susan Robertson Freeman, p. _____ Robertson, d. Salem, widow, d. April 4, 1867, age 97.

James Bennett, d. April 26, 1879.

Susan Bogart, husband Cato, d. July 20, 1882.

Cato Bogart, wife Susan, d. Feb. 21 1877, age 74.

Samuel Boston, widower, d. Feb. 17, 1879, age 73.

Melissa Ann Hogeboom, b. Moriah, NY, p. Alexander and Jane Ann Gansevoort, husband, Henry, d. Salem, Sept. 11, 1867, age 24, consumption

Alfred Morris, b. Saratoga Springs, p. Charles and Sarah Morris, d. Saratoga Springs, April 20, 1877, age 3

Sylvia Boston, d. 1842, disinterred from the Revolutionary War Cemetery in 1861 and buried in Evergreen Cemetery, according to the notes of Dr. Asa Fitch, Jr.

# PHOTO #1

**ORIGINAL CONDITION OF
AFRICAN GROUNDS AT EVERGREEN
CEMETERY
SALEM, NY**

## ORIGINAL CONDITION OF AFRICAN GROUNDS
## SALEM, NY

# PHOTO #2

## REFURBISHED CONDITION OF AFRICAN GROUNDS, SECTION P AT EVERGREEN CEMETERY SALEM, NY

# NEW AFRICAN GROUNDS GRAVESITE
# EVERGREEN CEMETERY, SALEM, NY

**PHOTO NEW FREEMAN GRAVESITES
WITH HEADSTONES AND WALKWAY**

# BETSEY FREEMAN AND
# SUSAN ROBERTSON FREEMAN
# HEADSTONES EVERGREEN CEMETERY

*(Courtesy W. A. Cormier)*

**Susan Robertson's gravestone.** *(Courtesy W. A. Cormier)*

# PHOTO #6

## NEW VAN VRANKEN/BURK GRAVESITE
## AND WALKWAY
## AFRICAN GROUNDS

# OLD REVOLUTIONARY WAR CEMETERY
# SALEM, NEW YORK

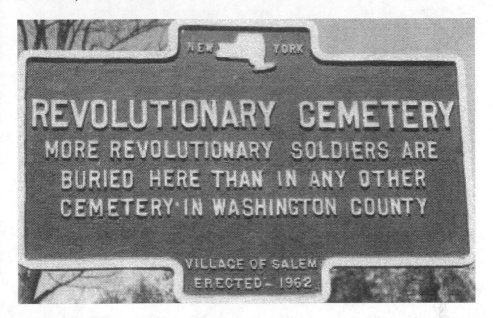

In the spring of 1766, Dr. Thomas Clark arrived with his Scotch-Irish Presbyterian congregation from Ballybay, Ireland. The two groups cooperated in settling this territory and soon determined that a common burying ground was needed. This burying ground was Salem's only public burying ground until the Evergreen Cemetery was established on March 5, 1859.

According to local history, the first burial was that of a Native American who wandered into the settlement and died. The first settler to be burial here was Solomon Barr. The location of these two graves is unknown. The earliest engraved tombstone is that of Abram Savage of the prominent Savage family. He died in 1769, and at age 17 was the youngest burial. The oldest person buried here was John McNish who died in 1821 at the age 104. The last burial was that of John E. Gillis who died in 1921.

Local legend has it that after the Battle of Saratoga in 1777, about 100 soldiers bodies were loaded like "cord wood" on wagons and brought to Salem for burial in one common grave in this cemetery. In addition to containing the bodies of many of Salem's earliest settlers, like James Turner, Hamilton McCollister and Joshua Conkey, the cemetery contains documented burials of 101 Revolutionary War soldiers. Consequently, this cemetery probably holds the greatest number of Revolutionary War soldiers in New York State. Overall, 1034 engraved tombstones are found here.

In 1810, a stonewall was erected to protect the cemetery from vandalism and the theft of gravestones. A cemetery supervisor was hired to manage the use of the cemetery. In 1933, outside the cemetery walls, the town and State of New York erected a monument in memory of the Revolutionary War soldiers buried there.

## VAN VRANKEN BURIALS AT REVOLUTIONARY WAR CEMETERY

On 22 April 1861, Sally Van Vranken, wife of Samuel Van Vranken, age 68 or 69, depending on the source, dies and is buried in the Revolutionary War Cemetery in Salem, NY. (Census records would show Sally to be 56 in 1861).

*DEATH NOTICES from WASHINGTON COUNTY,*
*WASHINGTON COUNTY PEOPLE'S JOURNAL*
*January 5, 1854—December 30, 1879 (Pg. 206)*

*VAN VRANKEN Sally abt 68y wife of Samuel in Salem, NY*
*April 22, 1861*

*Buried in the Revolutionary War Cemetery (Salem, NY) located by William A. Cormier (Historian Salem, NY). Stone inscribed: "Sally wife of Samuel Van Vranken, died April 22, 1861, age 69 years"*

Additionally, there are three (3) other members of the Van Vranken family buried at the Revolutionary War Cemetery in Salem, New York.[252]

1- Katherine Burk, dau. of James and Mary Matilda (Van Vranken) Burk, d. 30 Aug. 1857, age 4 years old;
2- Mary Matilda, dau. Samuel and Sally Van Vranken, wife of James Burk, d. 10 Apr 1861, 29y;
3- Samuel, son of James & Matilda Burk, d. 2 Nov 1868, 17y.

The proximity of the dates of Sally and Mary Matilda Van Vrankens' deaths, 12 days apart is probably due to some type of contagious disease that was commonly spread throughout New York State during this time period.

# PHOTO #9

**SALLY VAN VRANKEN AND
MARY MATILDA BURK GRAVESITES
OLD REVOLUTIONARY WAR CEMETERY
SALEM, NEW YORK**

# SALLY AND MATILDA'S GRAVESITES
## OLD REVOLUTIONARY WAR CEMETERY

# WASHINGTON COUNTY POORHOUSE CEMETERY

The Washington County Poorhouse Cemetery in Argyle contains the names of those "inmates" buried with headstones that had names engraved on them as well as those whose stones were only numbered. (Those names which correspond to numbered stones had been previously "lost", and in recent years were considered unknown.

As has been stated earlier, three members of our Family were at one tine housed at the Washington County Poorhouse, two of whom died while they were in residence at the facility. John Van Bronk, and his wife Susanna were admitted into the Washington County Poorhouse in Argyle, New York on 3 January 1865 for palsied and old age, respectively. John Van Bronk died at the facility on 10 April 1865 at the age of 88. Hannah/Roseanna was discharged on 12 April 1865 and moved in with her daughter Catharine, the wife of Eli Hazzard in Greenwich, Washington County, New York. She is later readmitted to the Washington County Poorhouse in 1868. No additional records exist for her. No record presently exists either for the burial of John Van Bronk after his death at the County Poorhouse. It is believed that the Poorhouse handled the arrangements of his burial but their records with respect to this event are non-existent.

James Peterman was the other member of our Family who died while a resident at the Washington County Poorhouse. James was Samuel's son-in-law and his daughter, Susanna's husband. He was admitted to the Poorhouse in 1903 at the age of 73 for Debility and old age. He died on 11 June 1903 and was buried at the Washington County Poorhouse Cemetery. . See document below for the official record of his death and the recording of his Burial Stone number within the Washington County Poorhouse Cemetery.

# WASHINGTON COUNTY (NY) POORHOUSE CEMETERY

## NUMBERED STONES – K- R

Note: Information in the last column came from the entry in the actual interment lists UNLESS it is in parentheses. The interment lists gave "nationality". However, any information in parentheses comes from an Inmate Registration Certificate which gives only " birthplace".

Click here for further information about Inmate Registration Certificates.

Note: Six stone numbers were never assigned (possibly broken before use?): 128, 139, 140, 169, 199. Four stone numbers were assigned twice -- highlighted below: 45, 104, 149, 178. The assignment of one stone (202) was too illegible to be read.

| STONE # | CERT # | LAST NAME | FIRST NAME | AGE | DEATH DATE | CAUSE of DEATH | COMMENTS | NATIONALITY or BIRTHPLACE |
|---|---|---|---|---|---|---|---|---|
| 87 | | PETERMAN | JAMES | 79 | 6/11/1903 | DEBILITY & OLD AGE | | |

## REFERENCE NOTES

248  Evergreen Cemetery Property Map, Evergreen Cemetery Record Book

249  Efforts were also made to contact and coordinate the "African Grounds" restoration with the African Burial Grounds Project in New York City. This linkage was an attempt to secure expert advice, service and recommendations with respect to the disposition, identification and restoration of the "African Grounds".

250  Evergreen Cemetery Record Book, pg. 366; Section P African Grounds, Map of the occupied part of Section P

251  Evergreen Cemetery, Salem, NY; African Grounds—Section P; List of Individuals

252  Revolutionary War Cemetery: Visitors' Catalog, Sally Van Vranken and Mary Matilda buried: Section 9 Row 2; Katherine and Samuel Burk buried: Section 9 Row 4.

# APPENDIX

# Appendix A

## ACT OF ATTAINDER OCTOBER 1779

# LAWS OF THE STATE OF NEW YORK, PASSED IN THE THIRD SESSION OF THE LEGISLATURE, HELD AT KINGSTON, IN ULSTER COUNTY.

## CHAPTER XXIV

*An Act for the Forfeiture and Sale of the Estates of Persons who have adhered to the Enemies of this State, and for declaring the Sovereignty of the People of this State, in respect to all Property within the same.*
*—Passed 22d October, 1779.*

Preamble

**Whereas,** during the present unjust and cruel war, waged by the King of *Great Britain*, against this State and the other United States of *America*, divers persons holding or claiming property within this state, have voluntarily been adherent to the said King, his fleets and armies, enemies to this State and the said other United States, with intent to subvert the government and liberties of this state and the said other United States, and to bring the same into subjection to the crown of *Great Britain*; by reason whereof, the said persons have severally justly forfeited all rights to the protection of this state, and to the benefit of the laws under which such property is held or claimed: *And whereas*, the public justice and safety of this state absolutely require that the most notorious offenders should be immediatly hereby convicted and attainted of the offence aforesaid, in order to work a forfeiture of their respective estates, and vest the same in the people of this state; *And whereas*, the constitution of this state hath authorized the legislature to pass Acts of attainder for crimes committed before the termination of the present war.

Persons by name, Ipso Facto, attainted of the offence of adhering to the enemies of the State, and their Estates forfeited to the People of this State.

**I.** *Be it therefore enacted by the People of the State of New York, represented in Senate and Assembly, and it is hereby enacted by the authority of the same,* That John Murray, earl of *Dunmore*, formerly governor of the colony of *New York*; William Tryon, Esq., late governor of the said colony; John Watts, Oliver De Lancey, Hugh Wallace, Henry White, John Harris Cruger, William Axtell, and Roger Morris, Esquires, *late members of the council of the said colony*; George Duncan Ludlow, and Thomas Jones, late justices of the Supreme Court of the said Colony; John Tabor Kempe,

Their estates
forfeited.

late attorney-general of the said colony; Willaim Bayard, Robert Bayard, and James De Lancey, *now or late of the City of New York*, Esquires; David Matthews, late Mayor of the said city; James Jauncey, George Folliot, Thomas White, William McAdam, Isaac Low, Miles Sherbrook, Alexander Wallace, and John Wetherhead, now or late of the said city, merchants; Charles Inglis, of the said city, clerk, and Margaret, his wife; Sir John Johnson, late of the county of *Tryon*, Knight and Baronet; Guy Johnson, Daniel Claus, and John Butler, now or late of the said county, Esquires, and John Joost Herkemer, now or late of the said county, yeoman; Frederick Philipse, and James De Lancey, now or late of the said county of *Westchester*, Esquires;

Frederick Philipse (son of Frederick) now or late of said county, gentleman; David Colden, Daniel Kissam the Elder, and Gabriel Ludlow, now or late of *Queen's* county, Esquires; Philip Skeene, now or late of the county of *Charlotte*, Esq.; and Andrew P. Skeene, son of the said Philip Skeene, late of *Charlotte* County; Benjamin Seaman, and Christopher Billop, now or late of the county of *Richmond*, Esquires; Beverly Robinson, Beverly Robinson the younger, and Malcolm Morrison, now or late of the county of *Dutchess*, Esquires; John Kane, now or late of said county, gentleman; Abraham C. Cuyler, now or late of the county of *Albany*, Esq.; Robert Leake, Edward Jessup, and Ebenezer Jessup, now or late of the said county, gentlemen; and Peter Du Bois, and Thomas H. Barclay, now or late of the county of *Ulster*, Esquires; Suannah Robinson, wife of the said Beverly Robinson, and Mary Morris, wife of the said Roger Morris; John Rapalje, of *Kings* county, Esq.; George Muirson, Richard Floyd, and Parker Wickkam, of *Suffolk* county, Esquires; Henry Lloyd, the elder, late of the State of *Massachusetts Bay*, merchant; and Sir Henry Clinton, Knight, be, and each of them are hereby severally declared to be, *Ipso Facto*, convicted and attainted of the offence aforesaid; and that all and singular the estate, both real and personal, held or claimed by them the said persons severally and respectively, whether in possession, reversion or remainder, within this State, on the day of the passing of this Act, shall be and hereby is declared to be forfeited to and vested in the people of this state.

The said persons banished from this State and declared Felons, without benefit of clergy, if found within it.

II. *And be it further enacted by the authority aforesaid*, That the said several persons herein before particularly named, shall be and hereby are declared to be for ever banished from this State; and each and every of them, who shall at any time hereafter be found in any part of this State, shall be, and are hereby adjudged and declared guilty of felony, and shall suffer death as in cases of felony, without benefit of clergy.

For the purpose of attainting other offenders.

Indictments to be found against persons either in full life, or deceased, in any county, without regard to that in which the offence was committed. Not necessary to state whether the offender is at the time in full life or deceased.

III. *And to the end*, That for the purpose aforesaid, convictions and attainders for the offence aforesaid, may, in pursuance of this act, be had against other offenders than those herein before particularly named; *Be it further enacted by the authority aforesaid*, That it shall and may be lawful for the grand jurors at any supreme court of judicature to be held for this state, or any court of oyer and terminer and general goal delivery, or general and quarter sessions ot the peace, to be held and for any county within this state, whenever it shall appear to such grand jurors by the oath of one or more credible witness or witnesses, that any person or persons, whether in full life or deceased, generally reputed, if in full life, to hold or claim, or if deceased to have held or claimed, at the time of their death respectively, real or personal estate within this state, hath or have been guilty of the offence aforesaid, to prefer bills of indictment against such persons as shall then be in full life, for such offence, and in relation to the offence committed by such persons in their lives time, as shall then be deceased, severally and respectively, notwithstanding that such offence many have been committed elsewhere than in the county for which such grand jurors shall be summoned. That in every indictment to be taken in pursuance of this act, the offence or offences shall be charged to have been committed in the county where the indictment shall be taken, notwithstanding such offence or offences may have been committed elsewhere; and it shall not be necessary to set forth specially, whether the several persons charged in such indictment were respectively deceased or in full life, or were reputed to hold or claim real or personal estate within this state. And on every such indictment shall be indorsed that the same was taken in pursuance of this act, and the day when the same was preferred into court.

Notices of indictments to be published by the Sheriffs.

**IV**. *And be it further enacted by the authority aforesaid*, That whenever and as often as any such indictment shall be taken, against any person or persons, the sheriffs of the respective counties where such indictments shall be taken, shall forthwith cause notices thereof, agreeable to such form as is hereinafter mentioned, to be published in one or more of the public newspapers within this state, for at least four weeks.

Forfeiture thereon by Default or on conviction, on Traverse, and judgment accordingly when the forfeited estates to vest in the people.

**V**. *And be it further enacted by the authority aforesaid*, That in every case of a neglect to appear and traverse agreeable to the sheriff's notice, the several persons charged in such indictment, whether in full life or deceased, shall respectively be and hereby are declared to be, and shall be adjudged guilty of the offences charged against them respectively. And the several persons who shall, in pursuance of this act, either by reason of such defaults, in not appearing and traversing as aforesaid, or upon trial, be convicted of the offence aforesaid, shall forfeit all and singular the estate, both real and personal, whether in possession, revision or remainder, held or claimed by them respectively, within this state, to the people of this state; and judgment shall accordingly be awarded in the supreme court of this state, against the said persons respectively. And such forfeitures, as well of the estates which were at the time of their death, respectively of persons deceased, as of persons in full life, at the time of conviction, shall be deemed to have accrued; and the estates accordingly attached to and vested in the people of this state, at and from the day charged in each respective indictment, most distant from the day of the taking thereof.

Proviso in favour of persons pardoned.

Proviso in favour of those who shall have taken the oath of allegiance before the 4th of April 1778, before whom, and how to operate.

*Provided, nevertheless*, That where a trial shall be had upon any indictment, the forfeiture shall in such case be deemed to have accrued from the day to be found by the verdict of the jury, by which such persons shall be respectively convicted, most distant from the day of the taking of the indictment; any other day to be charged in the indictment notwithstanding. *And provided further*, That the several persons who shall have been pardoned in pursuance of a declaration or ordinance of the convention of this state, passed the tenth day of May, in the year of our Lord one thousand seven hundred and seventy-seven, offering free pardon to such of the subjects of the said state, as, having committed treasonable acts against the same, should return to their allegiance; or, in consequence of any proclamation or proclamations heretofore issued by the commander-in-chief of the army of the United States of America, may respectively plead their pardons to indictments, taken in pursuance of this act, in like manner as they might or could do to indictments for high treason, taken in the ordinary course of law. *And provided further*, That each and every person, who shall at any time before the fourth day of April, in the year of our Lord, one thousand seven hundred and seventy-eight, have taken the oath of allegiance to this state, before the convention or councils of safety of this state; or before the committee of the said convention, appointed for enquiring into, detecting and defeating all conspiracies, which may be formed in this state, against the liberties of America; or the commissioners appointed for the like purpose, or a county, district or precinct committee; shall and may plead such taking the oath of allegiance in bar to any indictment, to be taken in pursuance of this act, for offences committed before the day on which they respectively took such oath.

All indictments on this law, taken in the other courts, to be returned into the Supreme Court, and there tried. On such trial, no greater number of witnesses necessary than in cases of felony.

**VI.** *And be it further enacted by the authority aforesaid*, That all indictments to be from time to time taken in pursuance of this act, at any court of oyer and terminer, or general goal delivery, or general or quarter session of the peace, shall, by the clerk of the said courts, respectively be returned, under their respective hands and seals, into the supreme court of this state, and shall be tried at the bar of the said court; and upon the trial of such indictment, no greater number of witnesses shall be required than are required by law in cases of felony, without benefit of clergy.

Sheriff's returns of the numbers of the newspapers in which their Notices were published, to remain as records of Court till Judgment.

**VII.** *And be it further enacted by the authority aforesaid*, That the several sheriffs shall, from time to time, respectively return, under their hands and seals, into the supreme court of this state, the several numbers of the newspapers containing the notices published by them respectively, there to remain as records of such notices, until judgments shall be had against the several persons named in such notices respectively.

Prosecutions not to be affected by defects of form. Indictments sufficient if generally charging Adherence to the enemy, fixing the times and places. The grand jurors to deliver into court the examinations of the witnesses. Defendants to have copies of Indictments and Examinations.

**VIII.** *And to the end,* That in prosecutions for the offence aforesaid, in pursuance of this act, no advantage may be taken of mere matters of form; and that the defendants may, notwithstanding, be fully apprized of the several matters charged against them; in order to their defence, Be it further enacted by the authority aforesaid, That it shall be sufficient in all indictments to be taken for the offence aforesaid, in pursuance of this act, to charge generally, that the several persons therein charged, did, on the several days, and at the several places therein mentioned, adhere to the enemies of this state, and the grand jurors shall, at the time they deliver any such indictment into court, deliver into court the examinations or depositions of the witness or witnesses, upon whose testimony such indictment was found, to be filed in court, together with the indictment; and the defendants shall respectively, upon application, be entitled to copies of the indictments against them respectively, and of such examinations or depositions; and the prosecutor on the part of the state, shall not, upon the trial, be permitted to give evidence of any overt acts, other than such as shall be charged in such examination or depositions; and the clerks of the several courts of oyer and terminer, and general goal delivery, and general or quarter sessions of the peace, shall return such examinations or depositions, into the supreme court, in like manner as is herein before directed, with respect to indictments, taken at the courts of oyer and terminer, and general goal delivery, or general or quarter sessions of the peace.

What overt acts shall be deemed evidence of High Treason.

**IX.** And be it further enacted by the authority aforesaid, That besides the several matters by the law of England, declared to be evidence and overt acts of high treason, in adhering to the King's enemies, and which are hereby declared to be evidence and overt acts of high treason, in adhering to the enemies of the people of this state, as sovereign thereof; the following matters shall be, and are hereby declared to be evidence and overt acts of adhering to the enemies of the people of this state, whereon and for which persons may, in pursuance of this act, be indicted and convictef for the offence aforesaid; *that is to say,* Being at any time since the *ninth day of July,* in the year of our Lord, one thousand seven hundred and seventy-six (the day of the declaration of the independence of this state within the same), in any part of the United States, not in the power or possession of the fleets or armies of the King of *Great Britain*, and afterwards voluntarily withdrawing to any place within the power or possession of the King of *Great Britain*, his fleets or armies; or being apprehended by order of, or authority from the commander-in-chief of the armies of the said United States; or, of or from the provincial congress, or conventions, or committees thereof, or councils of safety of this state; or the commissioners above mentioned, appointed for enquiring into, detecting and defeating all conspiracies which may be formed in this state against the liberties of *America*; or county, district, or precinct committees within this state; or by the supreme executive authority of this state, and confined within certain limits upon engagement, by parole or otherwise, not to go beyond such limits, and breaking such engagements, and voluntarily escaping to any place in the power of the fleets or armies of *Great Britain*; or being so confined as aforesaid, and afterwards permitted by proper authority to go to any place in the power of the fleets or armies of *Great Britain*, upon engagement to return within a certain given time; and not returning within such time, but afterwards remaining at any place within the power or possession of the fleets or armies of Great Britain.

**Preamble with respect to certain persons in the power of the Enemy.**

**Exemptions in their behalf.**

X. *And whereas*, divers persons, inhabitants and well affected subjects of this state, at the time of the declaration of the independence thereof, who had their fixed residence in the southern district of this state, were obliged, on the invasion of the said district by the enemy, to fly before their superior force, into parts of this, or some other or others of the said United States, and some of them having thereby abandoned all or the greatest part of their property, were so reduced as to have been respectively obliged, through absolute necessity and the want of sufficient habitations and the necessary means of support and subsistence, to return to their respective places of abode; and other of them, for the same cause, having deserted their habitations, and fled in manner aforesaid, have for particular reasons been permitted either by the commander in chief of the armies of the said United States, or other lawful authority, in the places to which they respectively fled, to return within the power of the enemy, where they also severally do reside; *Be it therefore further enacted by the authority aforesaid, and it is hereby provided*, That nothing in this act contained shall be constructed to extend or to affect the said persons, severally and respectfully, or any or either of them, except such of them as since his, her or their return to any place or places within the power of the enemy, has or have done any act or thing, which in judgment of the law would be construed, deemed and adjudged an adherence to the enemies of this state, and high treason against the people thereof, had such person or persons respectively, voluntarily and freely, and without any such cause as aforesaid, returned within the power of the enemy. In which case such return with the power of the enemy, and such act or thing as aforesaid, shall in judgment of law be construed, deemed, and is hereby declared to be adjudged an adherence to the enemies of the people of this state.

No attainder under this law to exempt from punishment in ordinary course.

**XI**. *And be it further enacted by the authority aforesaid*, and it is hereby provided, That no conviction or attainder in pursuance of this act, shall be construed to exempt any person or persons from being apprehended, tried, convicted, attainted and executed for high treason, according to the ordinary course of law.

Conveyances since 9th July, 1776, by any of the parties attainted by this act to be presumed fraudulent.

And proof of their being otherwise to lay upon the claimant.

**XII**. *And be it further enacted by the authority aforesaid*, That all conveyances and assignments of any real or personal estate, made or executed since the ninth day of July, in the year of our Lord one thousand seven hundred and seventy-six, by any or either of the persons, who are immediately convicted and attainted by this act; or any or either of the persons who shall be convicted or attainted in pursuance of this act; or any or either of the persons who shall be convicted or attainted of high treason, in the ordinary course of law, for offences committed during the present war, shall be presumed to be fraudulent and to have been made with intent to prevent a forfeiture of the estates by such conveyances or assignments respectively intended to be conveyed or assigned; and upon every trial wherein any such conveyance or assignment shall come in question, the burden of the proof shall lay upon the person or persons claiming under such conveyances or assignment, that the same was made and executed bona fide, for a valuable consideration, and not with intent to prevent a forfeiture as aforesaid.

Executory Devise and contingent remainders subjected to Forfeiture.

**XIII**. And be it further enacted by the authority aforesaid, That all titles, estates and interests, by executory devise or contingent remainder, claimed by any person hereby or by virtue of the law to be convicted, shall, on conviction, be as fully forfeited to all intents, constructions and purposes, in the land whatsoever, to the people of this State, as any other titles, claims, estates, or interests whatsoever.

Crown Lands, etc., vested in the People, and their Sovereignty and Seignory therein declared, from the 9th of July, 1776.

**XIV**. And be it further enacted by the authority aforesaid, That the absolute property of messuages, lands, tenements and hereditaments, and of all rents, royalties, franchises, prerogatives, privileges, escheats, forfeitures, debts, dues, duties and services, by whatsoever names respectively the same are called and known in the law, and all right and title to the same which next and immediately before the ninth day of July, in the year of our Lord one thousand seven hundred and seventy-six, did vest in, or belong, or was, or were due to the crown of Great Britain, be, and the same and each and every of them, hereby are declared to be, and ever since the said ninth day of July in the year of our Lord one thousand seven hundred and seventy-six, to have been, and forever thereafter shall be, vested in the people of this state, in whom the sovereignty and seignory thereof are and were united and vested, on and from the said ninth day of July, in the year of our Lord one thousand seven hundred and seventy-six.

Commissioners to be appointed for the sale of forfeited estates in each of the Great Districts of the State, at public vendue. How they are to proceed. Amended and altered 4th sess., ch. 13 and 51; 5th sess., ch. 45; 7th sess., ch. 64.

**XV**. And be it further enacted, by the authority aforesaid, That the person administering the government of this state for the time being, shall be, and he is hereby authorized and required, by and with the advice and consent of the council of appointment, to appoint, during the pleasure of the said council and commission under the great seal of this state, three commissioners of forfeitures, for each of the great districts of this state. That the said commissioners, or majority of them, shall be and hereby are authorized and required, from time to time, to sell and dispose of all real estates within their respective districts, forfeited or to be forfeited to the people of this state, at public vendue, to the highest bidder or bidders, and in such parcels as they shall from time to time think proper, first giving eight weeks' notice of each sale, in one or more public

Powers given commissioners by this act repealed, 7th sess., ch. 64, sec. 54.

Commissioners' Deeds to operate as Warranty Deeds.

newspapers in this state, containing a description as to the quantitiy, by estimation, of the lands or tenements to be sold, the situation thereof, and the name or names of the person or persons by the conviction and attainder of whom the said lands or tenements are deemed to have become forfeited; and to make, seal and deliver to the purchaser or purchasers respectively, good and sufficient deeds and conveyances, in the land, to vest the same in them respectively, and their respective heirs and assigns, upon such purchaser or purchasers respectively producing such receipt from the treasurer, as is hereinafter mentioned: That every such purchaser and purchasers shall, by virtue of such deeds and conveyances respectively, be so vested in title, seisin and possession of the lands and tenements so purchased, as to have and maintain in his, her or their name or names, any action for the recovery thereof, or damages relating thereto, any actual seisin or possession thereof, in other person or persons, notwithstanding: That every such deed and conveyance shall be deemed to operate as a warranty from the people of this state to the purchaser or purchasers respectively, and their respective heirs and assigns, for the lands and tenements thereby respectively granted and conveyed, against all claims, titles and encumbrances whatsoever; and such purchaser or purchasers respectively, and their respective heirs and assigns, shall, in case of eviction, have such remedy and relief upon such warranty, in such manner as shall be more particularly provided for in such further act or acts of the legislature, as are hereinafter mentioned.

Not to sell more than 500 acres in one parcel, and no more than one farm in one sale. No sales to be made before first October, 1780. Partly repealed by 3d session, ch. 51, passed 10th March, 1780.

*Provided,* That the said commissioners shall not be authorized to sell any lands in larger parcels than the quantity of five hundred acres in each parcel; that no more than one farm shall be included in one and the same sale; and that the sales shall be made in the county where the lands or tenements to be sold respectively lie. *And provided further,* That nothing in this law contained shall be construed, deemed, esteemed or adjudged to authorize the commissioners to be appointed by virtue hereof, to make sale of any of the lands, messuages, tenements or hereditaments hereby forfeited, or by virtue hereof to become forfeited, before or until the first day of *October* next; and that all such sales shall be, and the same hereby are wholly prohibited until that day.

Public Faith pledged to the commissioners for their pay and expenses by the Legislature.

**XVI.** *And whereas*, it is impossible at present to form an estimate of what will be a proper compensation to the said commissioners, for their services and expenses in executing the business hereby committed to them; *Be it therefore further enacted by the authority aforesaid*, That the public faith of this state shall be, and hereby is pledged to the said commissioners, for such allowance and compensation to them for their services and expenses (besides the expenses of surveyors, clerks, and other incidental charges) as shall hereafter by the legislature be deemed just and reasonable.

Not exceeding £2,000 advanced to the commissioners of each District for expenses.

**XVII.** *And be it further enacted by the authority aforesaid*, That the treasurer of this state shall be, and he is hereby authorized, out of the monies which now are, or hereafter may be in the treasury, to advance to the said commissioners for each district a sum not exceeding two thousand pounds, to defray the expenses of the business hereby committed to them.

Provision in favor of tenants of forfeited lands.

**XVIII.** *And whereas*, in many instances, lands, the reversion or remainder whereof is or may become forfeited to this state, are possessed by tenants who have, at considerable expense, made or purchased the improvements on the same, and which tenants have certainly, uniformly and zealously, since the commencement of the present war, endeavoured to defend and maintain the freedom and independence of the United States; *Be it therefore further enacted by the authority aforesaid*, That where lands, the reversion or remainder whereof is hereby, or may become forfeited to the people of this state, shall be possessed by any tenant of the character above described, and who or whose ancestor, testator or intestate, shall have made or purchased the improvements on the same, they shall continue in possession of their former rents, and be at liberty as heretofore, to transfer their improvements, until the fee simple of the said lands shall be sold, they paying their respective rents, and the present arrearages thereof in money, equal to the current prices of the articles of produce, in which their rents were heretofore paid, into the treasury of this state, if such rents were reserved in produce, or if reserved in money, then in so much money as will be equivalent to the price of wheat at seven shillings per bushel; and that when the fee simple of the said lands shall be sold by the commissioners, to be appointed in pursuance of this act, they shall cause such lands to be appraised by three appraisers, at what shall be deemed the then present value thereof, exclusive of the improvements thereon, at the time of appraising; that one of the said appraisers shall be elected by the commissioners, another by the tenant claiming the benefit intended by this clause, and the third by the said other two appraisers; that the said appraisers, previous to the making of such appraisement, shall each of them take an oath, and which oath the said commissioners are hereby authorized to administer, well and truly to appraise the lands held by such tenant, at what shall be deemed the then value thereof, exclusive of the improvements thereon; and upon payment into the treasury by such tenant of the sum at which such lands shall be so appraised within three months after the making of such appraisement, together with all arrearages of rents then due thereon; the commissioners shall convey the lands so appraised to such tenants, in like manner as if such lands had been sold at public vendue, and such tenant had appeared, and been the highest bidder for the same: *Provided*, That no person being a tenant himself, or of affinity or consanguinity to the tenant requiring such appraisement to be made, shall be an appraiser.

How tenants to avail themselves of the above provision.

**XIX**. *And in order that the commissioners may be enabled to determine* who are the proper objects of the benefit intended by the aforegoing clause, *Be it further enacted by the authority aforesaid*, That no tenant shall be entitled to such benefits, unless he or she shall, within one month after the same shall be required of him or her by the said commissioners, produce to them a certificate to be subscribed by at least twelve reputable inhabitants of the county, of known and undoubted attachment to the American cause, to be approved of by the commissioners, and which inhabitants shall severally declare upon oath, the truth of the matter by them certified, before a justice of the peace of the county who is hereby authorized to administer such oath, certifying that such tenant hath constantly and uniformly, since the said ninth day of July, one thousand, seven hudnred and seventy-six, demeaned himself or herself, as a friend to the freedom and independence of the United States; and that, as far forth as his or her circumstances would admit, taken an active and decisive part to maintain and promote the same.

**Memorandums in writing to be made of all sales, and given to purchasers.**

**XX.** *And be it further enacted by the authority aforesaid,* That whenever the said commissioners shall, within their respective districts, make sale of any lands, either at public vendue or upon such appraisement as aforesaid, and the commissioners, and the person or persons to whom such sale shall be made, having reciprocally subscribed a memorandum or note, in writing, of such sale; the commissioners shall immediately thereupon give to the person or persons to whom such sale shall be made, a certificate thereof, to contain the sum for which the lands purchased by such person or persons were sold, and if such sale was made upon such appraisement, then also of the arrearages of rent due on such lands. That the said person or persons to whom such certificates shall be given, shall, within three months from the date thereof, pay into the treasury of this state the sums in such certificates respectfully specified; and the treasurer is hereby required and authorized to receive the same, and to give to the said person or persons paying, duplicate receipts for the monies by them respectively paid; and the several persons to whom such receipts shall be given shall, upon their respectively producing and lodging with the said commissioners one of the said receipts, be entitled to deeds and conveyances for the lands by them respectively purchased.

**Commissioners to sue purchasers for non-performance of contracts.**

**XXI.** And be it further enacted by the authority aforesaid, That the Commissioners for the respective districts, shall and may, in their own names, commence and prosecute any suit upon a contract for the sale of any estate against any person or persons who shall have subscribed such note or memorandum in writing thereof as aforesaid; and all damages which shall be recovered by the said commissioners in such suits, shall be by them paid into the treasury of the state.

**All purchases in which commissioners shall be interested declared void. Each commissioner to take oath before entering on his office.**

**XXII.** And be it further enacted by the authority aforesaid, That all purchases made at such vendues by the said commissioners, or any or either of them, or by any other person, to or for the use of them, or any or either of them, shall be null and void; and that each commissioner, before he enters upon the execution of his office, shall appear before one of the judges of any of the counties within the district for which such commissioner shall be appointed, and take and subscribe the following oath, which such judge is hereby authorized and required to administer, viz:

Form of the oath.

I, *A. B.*, appointed a commissioner of forfeiture, for the district, do solemnly and sincerely swear and declare in the presence of Almighty God, that I will faithfully and honestly execute the said office in such manner as I shall conceive most for the benefit and advantage of the people of this state, according to the true intent and meaning of an act entitled "*An act for the forfeiture and sale of the estates of persons who have adhered to the enemies of this state, and for declaring the sovereignty of the people of this state, in respect to all property within the same.*"

No lands to be sold while in the power of the enemy.

**XXIII**. *And be it further enacted by the authority aforesaid*, and it is hereby provided, That the said commissioners shall not be authorized to sell any lands which, at the time of the sale thereof, shall be within the power of the enemy, any thing herein before mentioned notwithstanding.

The Treasurer, in his account of sales, to specify the Persons to whom the Estates respectively belonged, that debts due by them may be collected.

**XIV**. *And be it further enacted by the authority aforesaid*, That the treasurer of this state shall, in his accounts of the moneys arising by sales of forfeited estates, specify the names of the several persons to whom the several estates immediately before the forfeiture thereof were deemed to belong, as the same shall appear from the certificate of the commissioners; To the end, That when the lesislature shall, by future act or acts, to be passed for the purpose, provide for the payment of the debts due from the said persons respectively the amount of the moneys arising from the sales of their respective estates may with the greater ease be ascertained.

Forms of the several proceedings and conveyances under this law.

**XXV**. *And be it further enacted by the authority aforesaid*, That the forms of the several proceedings to be had in pursuance of this act, and of the deeds or conveyances, to be executed by the commissioners to be appointed in pursuance of this act, shall be as follows, that is to say:

(*The following forms are here omitted,—to wit:*)
"Form of the Notices by the Sheriff."
"The Form of a Record where Judgment shall be entered by Default."
"Form of a Record where a Trial shall be had."
"Form of a General Verdict."
"Form of the Conveyances from the Commissioners."

Forms of proceedings not herein particularly described to be similar to those in cases of Felony without benefit of Clergy.

On Traverse by Representatives of a dead person, the Proceedings to be the same as if he was living.

And that all the forms of Proceedings in Prosecutions for the offence aforesaid, to be had in pursuance of this Act, other than such as are hereby otherwise specially directed, shall be, as nearly as may be, similar to the forms of the Proceedings in cases of Felony without benefit of Clergy, except that the word, or words, "Offence," *or* "Offences," (as the case may be) shall be used instead of the word, or words, "Felony," or "Felonies," and that when a Traverse shall be put in by any person or persons claiming any Estate or Interest, under a person deceased as aforesaid, all and singular the Proceedings and Proceses, shall, notwithstanding, be of the same form as if the respective persons charged in the several Indictments had been severally in full life, and had in their own respective proper Persons, appeared and traversed; and for the want of such Traverse, as if such Person had made default in full Life.

Representatives on affidavit of interest to be permitted to traverse.

After traverse any other person applying on affidavit, may be admitted to join in the defence.

**XXVI**. *And be it further enacted by the authority aforesaid*, That each and every person, or persons, claiming an Estate or Interest, under any person deceased, shall, and may, upon affidavits of such claim, and of the death of the person under whom such claim shall be made, to be read and filed in court, be admitted to traverse the indictments against the persons under whom they so respectively claim. That in every case of such traverse as last aforesaid, no trial shall be had thereon until after the expiration of the time herein before limited for putting in such traverse. That where two or more persons shall appear at one and the same time, and produce such affidavit, and thereupon apply to be admitted to traverse, the court may compel such persons to join in the traverse; and that where any person or persons, so claiming as aforesaid, shall have been admitted to traverse, and shall have traversed accordingly, and any other person or persons shall afterwards apply to be admitted to traverse, the person or persons so afterwards applying having respectively produced such affidavit of a claim as aforesaid, shall, upon the trial of such traverse, be permitted to employ counsel, produce witnesses, sue forth subpœnas, for the attendance of witnesses, cross-examine the witnesses on the part of the state, and do every other act and thing, in and about a defence, in like manner, and as fully as the person or persons by whom the traverse shall have been put in.

# BIBLIOGRAPHY

# BIBLIOGRAPHY

## BOOKS

- Anderson, G.B., Our County and its People, The Saratogian, The Boston History Company, Publishers, 1899
- Archdeacon, Thomas, *New York City, 1664-1710, Conquest and Change*, (Tthaca, NY: Cornell
- Berlin, Ira, Many Thousands Gone, (Boston: The Belknap Press of Harvard University Press, 1998)
- Beyer, Richard, *"Slavery in Colonial New York." Journal of American History, (1929)*
- Blackburn, Robin, *The Overthrow of Colonial Slavery*, Verso( New Left Books, 1998)
- Bloch, Herman D., *The Circle of Discrimination: An Economic and Social Study of the Black Man* Documents Relative to the Colonial History of the State of New York. 15 vols. Albany: Weed, Parsons & Co., 1853-1887
- Brown, William H., History of Warren County, New York: 1963
- Edward S. Abdy, "Journal of a Residence and Tour in the United States", Vol. 2, (London, 1835)
- Ewing and Mike Wallace, *Gotham: A history of New York City to 1898*, (Oxford Press), 1999
- Fitch, Dr. Asa, A Historical, Topographical & Agricultural Survey of the County of Washington, New-York State Agricultural Society, 1849
- Flick, Alexander Clarence, Loyalism in New York during the American Revolution (1901) Columbia University Press

- Flick, Alexander Clarence, Loyalism in New York During the American Revolution. Studies in History, Economics, and Public Law vol. 14 no. 1. Edited by the Faculty of Political Science of Columbia University. New York: The Columbia University Press, 1901
- Freeman, Rhoda Golden, *The Free Negro in New York City in the Era before the Civil War* (New York:
- GA: University of Georgia Press, 1991)
- Greene, Evarts B., and Harrington, Virginia D., *American Population Before the Federal Census of 1790. New York: Columbia University Press, 1932; reprint ed., Gloucester, Mass.: Peter Smith, 1966*
- Greenwood, Bea, comp, *Reflections and Recollections of the Town with a Past: Warrensburg* (2002)
- Gronowicz, Anthony, *Race and Class Politics in New York City Before the Civil War* (Boston: Northeastern Garland Publishing, 1994)
- Gutman, Herbert G., *The Black Family in Slavery and Freedom, 1750-1925. New York: Pantheon Books, 1976*
- Hammersley, Sydney Ernest, The History of Waterford, New York, 1957
- Hammond, Jabez D., *History of Political Parties in the State of New York* (Buffalo: Phinney and Company, 1850), vol. 1
- Harris, Leslie M., In the Shadow of Slavery: African Americans in New York City, 1626-1863, (Chicago: University of Chicago Press, 2003)
- Haskell, David C. and Edythe L. *A History of Stony Creek, New York,* 2 vols (1991-96)
- Higginbotham, A. Leon, Jr., *In the Matter o f Color Race and The American Legal Process: The Colonial Period. New York: Oxford University Press, 1978*
- Hoffer, Peter Charles, *Law and People in Colonial America,* (Baltimore, MD: The John Hopkins University Press, 1998)
- Holden, A. W., *A History of the Town of Queensbury, in the State of New York with Biographical in New York* (New York: New York University Press, 1969)
- Johnson, Crisfield, "History of Washington County, New York, Everts & Ensign, Philadelphia, pub. [from old catalog] Philadelphia, Everts & Ensign, 1878
- Journals of the Assembly of the State of New York. Sessions 8, (1785, 1797-1829), New York State Library
- Journals of the Senate of the State of New York. Sessions 8, (1785, 1797-1815), New York State Library

- Lincoln, Charles; Johnson, William; and Northrup, A. Judd, eds. The Colonial Laws of New York from the Year 1664 to the Revolution, 5 vols, Albany: James B. Lyon State Printer, 1896
- *Many of its Distinguished Men, and Some Account of the Aborigines of Northern New York,* Joel Munsell, Albany, NY, 1874.
- Metcalfe, Ann Breen, *The Schroon River: A History of an Adirondack Valley and Its People* (2000)
- McManus, Edgar J., Black Bondage in the North, Syracuse University Press, 1973
- Meyers, Carol M., ed. Early New York State Census Records, 1663-1772, 2d ed. Gardenia, Calif.: RAM Publishers, 1965
- Northup, Solomon, *"Twelve years a slave. Narrative of Solomon Northup, a citizen of New-York, 1853"*,
- O'Callaghan, Edmund, ed. *The Documentary History of New York State. 4 vols. Albany: Weed, Parsons & Co., 1849-1851.* Low, Son & Company, 47 Ludgate Hill., 1853)
- Pearson, Jonathan, Contributions for the Genealogies of the Descendants of the First Settlers of the Patent and City of Schenectady, from 1662 to 1800 (Albany, NY: J. Munsell, 1873
- Phillips, Ulrich B., *American Negro Slavery, (New York,* 1918)
- Quarles, Benjamin, Black Mosaic: Essays in Afro-American History and Historiography, 1988
- Smith, H. P., Edited, *History of Warren County, with illustrations and Biographical Sketches of Some of its Prominent Man and Pioneers..* D. Mason & Co., Syracuse, NY. 1885
- Stewart, L. Lloyd, A Far Cry From Freedom: Gradual Abolition (1799-1827), AuthorHouse, 2006
- Stone, William, Washington County, New York, Its History to the Close of the 19th Century, 1904
- Sylvester, Nathaniel Bartlett, History of the Villages and Towns of Saratoga County, New York, 1878
- Sylvester, Nathaniel Bartlett, History of Saratoga County, New York, 1878
- The Documentary History of New York State. 4 vols. Albany: Weed, Parsons & Co., 1849-1851
- The Encyclopedia of New York State, editor in Chief: Peter Eisenstadt, Managing Editor: Laura-Eve Moss, 2005, Syracuse University Press
- Thomas, Hugh, *The Slave Trade,* (NYC: Touchstone, 1997)
- Thomas, Lester S., Timber, Tannery and Tourists: Lake Luzerne, Warren County, New York, 1979
- Truth, Sojourner, *Narrative of Sojourner Truth,* 1850, Boston

- Whipple, Janice M., *Stony Creek: Then and Now* (1980)
- White, Shane, *Somewhat More Independent: The End of Slavery in New York City, 1770-1810* (Athens, GA: University of Geogia press, 1991)
- Williams-Myers, A. J., *Long Hammering*, (Trenton, NJ: Black World Press, 1994)
- Yoshpe, Harry Beller, The Disposition of Loyalist Estates in the Southern District of the State of New York, Columbia University Press, 1939
- Young, Alfred E. *The Democratic Republicans of New York: The Origins, 1763-1797* (Chapel Hill, University of North Carolina Press, 1967)
- Zilversmit, Arthur, *The First Emancipation: The Abolition of Slavery in the North*, (Chicago: The University of Chicago Press, 1967)

## ARTICLES

- Adolph Phillipse, Manor of Philipsburgh. Inventory and Administration of Estate, 1749-1763, New York State Archives
- Adolph Phillipse's Probate Inventory, 2 February 1750, New York Public Library, American History, The Collection—Newly Discovered Documents
- Anderson, G.B., Our County and its People, The Saratogian, The Boston History Company Publishers, 1899
- Bevier, Ann, Account Book, 1802-1812, *Philip Dubois Bevier Family Papers (1685-1910)*
- Bloch, Julius; Hershkowitz, Leo; and Scott, Kenneth. "Wills of Colonial New York, 1736-1775." *National Genealogical Society Quarterly* 54 (June 1966)
- Board of Education. *"The Black Man on Staten Island." The Black Man in American History. Staten Island Institute of Arts and Sciences*
- Bruns, Roger A., *A More Perfect Union: The Creation of the United States Constitution*, published for the Collection, Huguenot Historical Society of New Paltz, NY, Inc.
- Corbett, Theodore, Saratoga County Blacks, 1720-1870, *The GRIST MILL*, Quarterly Journal of the Saratoga County Historical Society, vol. XX, no. 3, 1986
- Cormier, William, *Salem's Forgotten African Americans*, The Journal of the Washington County Historical Documents
- Dodge, Roberta, Van Vranken Van Frank Genealogy, 2005, (via FamilySearch.com)

- *"Dutch Systems in Family Naming."* National Genealogical Society Special Publication no. 12 (May 1954)
- "Early New York Inventories of Estates." National Genealogical Society Quarterly (June 1965): New York State Archives
- Frederickson, George M. *"The Gutman Report: The Black Family in Slavery and Freedom: 1750-1925."* New York Review of Books, 23, no. 15 (September 30, 1976)
- GLC08893, Population of the State of New York, ca. 1800, *The "Three-Fifths Clause"*, Archive of The Past Gilder Lehrman Institute of American History
- Gilder Lehrman, *The Origins and Nature of New World Slavery*, Abolition
- Goodfriend, Joyce D. *"Burghers and Blacks: The Evolution of a Slave Society at New Amsterdam."* New York History, 59, no.2 (April 1978)
- Hebron (Washington County) Town Record Book, 1784-1845, Office of Town Clerk, 11/28/75, New York State Archives
- History of Washington County, New York; Some Chapters in the History of *the Town of Easton, N.Y.*, Washington County Historical Society, 1959 National Archives Trust Fund Board.
- Jones, Katherine Butler, "They called it Timbucto", *Orion Magazine*, Winter 1998
- Journal of the Assembly of New York State, 1785
- Journal of the Senate of the State of New York, 1811
- Kennedy, Ellen, "History of the Town of Half Moon," www. townofhalfmoon.org/history
- Kruger, Vivienne, *Slavery In New York*, "BORN TO RUN: The Slave Family in Early New York, 1626 to 1827", Butler Library, Columbia University, New York, New York, USA http://www.columbia.edu/, 2007
- McCarl, Dr. Henry, Beyond Face Value, Economic Environment, *(www.cuc.lsu.edu/economics)*
- New York Gazette and Weekly Post Boy, March 26, 1749 and July 20, 1747
- *New York Spectator*, April 19, 1815
- New York State Secretary of State, Article II, Second Constitution of the State of New York, 1821
- *New York Journal and Patriotic Register*, March 16, 1799
- Northrup, Judd, Slavery In New York, State Library Bulletin—History No. 4, Albany, University of the State of New York, 1900

- Perry, Kenneth, Compiled and Edited, "Some Notes Towards History and Genealogy of the African American Population of Washington County, New York," February 2005
- Ratner, Vivienne L. "The Hastings Men." *The Westchester Historian.* (Summer 1972)
- "Records of the First United Presbyterian Congregation in the Village of Cambridge, Washington County, N.Y" Transcribed by: The New York Genealogical and Biographical Society; Edited by: Royden Woodward Vosburgh, New York City, March 1917
- Report of the Sales by Commissioner of Forfeiture for the Eastern District of New York; Alexander Webster Commissioner, Oct. 1784, New York State Archives
- Revolutionary War Cemetery: Visitors' Catalog, Sally Van Vranken and Mary Matilda buried: Section 9 Row 2; Katherine and Samuel Burk buried: Section 9 Row 4
- Roth, Eric J., The Society of Negroes Unsettled: The History of Slavery in New Paltz, NY, May 2001, Huguenot Historical Society Library and Archives, www.hhsnewpaltz.net/library_archives/topics of *nterest/slavery.htm*
- Scherer, John L., Community News: *'A BIT OF HISTORY:* Slavery in Halfmoon, March, 1999
- Scherer, John, L, Community News: *'A BIT OF HISTORY:* "Several Local Families Once Thrived Using Slave Labor,"
- Swain, Charles B., "Black's roots in Albany: Old as Fort Orange", Viewpoint, Times Union Newspaper,
- Feb. 19, 1983
- *The Dutch Imprint,* Cross Roads & Cross Rivers: Africans at Phillipsburg Manor, Upper Mills, (*www.hudsonvalley.org*)
- "The Negro Vote in Old New York." *Political Science Quarterly 32 (1917)*
- —Thornton, Dave, Up from . . . Slavery in the Cambridge Valley, Historical Perspectives, Cambridge, NY,
- 2002
- Town of Salem Minutes 1790-1826, Washington County Clerk's Office, 1992, Washington County Archives
- Unpublished MSS Evergreen Cemetery Property Map, Evergreen Cemetery Record Book
- Washington County Town Clerks' Records of Births, Deaths, and s. 1X47 1849," Keel 289
- Wells, Robert V. "The New York Census of 1731." *New-York Historical Society Quarterly 57 (July 1973)*

- Yoshpe, Harry. "Record of Slave Manumissions in Albany, 1800-28." Journal of Negro History, 26, no.4 (October 1941)

## NEW YORK STATE LAWS

CHAPTER 32, LAWS OF THE STATE OF NEW YORK: "An Act for Raising Two Regiments for the defense of this state on bounties of inappropriate lands," March 20, 1781, 4th Session

CHAPTER 64 of the Laws of New York State of 1784, "An Act for the speedy sale of the confiscated and forfeited estates within this state and for other purposes therein mentioned," May 12, 1784

CHAPTER 58 OF THE LAWS OF 1786; "An Act further to amend an act entitled, "An Act for the speedy sale of the confiscated and forfeited estates within this state,' May 1, 1786, 9th Session

CHAPTER. 45 of the Laws of 1816: "An Act concerning the maintenance of certain persons, formerly slaves," March 22, 1816, 39th Session,

CHAPTER XXIV OF THE LAWS OF THE STATE OF NEW YORK, PASSED IN THE THIRD SESSION OF THE LEGISLATURE, HELD AT KINGSTON, IN ULSTER COUNTY; *An Act for the Forfeiture and Sale of the Estates of Persons who have adhered to the Enemies of this State, and for declaring the Sovereignty of the People of this State, in respect to all Property within the same.—Passed 22d October, 1779.*

CHAPTER 62 of the Laws of 1799 of New York State, Gradual Abolition Act

CHAPTER 40 of the Laws of the State of New York of 1804

CHAPTER188 of the Laws of 1817 of New York State

## UNITED STATES FEDERAL CENSUS RECORDS

- U.S. Census Office. *"Aggregate Amount of Each Description of Persons Within the U.S.A., 1810."* Washington, D.C.: n.p., 1811. Document Center, Lehman Library, Columbia University, reel F-a68, U.S. Census of Population, 1800-1830
- U.S. Census Office. *"Second Census of the U.S., 1800—Schedule of the Whole Number of Persons in the District of New York." Return of the Whole Number of Persons Within the Several Districts of the U.S. Washington, D.C.: Printed by order of the House of Representatives, 1801.*
- 1790 Bureau of Census Black Heads of Families, Century of Population Growth

- U.S. Bureau of the Census. *Negro Population in the United States,1790-1915. n.p., 1918; reprint ed., New York: Arno Press, 1968*
- U.S. Bureau of the Census *Population Schedules of the First Census of the United States, 1790. Washington, D.C.: 1965*. New York Public Library
- U.S. Bureau of the Census *Population Schedules of the Second Census of the United States, 1800. Washington, D.C.: 1959*. New York Public Library
- U.S. Bureau of the Census *Population Schedules of the Third Census of the United States, 1810. Washington, D.C.: 1958*. New York Public Library.
- 1810 U.S. Federal Census: "A Statement of the ARTS AND MANUFACTURES OF the United States of America for the year 1810: Digested and Prepared by: Tench Coxe, Esquire, of Philadelphia, Philadelphia, Printed by A Cornman, June, 1814, Bureau of the Census Library
- 1810 U.S. Federal Census: "A Series of Tables of the Several Branches of AMERICAN MANUFACTURES, Exhibiting Them in every County of the Union, So Far As THEY ARE RETURNED IN THE REPORTS OF THE MARSHALLS, AND OF THE SECRETARIES OF THE TERRITORIES AND OF THEIR RESPECTIVE ASSISTANTS, IN THE AUTUMN OF THE YEAR 1810: Together with Returns of certain doubtful Goods, Productions of the Soil and Agricultural Stock, so far as they have been received. Bureau of the Census Library
- 1790 U.S. Federal Census, *Population Tables*
- U.S. Bureau of the Census *"A List of the Number of Inhabitants, Both Whites and Blacks of Each Species, Within the Province of New York, 1737."*
- U.S. Bureau of the Census *"An Account of the Number of Inhabitants of the Province of New York, Taken 4 June 1746*
- U.S. Bureau of the Census *""An Account of the Number of Inhabitants in the Province of New York, Taken 10 May 1749."*
- U.S. Bureau of the Census *"General List of Inhabitants in the Province of New York, Extracted from the returns of the Sheriffs in the Several Counties, 16 February 1756*
- U.S. Bureau of the Census *"Population of the Colony of New York, By Counties: 1698.*
- U.S. Bureau of the Census *"Male and Female Population of the Colony of New York, in Certain Age Groups, By Counties, 1703*
- U.S. Bureau of the Census *"White and Slave Population of New York, in Certain Age Groups, By Sex, According to the Partial Census of 1712*

- U.S. Bureau of the Census *"White and Negro Population of the Province of New York, Distinguished as Children and Adults, By Sex: 1723*
- U.S. Bureau of the Census *"An Account of the Number of Inhabitants of the Province of New York, Taken 4 June 1746*
- U.S. Bureau of the Census *"An Account of the Number of Inhabitants in the Province of New York, Taken 10 May1749*
- U.S. Bureau of the Census *"List of Inhabitants in the Several Counties in the Province of New York, Taken in the Year 1771*
- U.S. Bureau of the Census *"White and Slave Population, and Indians Taxed in New York, in Certain Age Groups, B Sex: 1786*

# NEW YORK STATE OFFICE OF THE COMPTROLLER

- Office of the State Comptroller, Albany, Day Book No. 2, August 13, 1801 to January 8, 1803, New York State Archives
- Office of the State Comptroller, Albany. Ledger A, 1797-1806. Accountant Ledger, 1797-1837. Accession Number 233, New York State Archives
- Office of the State Comptroller, Albany, Day Book No. 3, January 11, 1803 to November 9, 1803, New York State Archives
- Office of the State Comptroller, Albany, Day Book No. 4, November 10, 1803 to January 9, 1805, 231. All three Day Books are catalogued as Manuscript No. 310, New York State Archives, Albany, N.Y.
- New York State Comptroller's Office Revolutionary War Accounts and Claims, Overview of the Records New York (State). Comptroller's Office Revolutionary War accounts and claims,1775-1808, New York State Archives
- New York State Comptroller's Reports, January 25, 1798-January 14, 1829, Journals of the Assembly of New York State. Sessions 21-52, 1798 to 1829,. New York State Archives

# INDEX

## A

abandoned children, 89

Abandonment Program, 88–89

Abdy, Edward S., 168, 175, 299
  *Journal of a Residence and Tour in the United States*, 168

abolition, 7, 16, 21, 25–26, 47, 56, 68, 72, 86–93, 103–4, 107, 146, 160, 162–66, 171–72, 174–75, 181–83, 198, 204, 206–7, 211–12, 219, 301–3, 305

abolitionists, 26, 86, 171

Act of Attainder, 77, 80

Act of Forfeiture, 111, 184

"An Act relative to slaves and servants," 160

Addersey Lodge, Northamptonshire, 84

African American, 5, 13–14, 16, 24, 45, 47, 157, 164–65, 174, 179–81, 208, 219, 250, 252–54, 300, 302

African-American historical research, 194

african descendant landowners, 148, 150

African descendants, 9, 44, 48–49, 56–58, 60–62, 66, 68–71, 75, 81, 93, 99, 125–26, 129, 144, 146–48, 160–70, 179–80, 182–83, 186–87, 193, 201, 207, 213, 253

African Grounds, 10, 19, 44, 229, 254, 256–59, 261–65, 268, 277

African origin, 15, 253

agricultural production, 24, 61, 109, 182

agricultural production and home-manufacturing, 109

agriculture, 14, 47, 110–11, 155, 184, 201, 227

Albany, New York, 198, 236–37, 239, 245–46

*Albany Argus*, 86

Albany County, 32–33, 65, 77, 111, 184, 198–99, 205, 212, 222, 236, 283

Albany Dutch, 198

Alexandria, 126

America, 16, 21, 24, 43, 61, 70, 72, 84–85, 100, 107, 139–40, 155, 170, 174, 179, 187, 192, 196–97, 201, 203, 207, 218, 220, 228, 252, 282, 286, 288, 300

American Citizen, 84, 140, 164

American forces, 69–70

American historians, 22

American Independence, 160

American Revolution, 33, 70, 95, 101, 103, 299–300

Americans, 13–14, 21, 33, 41, 45, 69, 75, 84, 118, 140, 157, 174–75, 219, 250, 299–300, 302

American seamen, 139–40
Amy, 92
Argyle, New york, 40, 195–96, 213, 222–26, 244, 246, 250, 275
aristocracy, 164
Armstrong, Thomas (major), 44, 101
army occupation, 69
Arqyle, 40
Ashley, McGeorge, 91
attainded, 77
auditors, 74, 83
August 1st, 160

**B**

Barnes, John (captain), and his Rangers, 44
Barnstable County, 60
Barrack Master General's Department, 70
Bayard, Robert, 76, 283
Becker, Jack, 92
Becker, Peter, 92
Bennington County, 60
Bergen County, New Jersey, 60
Bevier, Ann, 162, 174
Bill to Prevent Frauds at Elections, and For Other Purposes, 166
birth record, 194
Black Box, 16
black hole, 15
Bloch, Herman, 165
  Circle of Discrimination, The, 165
Boston, Samuel, 44, 261
Brazil, 140
Britain, 14, 138–39, 141, 186, 282, 288, 290
British, 13, 40, 61, 69–71, 73–75, 95, 101, 111, 138–41, 160, 184–85
British forces in America, 70
British lines, 70, 75

British loyalists, 61, 111, 184
British sympathizers, 75
British troops, 80
British withdrawal, 80
Bucktail Republicans, 167–68
Burgoyne (general), 41
burial grounds, 252–53, 277
Burlington, Vermont, 110
Burns, Roger A., 172

**C**

Cambridge, New York, 15, 32–33, 40, 93–98, 104, 110, 117, 119, 211, 219, 225, 229–33, 239, 244–45, 257, 304
Camden Valley, 40
Cameroon, 15, 228
Canada, 32, 61, 109, 139, 163
canal system, 110
Canastagione, 200
capitalism, 13
capitalist business, 13
capitalist farming, 47
carding, 120–22, 125
Catskill, New York, 110
cemeteries, 8, 252–54, 257, 271–72
census collection error, 68
census data, 60, 68, 163, 182
census of 1825, *15, 147, 187, 212*
census of 1855, *182*
census records, 60, 64, 92, 149, 182, 194, 198, 206, 211, 213, 223, 233–34, 272, 301, 305
census reports, 47, 57, 182, 195, 212–13
certificates of debt, 74
Champlain Canal, 109–10
Champlain Valley, 109
Charlotte (queen), 32–33
Charlotte County, New York, 24, 32–33, 60, 111, 184, 283
cheap labor, 61, 183, 185

*Circle of Discrimination, The* (Bloch), 165, 175, 299

citizenship
second-class, 13, 23, 157, 180
second- or third-class, 163
true, 23

City of Albany, 198, 207

civil rights, 13, 77, 168

Civil War, 14, 164, 170–72, 174, 194, 235, 250, 300

Clark, Thomas (doctor), 271

Clarke, R. (assymblyman), 169

cleaning, 120–21, 123–24

Clifton Park, New York, 198–200, 206, 219

Clinton, Sir Henry, 70, 101, 283

Clinton County, 32, 45, 65, 70, 101, 239, 283

Close, Solemon, 69, 100

cloth, home-manufacturing of, 185

Cole, Harry, 213–14

collateral damage, 139

colonial armies, 69

colonial era, 13

colonialists, 71–72

colonials, 69, 71, 75, 84, 95, 167, 218, 302

Columbia County, 124

Commissary General's Provision Department, 70

Commissioners of Forfeiture, 77, 81, 83, 103, 111, 295, 304

commissioners of forfeitures, 72, 74–77, 79–80, 290

Commissioners of Sequestration, 73–75, 78

Commissioners of Specie, 74

confiscated estates, speedy sale of the, 74

Confiscation Laws, 6, 74, 83

congressional bills of credit, 74

Congress of the United States, 73, 77, 83

Constitutional Convention, 75, 163, 165, 172

Constitutional Convention of 1821, *163*

Continental Army, 69, 73

Continental Congress, 74

cotton, 118, 123–25, 141, 171, 183, 185, 195, 223
cleaned and de-seeded, 123

cotton gin, 123

Council of Revision of the New York State, 166–67

county archivists, 181

County of Washington, New York, 32–33, 41, 43, 91–92, 98, 254, 299

crops, 109, 141, 186

Cuff, 91, 261

Cumberland county, 32, 60, 65, 77

Cutshall-King, Joseph A., 20, 43

**D**

Dean, John, 92

Deane, 204–5

death notices, 229, 272

De Lancey, James, 78, 283

DeLancey, Oliver, 71, 85, 282

Democratic Republican, 164

depression, 6, 138–39, 141–42, 144, 146–47, 165, 185–87, 253

Depression of 1807–1814, *138, 146, 185, 187*

DeRidder, Simon, 92

DeRidder, Walter, 92

discrimination, 15–16, 22, 24, 86, 144, 162, 165, 168, 170, 175, 179–80, 197, 299
politics of, 164

disenfranchisement, 7, 16, 165, 167, 169–70

disrupted enslavement system, 71

diversified manufacturing, 171

DNA, 15, 228
Dresden, New York, 40
Dukes County, 60
Dunlap, John, 96
Dutch, 40–41, 47, 80–81, 92, 95, 103, 198, 200, 202, 304
Dutchess County, 57, 65, 69, 73, 77, 283
Dutch farmers, 47
Dutch patroons, 80
Dutch privateers, 80
Dutch traders, 198
Dutch West India Company, 81, 202

E

Eastern District, 83, 103, 111, 304
Easton, New York, 32–33, 40, 92, 95, 104, 147, 303
economic boom, 6, 107, 111, 125, 138, 146, 148, 182–84
economic boom of 1810, *107*
economic depression, 138, 141
economic deprivation, 14
economic independence, 187
economic opportunity, 26
economic recovery, 140, 186
economic viability and sustainability, 22
economy, 13–14, 19, 21–22, 24, 47, 56, 72, 107, 109–10, 138–41, 144, 147, 170, 183–87, 201
  scales of, 24
emancipation, 7, 14, 16, 44, 56–57, 75, 86, 93, 160–62, 165, 170–71, 193, 219, 302
Emancipation Day, 160
Emancipation Proclamation, 171
embargo, 139–40
Embargo Act of 1807, *139*
Embargo of 1804, *165*
Empire State Building, 21

employment, 13, 64, 108, 142, 144, 162, 164–65, 171, 181, 183, 186
employment opportunities, 64, 142, 144, 186
*Encyclopedia of New York State, The*, 100, 126, 157, 301
England, 26, 32–33, 40–41, 43, 60–62, 84–85, 139–41, 182, 185, 224, 287
English immigrants, 40
enlistment, 6, 69, 71, 75, 250
enlistment of men of African descent, 69
Enslaved Labor Force, 7, 200
enslaved population, 24–26, 56–57, 70, 146, 163, 197–98, 204, 206–7
enslavement, 7, 15–16, 21–27, 47–48, 60–61, 64, 68–69, 71–72, 80, 86, 90, 93, 96–97, 99, 144, 146–48, 154, 160, 162–65, 168, 170–72, 179–81, 183, 186, 193–97, 200, 202–3, 206–7, 219, 228, 231, 233, 250
  brutality of, 23, 61
  status of, 202
enslavers, 25–26, 69–72, 75, 86–93, 146, 163, 171, 182, 194–95, 197, 200–204, 229
Epps, Bella (Bama) Davis, 236, 238, 245
Epps, Charles Albert, 236–37, 245
Epps, Ida Mae, 236–37, 245
Epps Family, 233–34, 237
equality, 23, 86, 160, 168, 197
Erie Canal, 21, 109, 141, 185
escape, 61, 71
Essex County, 32, 60
Europe, 138–39, 147, 163, 171, 185
European immigrants, 144, 186
Europeans, 202
Evergreen Cemetery, 10, 19, 44, 214, 229, 254–57, 261–62, 264–65, 267, 271, 277, 304
exodus, 25

# F

family life development, 51
family members, reunion of, 64
farm commodities, 47
farm creation, 109
farmers, 41, 47, 61, 77–81, 98, 109, 111, 117, 119–20, 123, 141, 148, 184, 186, 198, 224
farming, 24, 41, 47, 64, 144, 186, 196
farms, 23, 33, 51, 78–79, 95, 109, 126, 154, 171, 183, 195–96, 200–202, 204, 207, 212, 223, 228, 233, 291
Federal Census, 24, 100, 107, 183, 196, 202, 211–12, 223–24, 227, 300, 306
Federal Census of 1800, *24*
Federal Census of 1810, 100, *107*
Federalists, 86–87, 140, 164, 166–68, 171
fiber, 117–18, 123, 157
final abolition, 16, 160, 164–65
finishing, 120, 122, 124
First Presbyterian Church, 99
First United Presbyterian Congregation, 211, 219, 225, 304
Fisher, Donald, 85
Fitch, Asa (doctor), 44, 119, 157, 261
  *Survey of Washington County*, 119, 157
flannel, 41, 110, 149
flax, 110, 117–18, 125, 141, 157, 185–86
flaxen, 114, 184
flaxen goods, 114
fledgling factories, 23
fleece, 119–21, 141
Flora, 92
Forage Department, 70
forfeiture legislation, 111, 184
Fort Ann, 40, 43
Fort Anne, 40
Fort Edward, New York, 40, 109–10

Fort Nicholson, 40
Fort Saratoga, 40
Fort's Ferry, 199, 204
Fort Ticonderoga, 43
foster care system, 16
France, 138–39
free citizens, 166
free citizens of African descent, 16, 24–26, 56
free colored, 24–25, 195, 214
free communities of African descent, 126, 186, 252
freedmen, 14, 71, 86, 165
freedom, 14, 16, 24, 26–27, 65, 69–71, 76, 93, 104, 144, 161–62, 166, 174, 179–81, 197, 235, 292–93, 300–301, 303
"freedom, justice, and equality" for all men, 197
freedom, proof of, 166
freedom initiatives, 56, 183
freedom policies, 69
Freedom Provisions, 6, 75
free labor, 171–72, 202
free land lottery, 25
freemanship laws, 163
free men and women, 23, 111
free people, 69, 169
freeperson of African descent, 180, 194
French, 17, 40, 139–40, 163, 228
French and Indian War, 40
French Canada, 163
Fugitive Slave Law, 61
full citizenship, 23, 170
  privileges of, 170
fulled-cloth, 41, 110, 125, 185
fulling mills, 114, 124–25, 184
fulling process, 124

## G

Garvey, James, 91

Genealogy, 8, 193, 218–20, 222, 301–2, 304

generations, 12, 15, 104, 154, 180, 187, 193, 238, 252

geopolitical conditions, 56, 107

George III (king), 32

German Moravians, 40

Germany, 163

Gloucester, 65, 300

grading, 120

gradual abolition, 16, 25–26, 47, 56, 86–93, 103–4, 107, 146, 160, 163, 166, 181–83, 198, 204, 206–7, 211–12, 301, 305

Gradual Abolition Act, 25–26, 47, 56, 86, 88–90, 92–93, 146, 160, 182, 204, 206–7, 211–12, 305

Gradual Abolition Law, 26, 47, 89–91, 107, 160, 183, 198, 211

Gradual Abolition Law of 1799, 89–90, 160

gradual emancipation, 14

grandchildren, 15, 20, 192, 195, 224, 234, 240

Grandmother, 12, 15, 20, 234, 236, 238, 241

Granville, New York, 40, 110, 119, 126, 250

Gravesend, Long Island, 70

Great Britain, 14, 138–39, 141, 186, 282, 288, 290

Great Compromise, 172

Green Mountains, 32

Greenwich, New York, 32–33, 40, 104, 147, 225–26, 250, 275

Gronowicz, Anthony, 164, 174

## H

Halfmoon, 197–200, 206, 218–19, 304

Half Moon, 7, 9, 197–98, 200, 202–4, 206–8, 212, 218–19, 303

Half-Moon, 198–99

Half-Moon Point, 198

Ham, Henry, 94

Hammersley, Sydney Ernest, 250, 300

Hampton, New York, 40, 110

Hannah, 94, 211–12, 220, 223–25, 228, 244, 261, 275

Harlem Heights, 70

Hartford, New York, 40, 222

Hartwell Manor, 84

hatteries, 114, 125, 184

Haver (Peebles) Island, 198

Haynes, 60

Hazzards, 60, 196, 224–26, 246, 250, 275

Hebron, New York, 40, 93, 104, 110, 261, 303

historical memory, 15

historical mysteries, 22

historical societies, 22, 181

history of people of African descent, 16, 22, 27, 181, 197, 206, 211

Hoffnagle, Michael, 85

home-manufactured products, 149, 154

home-textile manufacturing, 24

hostile and violent homeland, 187

Hudson and Mohawk Valley farmers, 109

Hudson Falls, 40

Hudson Flatts, New York, 195

Hudson River, 21, 41, 109–10, 198, 236

Hudson Valley, 141, 186, 203

human bondage, 26

human dignity, 14

human enslavement, 16, 23–25, 48, 80, 97, 197

# I

immigrants, 40, 144, 162, 165, 171, 186, 196
immigration, 165
Indian Africans, 80
Indian Ocean, 80
industrial economy, 47
industrial revolution, 117, 171
industries
  agricultural and textile, 141, 186
  labor intensive, 114, 184
  timber-related, 110, 184
Ireland, 163, 227, 246, 271
Irish Republican, 164
Ithaca, New York, 110

# J

Jackson, 15, 32–33, 40, 94, 169, 195, 211, 222, 237, 245, 250
Jacksons, 60
Jefferson, Thomas (president), 138–40, 165, 185
Jessup, Edward and Ebenezer, 85
Jim Crow, 13, 16, 170
jobs, menial of, 144, 186
Johannesburg, 126
Johnson, Crisfield, 45, 93, 104, 109, 156, 219
Jones, David, 85
Jones, Jonatahn and Daniel, 85
Jones, Jonathan, 85
*Journal of a Residence and Tour in the United States* (Abdy), 168, 175, 299
*Journals of the New York State Assembly and Senate*, 76

# K

Kemp, John Tabor, 85
Kingsbury, 40, 110, 224, 226, 250
Kissam, Daniel, Sr., 76, 283
Kwanzaa, 15

# L

laborers, 13, 70, 114, 125, 148, 162, 164, 185, 201, 223, 227–28
Lake Champlain, 43, 84, 109–10
land ownership, 64, 147–48, 154, 213, 223
lands
  appropriated, 74
  availability of, 114, 185
  forfeited, 74, 77, 83, 85, 111, 125, 184, 220, 292
  speedy sale of the, 83
landscapes, non-traditional, 253
Lansingburgh, 110, 218, 224, 227, 231–34, 238–39, 244, 246, 257, 261
Lasing, Gerrit, 92
Latimer, 196, 230–31, 244
Lecky, 78
legal confiscation, 73
Lincoln, Abraham, 171–72, 235, 301
linen, 111, 117–18, 125, 149, 157, 183, 195, 223
Livingston (chancellor), 119
London, 84, 91–92, 175, 299
Long Island, 70
Lotte, 92
Louisiana Purchase, 142
Loyalist property
  confiscation of, 74
  forfeited, 73, 77, 83
Loyalists, 43, 61, 70–78, 83, 101, 103, 111, 184
Lydius, John Henry (colonel), 40

# M

MAAT, 192
Madagascar, 80
Maine, 24, 60
maintenance and support, 88–89, 182
Manhattan, 21, 47
man-made disasters, 56
Manor of Philipsburg, 80–81
manufacturing, 24, 47, 51, 64, 109–11, 115, 118, 120, 123, 125, 141, 144, 171, 182–86
manufacturing labor, 144, 186
manufacturing plants, 183
manumission, 26, 44, 47, 71, 75–76, 86, 89, 92–93, 98, 102, 107, 174, 182–83, 198, 206–7, 211
Manumission Provisions, 6, 47, 68, 86, 89, 107, 182–83, 198, 206–7, 211
manumit, 25, 89, 93, 98–99, 146, 182
manumitted, 44, 71, 75, 89, 92, 96, 99, 147, 163
Marbletown, 162
Mary Peterman, Anna, 233, 236, 245
Massachusetts, 24, 60
McAuley, William, 94, 97
McCleary, John (colonel), 44
McClellan, Frank, 95
McManus, Edgar J., 163
Mecca, 64
Mechanicville, 198
merchants, 13, 283
Merino sheep, 119–20
messengers, 70
Middle Atlantic States, 109, 140–41
Middle Passage, 15
Middlesex, 60
migrants, 40, 57, 60–61
migrant workers, 48, 144, 186
migrate, 25, 56, 212
migrates of African descendant, 60

migration, 5, 14, 21, 23–27, 29, 43, 46, 48, 51, 56–57, 60–61, 64–65, 73, 86, 99, 107, 111, 125, 146–48, 181–83, 187, 211
  significant, 51
migration pattern, 48
migratory, 14
military service, 41, 69, 138
Military Tract, 83
militia, 69, 71, 73–74, 83
mining, 56, 110
Mink, 204–5
Mohawk River, 198, 200
Mohawks, 40, 198–200
Mohawk Valley, 109, 199
Mohicans, 40
Montgomery County, 32–33, 65, 241
Montreal, 109
Morris, Roger, 78, 282–83
Motts, 60
mystorian, 22

# N

Nann, 204
Native Americans, 41, 80, 198, 271
negrophobia, 163
newborn children, 26
New England, 9, 26, 40–41, 60–62, 139–41, 182
New Englanders, 26, 32–33, 47, 60, 118
New England shipping interests, 139
New Hampshire, 24, 60
New Jersey, 60
New Netherland, 81, 202
New Paltz, 162, 174, 302, 304
New Perth, 40
New Spain, 80
New World, 47, 72, 84, 117, 175, 196, 252, 303
New World markets, 47

New World Order, 72

New York, upstate, 8–9, 14, 19, 21, 24–26, 47–48, 65, 90, 111, 126, 196–97, 199, 201, 206–7, 247

New York City, 21, 70, 80, 100–101, 109, 163–64, 166–68, 174, 219, 225, 277, 283, 299–300, 302, 304

New York Colony, 182

New York Constitutional Convention, 165

New York Genealogical and Biographical Society, 211, 219, 225, 304

New York Journal and Patriotic Register, 164, 175

New York Manumission of Slaves Statute of 1785, *44*

New York Provincial Convention, 73

New York Society for the Encouragement of Faithful Domestics, 165

New York State, 6, 9, 12, 14–16, 19–27, 32, 45, 47–48, 51, 56–58, 60, 62, 65–66, 68, 71, 73–79, 81, 83–84, 86–88, 90, 92–93, 99–104, 106–7, 111, 114, 119, 123–26, 138, 144, 146–48, 157–58, 160, 162, 164–68, 170, 172–75, 179–85, 187–88, 192–93, 195–98, 200, 206, 211–14, 219–20, 223, 227, 230, 235–36, 254, 271–72, 282, 299–305, 307

New York State Constitution of 1777, *73*

New York State Constitution of 1821, *168*, *170*

New York State Gradual Abolition Act, 211–12

New York State Gradual Abolition Act of 1799, *211*

New York State history, 23, 25, 144, 179, 213

New York State Legislature, 47, 74, 77, 83, 86, 160, 166

New York State Library and Archives, 181

*New York State's Crime Against Humanity*, 16

New York State's Gradual Abolition Act, 25–26, 47, 56, 86, 88–90, 92–93, 146, 160, 182, 204, 206–7, 211–12, 305

New York State's Gradual Abolition Law, 107, 183, 198

New York State sponsored compensated abolition program, 88

Niskayuna, 198–200, 204, 206

non-citizen status, 194

Norfolk County, 60

northern states, 13–14, 25, 47, 87, 163, 171–72, 174

Northern Turnpike Company, 110

Northrups, 60

Northup, Solomon, 170, 175, 301

   *Twelve Years a Slave*, 170

**O**

occupation, 69–71, 234

Office of Auditor-General, 73

Ohio, 120

Old Burying Ground, 44

Old Town of Cambridge, 93

oppression, 23, 72, 161

Orange, 60, 65, 69, 73, 77, 198, 218, 304

Orange County, 60, 65, 69, 73, 77, 198, 218, 304

origination, 27, 56, 194

origination points, 56

out-of-state African descendants, 60

Outreach Committee for the Cathedral of All Saints, 240

outsider, 163

Overseers of the Poor, 88–90, 92–93

ownership, 64, 69, 76, 78, 92, 154, 165, 213, 223

## P

Palmer, Abiather, 147
Panic of 1819, *165*
Pennsylvania, 60, 120, 241
Perry, Henry, 19, 95, 218–19, 304
Peterman, James, 232, 275
Philipsburgh, 70, 302
Philipse, Adolphus, 80
Philipse, Frederick, 76–77, 80–81, 283
plantations, 23, 183, 196, 201, 212
Plymouth, 60
poorhouses, 162, 222–26, 232–33, 244, 275
Poor Master, 91–92
population, 5, 17, 20, 24–26, 41, 43, 47–48, 51, 56–57, 60, 64–65, 68, 70, 100, 109, 114, 125–26, 141, 143–46, 148, 157, 161–65, 171–73, 175, 182, 186–87, 198, 202–4, 206–7, 218–19, 228, 240, 252, 300, 303–7
Port of New York, 21, 109
pot and pearl ashes, 109
potash, 109
poverty, 14, 157, 165
pre-emancipation, 16
private vessels, unregistered, 71
production
  capitalistic approach to, 144, 186
  capitalistic system of, 22
  labor intensive, 114, 183, 185
  mechanics of, 24
production and processing of products, 183
production mills, plants, 125
property, 14, 23, 41, 70–71, 73–75, 78, 80–81, 84, 86, 95, 97, 102, 111, 148, 156, 165, 168, 171, 179, 181, 184, 188, 195, 199–200, 203–4, 223, 254, 282, 288, 295, 304–5
  forfeiture of, 73

prosperity, 41, 107, 171, 183, 187
Proudfit, Ebinezer, 91
Provincial Congress, 73–74, 77, 83, 288
public accommodations, segregation in, 165
Purdy, Ebenezer, 71
Putnam, 40, 78
puzzle management, 56

## Q

Quack Boston, 44, 147
Quarles, Benjamin, 100, 171
Quarter Master General's Department, 70
Quebec City, 109
Queen Anne's War, 40
Queens County, 65, 80

## R

racial discrimination, 15, 24, 168, 197
  dehumanizing and sordid practices of, 24
racism, 144, 154, 167–68, 180
Rapalje, John, 76, 85, 283
real estate, 78, 80, 213, 224, 290
reapportionment, 47
reconstruction, 164
regiment, 69–70, 226
*Register Newspaper*, 119
relocation, 47–48, 57, 107, 146, 183, 211
Rensselaer County, 228, 232
Rensselaerwyck, 198
"Report of the Sales by Commissioner of Forfeiture for the Eastern District of New York, October 1784 to August 1788," *111*
repositories and archives, 56
republic, 13–14, 126

Republicans, 86–87, 103, 140, 164–69, 175, 302
Republic of South Africa, 126
Revolutionary War, 41, 44, 60–61, 65, 69, 73, 77, 95, 100–101, 103, 163, 220, 229–31, 250, 261, 271–72, 277, 304, 307
Revolutionary War Cemetery, 44, 229, 261, 272, 277
Rexford, 204
Rhode Island, 60, 86
Richmond County, 57, 65, 80, 283
right of tenants, 78
right to vote, 13, 165–68
Rochester, 161
Royal Navy, 139–40
Rupill, Ebinezer, 91
Rycksen, 199–200

S

Salem, 10, 15, 19, 40, 44–45, 69, 90–92, 98–99, 104, 110, 119, 147, 157, 195–96, 213–14, 220, 223–24, 227–32, 244–45, 250, 253–54, 257, 261–62, 264–65, 271–73, 277, 302, 304
Salem Bedeau, 98
*Salem Press*, 44, 229
Samuel, 94, 192, 196, 211, 214, 225, 227–29, 257, 272
Sandy Hill, 110
Santa Domingo, 164
Saratoga County, 9, 32, 40, 110, 193, 197–203, 205–8, 212, 218, 227–28, 231, 236, 246, 261, 271, 301–2
Savage, Edward, 92
Schenectady, 193, 198–99, 212, 238, 301
Schenectady County, 193, 212, 301
Schenectady Dutch, 198
schools, segregated, 165

Schuyler, Jim, 147
Schuyler, Johannes, 201
Schuyler Flatts, 201
Schuylers, 201
scientific racism, 167
Scotch, 32, 41, 271
scouts, 70, 201
Searling, Hezakiah, 110
sequestration, 73–75, 77–78, 80, 83
settlement, 7, 40–41, 51, 60, 83–84, 142, 147–48, 154, 184, 197–99, 206, 211, 271
shearing, 120
sheep, 24, 41, 119–22, 141, 195, 223
sheep farming, 24
sheep raising, 141
Sherwood, Seth, 84
siblings, 15
Simpson, David, 94, 99
Sint Sink Native Americans, 80
Skene, 40, 43–44, 78, 84–85
Skene, Andrew P., 84
Skene, Philip, 43, 84
Skene, Phillip (colonel), 40, 44
Skene, Phillip (major), 40, 44
Skenesborough, 40, 43–44, 84–85
slave advertisements, 195
slavery, 13, 17, 44, 94–95, 103–4, 161–63, 169, 171–72, 174–75, 218–19, 235, 299–304
slave schedules, 194–95
slave trade, 16–17, 103, 229, 301
slavocracy, 165
Slyboro, 126
Smith, Anabel "Mamoo," 11–12, 238–41, 246
social and economic advancement, 180
social and economic status, advancement in the, 68
South Africa, 126, 157
Southern District, 81, 302

Southerners, 171–72
southern states, 13–14, 16, 170, 172, 197
Soweto, 126
Spanish colonies, 140
Spanish Merino sheep, 120
specie, value as, 74, 77
speculators, 74, 78
spies, 70
spinning, 120–21, 157
state and continental currency, 74
Staten Island, 70, 302
State of New York, 22–23, 25–26, 48, 56, 65, 68, 76, 79, 81, 84, 92–93, 98, 104, 111, 114, 167–68, 175, 184, 219–20, 254, 272, 282, 299–300, 302–3, 305
  support and maintenance provided by the, 81, 144, 146
state treasurer, 83
statutorily enslaved children, 93
statutory slaves, 162
Steward, William, 161
Stewart, L. Lloyd, 16, 301
  Far Cry from Freedom, A, 16, 104, 301
Stillwell, Jeremiah, 93, 96, 98
Stilwell, Jeremiah, 99
subsidy, 81, 88–89
subsistence employment, 144, 186
subsistence farming, 144, 186
Suffolk County, 57, 65, 80, 283
suffrage, 165, 169–70
"support by the state of those freed by the law," 76
Survey of Washington County (Fitch), 119, 157
survival employment, 186
sweat-shopped, 23
Sylvia, 44, 91, 261

T

Tammany Hall, 164, 175
tanneries, 114, 125, 184, 301
terrorism, 21
textile manufacturing, 24, 64, 184
Theall, Charles (of Rye), 71
Thompson, Thomas, 94
Thornton, Dave, 94, 104
Thread, 118, 121
"three-fifths of a man" clause, 172
Tikar people, 15, 17, 228–29
Tories, 69, 73, 75, 77–78, 83
tow-cloth, 111
town clerk, 88, 90–91, 93, 104, 303
Town of Jackson, 32, 94, 211
Town of Salem, 90, 254, 304
Town of Yonkers, 81
Township, 126
Tozer, Elishama, 85
trade embargo, 138, 140, 185
trading of Africans, 81
transporting products, 109
Troy, 110, 230, 232, 234, 236–39, 244–46
Tryon County, 32
Twelve Years a Slave (Northup), 170
Twin Towers, 21

U

Ulster County, 57, 65, 69, 73, 102, 156, 188, 282–83, 305
underground railroad, 26, 61, 231, 233
Underhill, William, 71, 101
United States, 7, 73–74, 77, 83, 101, 107, 118, 120, 123, 138–41, 144, 155, 160, 168, 170–72, 175, 185–87, 197, 220, 244, 252, 282, 286–88, 292–93, 299, 302, 306

United States Constitution, 170, 172, 175, 302
United States Constitutional Convention of 1787, 172
urban centers, 14
urban migration, 14

**V**

Van Boeckhoven, Claes Janse, 199–200
Van Bronk, John, 192, 195–96, 222–24, 226–27, 275
Van Buren, Gerrit, 92
Van Buren, Martin, 92, 167
Van Curler, Arendt, 199
Vandenberg, Cornelius, 92
Van Ness, Philip, 95
Van Olinda, Pieter Danieke, 199
Van Rankin, 195, 223, 226
Van Schaick, Harry, 94
Van Schaick, Jacob, 92
Van Vechten, Cornelius, 202
Van Vrancan, 212, 220, 225
Van Vrank, 15, 195–96, 212, 223
Van Vranken (unknown), 213, 220, 222, 244, 250
Van Vranken, Adam, 204–5
Van Vranken, Andreis (Andrew), 208
Van Vranken, Anneka, 203
Van Vranken, Catherine, 225, 227, 246
Van Vranken, David, 208
Van Vranken, Francis, 15, 154, 195–96
Van Vranken, Hannah/Elizabeth, 211–12
Van Vranken, Janatie, 202
Van Vranken, Johannes, 15, 192, 195, 213
Van Vranken, Maus, 204–5
Van Vranken, Ryck Claes, 199
Van Vranken, Ryckert, 200, 203–4
Van Vranken, Ryckert Claase, 200, 208

Van Vranken, Samuel, 192, 214, 218, 224, 227–29, 232, 244, 257, 261, 272
Van Vranken, Susannah, 231, 233, 245
Van Vranken family, 7, 27, 89–90, 189, 191–93, 195–98, 206–8, 211, 213, 219–20, 222, 242, 272
Van Vrankens, 7, 9, 14–15, 26–27, 86, 89–90, 154, 187, 189, 192–93, 195–209, 211–15, 218–20, 222–33, 242–47, 250, 252–53, 257, 261, 268, 272–73, 277, 302, 304
Vanvronk, 212
Van Vronk, 195–96, 211–13, 223–25, 227
Van Woak, Francis, 195, 211–12, 222
Van Woort, Peter, 92
Vermont, 24, 26, 32, 60, 71, 110–11, 119–20, 182, 184, 219
Vischer Ferry, 202, 204–5
Vischer's Ferry, 199
Vischers Ferry, 200

**W**

wage distribution, 13
wage laborers, 13
Wall of Enslavement, 206
Waltham, Massachusetts, 141
War of 1812, *117*, *140–141*, *147*, *164–186*
Warren County, 32, 41, 203, 222, 239, 299, 301
Washington, George, 172
Washington County, 5–10, 14–15, 19–21, 24–27, 29, 32–34, 39–41, 43–45, 47–49, 51–52, 56–57, 60–61, 64–65, 68, 73, 83–86, 90, 92–94, 98–100, 103–4, 106–11, 114–15, 117, 119, 122–27, 129, 138, 140–41, 144, 146–48, 150, 154, 156–58, 180–87, 193, 195–98, 206, 208, 211–15,

219–20, 222–30, 232–33, 244, 246, 250–54, 272, 275, 299–304

economic transformation of, 125

Washington County, New York, history of, 45, 104, 109, 156, 219, 300, 303

Waterford, 110, 198, 233–39, 245–46, 250, 300

water routes, 110

weaving, 120–22, 124, 157

Webster, Alexander, 83, 103

Weeks, John, 147

Wekquaesgeeks, 80

Wells, Austin, 94, 96–97

Wendell, Cornelius, 95–96

West Africa, 15, 17, 228

Westchester County, 70–71, 80, 283

White Creek, 32–33, 40, 95, 119

Whitehall, 40, 43–44, 84–85, 91, 109–10

white landowners, 13, 154

Whiteside, James, 117

Whiteside, William, 95

Wickham, Parker, 76

Widedale, Lincoln, 92

Williams, Dina, 91

Williams, John, 85, 91–92, 228

Wilson, Nathan, 91–92, 119

Winne, Daniel, 92

wolves, 119

Woods, Charles, 91

wool, 24, 110, 114, 117, 119–22, 125, 141, 149, 184–86

Worchester County, 60

working conditions, 23, 170

World Trade Center, 21

worsted yarns, 121–22

## X

xenophobia, 179

## Y

YMCA, 240

York, 60

York County, 60

Yoshpe, Harry B., 74, 78, 101–3, 302, 305

Younglove, John, 95, 98

## Z

Zambo, 164